Register N
Access t

MW00790469

Your print purchase of *Positive Psychology 101,* **includes
online access to the contents of your book**—increasing
accessibility, portability, and searchability!

Access today at:

**http://connect.springerpub.com/content/book/978-0-8261-2698-6
or scan the QR code at the right with your smartphone
and enter the access code below.**

RKW98E1J

*Scan here for
quick access.*

LS

SPRINGER **PUBLISHING COMPANY**
View all our products at springerpub.com

The
Psych
101
Series

James C. Kaufman, PhD, Series Editor
Department of Educational Psychology
University of Connecticut

Philip C. Watkins, PhD, is a professor of psychology at Eastern Washington University. He received his PhD in clinical psychology from Louisiana State University in 1991, where he worked with Andrew Mathews and Don Williamson. His initial research focused on memory biases in depression; however, for the last 15 years he has concentrated his energies on the psychology of gratitude. He developed one of the most utilized measures designed to assess the trait of gratitude (the GRAT), and his initial research dealt with the relationship of gratitude to happiness. He has now moved on to investigating *how* gratitude enhances well-being. Dr. Watkins has authored a number of peer-reviewed articles and chapters, and his research program in gratitude culminated in his book *Gratitude and the Good Life*, which was published in 2014. He has served on several editorial boards and was an associate editor for *The Journal of Positive Psychology*. Dr. Watkins's work in gratitude has been highlighted in the national media in such publications as *The Wall Street Journal, Self, Redbook, Ladies' Home Journal,* and *Psychology Today*.

Positive Psychology

101

Philip C. Watkins, PhD

SPRINGER PUBLISHING COMPANY

NEW YORK

Springer Publishing Company, LLC
11 West 42nd Street
New York, NY 10036
www.springerpub.com

Acquisitions Editor: Nancy S. Hale
Composition: Amnet

ISBN: 978-0-8261-2697-9
e-book ISBN: 978-0-8261-2698-6

15 16 17 18 19 / 5 4 3 2 1

Library of Congress Cataloging-in-Publication Data

Watkins, Philip C. (Philip Charles), author.
  Positive psychology 101 / Philip C. Watkins, Ph.D.
    pages cm
  Includes bibliographical references.
  ISBN 978-0-8261-2697-9 (print : alk. paper) — ISBN 978-0-8261-2698-6 (e-book)
1. Positive psychology. I. Title.
  BF204.6.W38 2015
  150.19'88—dc23

                                                                    2015021621

Special discounts on bulk quantities of our books are available to corporations, professional associations, pharmaceutical companies, health care organizations, and other qualifying groups. If you are interested in a custom book, including chapters from more than one of our titles, we can provide that service as well.

For details, please contact:
Special Sales Department, Springer Publishing Company, LLC
11 West 42nd Street, 15th Floor, New York, NY 10036-8002
Phone: 877-687-7476 or 212-431-4370; Fax: 212-941-7842
E-mail: sales@springerpub.com

Printed in the United States of America by Gasch Printing.

To the one who has been my wonderful positive
psychology coach these last 30 years:
Leslie Annie Watkins

Contents

CONTENTS

Preface

ittle did I know how much that e-mail invitation from Bob Emmons was to change my academic career. In the fall of 2000, Bob invited me to participate in the Kindling the Science of Gratitude seminar and this proved to be my baptism, so to speak, into positive psychology. Because Bob and I are now collaborating on developing a research program on the relationship between joy and gratitude, I look fondly back on that workshop and how Bob has been an encouragement to me over the years. My research into gratitude has been such a fun ride, and in many ways this book is the result of this involvement.

This book is not just about gratitude, of course, but about all the exciting aspects that have been investigated in the science of positive psychology. So much has happened in this field over the last 15 years that a book of this length cannot hope to cover it exhaustively, but I believe that I have captured the significant themes of this movement. This text is aimed primarily at college students interested in psychology; however, I believe it will also be helpful for graduate students and doctoral-level psychologists who would like an introduction into positive psychology.

One of the reasons that the interest in positive psychology has increased so much in recent years is that people are interested in happiness, and they're interested in enhancing their well-being. As we will see, positive psychology is more than just the science of happiness, but the bulk of research and interest in this area has been in the study of happiness, and so I have chosen to make that the focus of this work as well. People find happiness to be intrinsically interesting, and that's one reason why I believe you'll find the content of this book to be intriguing, sometimes surprising, and most of all applicable to your life. My hope is that you will find this journey of positive psychology to be as exciting as I have.

The chapters in this book may be divided into three major sections. First, in Chapters 1 and 2, I introduce some foundational concepts and then describe the strengths and virtues researchers into positive psychology have chosen to study. Chapters 3 through 7 are the heart of the book, and explore major questions about happiness. In Chapter 8 I offer some conclusions and insights into the past and the future of positive psychology. My take-home message here—and in the entirety of the volume—is simply that happiness matters.

One of the things you will find throughout this book is that gratitude matters to your happiness. And in that spirit, I feel overwhelmed with all of those who have contributed to my work. The support of my university has been wonderful at several different levels, from my dean Vickie Shields to my chair Nick Jackson, and perhaps most of all to my colleague Russell Kolts. To all these people I owe a deep debt of gratitude. Russell and I are different in many ways, but he has always given me the support and confidence that I need from friends to carry me through a significant project like this. And I can't forget all the wonderful students at Eastern Washington University with whom I have had the privilege to work. I am consistently impressed with how many excellent and highly motivated students we have here at Eastern, and their interest in happiness and positive psychology has been inspiring to me. I have found that students at Eastern are genuinely motivated to learn, and their passion for psychology has kept my spirit alive.

As I think about the important individuals who have contributed specifically to this book, my mind always goes to two people: David Myers and Bob Emmons. Although I know Dave only from a distance, his work—more generally in psychology and specifically in the study of happiness—has been extremely important for me. Indeed, his book *The Pursuit of Happiness* (Myers, 1992) was pivotal for my initiation into the science of happiness, and almost 25 years after it was published I still find it to be a wonderful read. They say you shouldn't have any heroes who are still living, but for me, David Myers is one of my heroes of psychology.

My friendship and collaboration with Bob Emmons in the science of gratitude have been enduring sources of encouragement for me. Bob is one of the busiest people I know, and yet he always seems to have time to discuss issues on gratitude research with me. Everyone should be so lucky as to have someone as balanced and positive as Bob to offer support in one's research.

I'm also very grateful to my fellow gratitude and positive psychology researchers. At the beginning of this project, I e-mailed a number of them about what they felt to be the most important work in positive psychology. I was amazed at how much time each one of these individuals took to provide sage advice on this matter—often with articles and links included. I'm consistently surprised how researchers in positive psychology seem to be so supportive and noncompetitive, and for this too I'm very grateful. So here's another big thanks to those who have contributed to this text by offering their time and expertise. Sara Algoe, Alex Wood, Mike McCullough, Giacomo Bono, Nate Lambert, and Jeff Froh, among others, were so generous with their time.

And of course, I am filled with thanks as I think about the contributions of my family to this book. My wonderful children, Josh, Claire, and Meghan, have been an unending source of joy in my life, each one in his or her own way. They have been so important in keeping me focused on the positive in my life. They constantly remind me of the importance of play, and I appreciate how much they have sacrificed so that this project could be completed (mostly in terms of tolerating their father's grumpiness).

Whether they're right or not, I still appreciate their consistent encouragements that let me know that I'm not as bad a father as I sometimes think I am. My son is a budding actor, and often in his acknowledgments in the playbill he writes: "I thank God who puts up with all my shenanigans." That's a great reminder for me too, and it fills me with gratitude when I think of the bounty with which the Giver of all good has blessed me. And to be sure, the greatest blessing and the greatest support through all my endeavors have been from my wife, Leslie. I often suffer from bouts of a lack of confidence, but she is always there to pick me up, in so many ways. Her support and provision for me have been so constant these last 30 years that it is easy to take these extraordinary benefits for granted. It is good to reflect on all that she has given me.

Perhaps one of my favorite scientists in the history of psychology is Edward Tolman. In the midst of the behavioral zeitgeist, Tolman was still willing to talk about that ultimate of all behavioral anathemas: cognition. I have often reflected on why Tolman is so appealing to me. Perhaps it was because he knew enough to not take himself so seriously at a time when psychology was so bent on doing *serious* behavioral science. Indeed, at his retirement he concluded:

> The best that any individual scientist . . . can do seems to be to follow his own gleam and his own bent, however inadequate they may be. In fact, I suppose that actually this is what we all do. In the end, the only sure criterion is to have fun. And I have had fun. (Hergenhahn, 2009, p. 428)

And I must say, that is what my ride in positive psychology has been thus far: fun. Perhaps we now need to initiate a science of fun. If "the only sure criterion is to have fun," my hope for you is that your introduction into positive psychology will be fun. Here's to having some fun with this book.

REFERENCES

Hergenhahn, B. R. (2009). *An introduction to the history of psychology* (6th ed.). Belmont, CA: Wadsworth.

Myers, D. G. (1992). *The pursuit of happiness: Discovering the pathway to fulfillment, well-being, and enduring personal joy.* New York, NY: Avon Books.

Positive
Psychology
101

Foundational Concepts and Issues of Positive Psychology: The What and Why of Happiness

don't think that my positive psychology story is all that unusual. In the mid-1990s I was happily engaged with investigating memory biases in depression (e.g., Watkins, 2002; Watkins, Martin, & Stern, 2000), but had been tinkering with a psychological approach to gratitude. My early gratitude research involved creating a questionnaire measuring gratitude, and conducting simple correlational studies with this scale. But as my research in depression started hitting some dead ends, the results with gratitude just kept piling up. It seemed that study after study showed that gratitude was related to desirable human characteristics. Then two important events shifted my research focus from depression to gratitude. First, I lost the election for my second term as chair of the psychology department. Second, Martin Seligman won a landslide victory as president of the American Psychological Association. I now view the first event—my "loss"—as the highlight of my career, for it redirected my time and energy back to what I love doing most: teaching and research, and this afforded me the time to dive into the psychology of gratitude. In the second event, Seligman found a theme for his presidency, and that theme was what would be called *positive psychology*. More about that second event later, but these two occasions coincided to launch me into gratitude research, which has been a very fulfilling pursuit for me. Like many other positive psychology researchers, my research was transformed from a focus on human suffering to human flourishing.

Of course, just because the field of positive psychology has been good for me does not mean that it should be a valued pursuit for you, or for psychology as a discipline. However, in this chapter I will try to show you how positive psychology is in fact important to psychology as a whole. But first we need to define some basic concepts before we discuss the value of this field.

FOUNDATIONAL CONCEPTS IN POSITIVE PSYCHOLOGY

Positive Psychology

Before jumping into the arena of positive psychology, we first need to agree on some basic definitions. In any scientific endeavor, foundational definitions can raise thorny issues, and positive psychology is no exception. First and foremost: What is positive psychology? Although every author seems to take their own approach, there is really a unity in the diversity of positive psychology definitions. First, all definitions of positive psychology involve science. From the beginning, positive psychologists wanted their endeavor to be based on scientific investigation. For me, this was an important emphasis, as you will see when we explore the history of happiness later. Second, all conceptions of positive psychology involve something to do with the "positive side of life" (Seligman, 1998, p. 5), which is clearly contrasted with the negative side of life. The positive side of life seems to go by many names, such as happiness, flourishing, thriving, a worthwhile life, a meaningful life, a fulfilling life, or "what goes right in life" (Peterson, 2006, p. 4). Nevertheless, all of these conceptions seem to refer to the same thing, without really defining what that positive thing is. Implicit in most definitions—and explicit in some—is the understanding that positive psychology studies human strengths and how we can build them. But even here, the emphasis on strengths is how they can be used so that individuals and communities may flourish.

So what is positive psychology? I would like to offer a fairly simple definition, and then follow it up by trying to define and illustrate the components of this description. *Positive psychology is the scientific study of the good life*. Of course, this definition suffers from the same problem as the other definitions; it begs for the answer to the question: What makes a life *good*? As before, various terms have been offered to help us understand the good life. For example, a life well lived is a commonly used phrase (e.g., Compton & Hoffman, 2013, p. 3). From a philosophical approach, Honderich (1995, p. 322) suggests that the study of the good life involves the study of the factors that "contribute to a well-spent or happy human life." As we will see later, philosophers do not always mean what we mean when they talk about happiness; however, this definition of the good life highlights happiness, and indeed that is an important emphasis of this book. The problem with words such as *good, well lived*, and *well spent*, is that we don't really know what is meant by "good" and "well." Because these words seem to have a value component to them, positive psychologists have attempted to define these concepts personally and subjectively. In other words, because we didn't want to prescribe to people what a "well-lived life" would look like, we have taken the approach of simply asking people: "Does life feel good to you?" As some have argued, we really can't take the moral/value aspect out of the discussion of the good life, and as it turns out, this is not as problematic as it might seem (Kristjansson, 2010). So what is *the good life*? Very simply, it's a life of happiness and flourishing. But what makes a life flourish? What makes a life well lived? Here I think Seligman's approach gives us clear direction; the good life is one where you use your strengths and resources effectively to produce pervasive happiness and enduring satisfaction (Seligman, 2002, p. 13).

So if positive psychology is the scientific study of the good life, what do positive psychologists study? There are three basic areas or dimensions in which positive psychology is interested (Seligman & Csikszentmihalyi, 2000): positive subjective states, positive psychological traits, and positive institutions. The study of *positive subjective states* involves two related but distinct areas of study: positive emotions and subjective well-being (SWB). I will explain SWB later; however, although positive emotions are very important to SWB, they are really distinct areas of study. *Positive psychological traits* are the morally valued strengths and virtues that lead to a fulfilling life. We will explore these traits in greater depth in Chapter 2. *Positive institutions* involves the study of things that contribute to more healthy communities, be they cities, workplaces, universities, or families. So what is positive psychology? Positive psychology is the science that studies positive subjective states, positive psychological traits, and positive institutions. Positive psychology is the scientific study of the good life. And in positive psychology the study of the good life is the science of happiness and flourishing. Clearly, the study of happiness is an important focus of positive psychology. So what is happiness?

Happiness

Happiness seems to be one of those terms that people understand until they try to define it. Indeed, defining happiness has turned out to be much more contentious than defining positive psychology. Even in philosophy, defining happiness is a troublesome issue. As the philosopher Kristjan Kristjansson summarizes the debate: "There is hardly a muddier concept in the over 2,000-year history of philosophy itself than that of happiness" (2010, p. 300). The first problem to confront us is that we use the term in different ways in our day-to-day speech. If I say, "Your compliment of my lecture makes me happy," that is a very different use of *happy* than saying "Bethany is a very happy person." In the first case, I'm simply referring to how I am feeling in the moment, whereas in Bethany's case, I'm alluding to a more enduring form of happiness. As we will see, when people discuss happiness— whether or not they are psychologists—they are usually referring to the more enduring type, and that is the form of happiness that I will emphasize in this book.

Positive psychologists often refer to two types of happiness: hedonic and eudaimonic. Briefly, *hedonic happiness* refers to how happy you feel whereas *eudaimonic happiness* involves being true to your authentic self. Researchers interested in eudaimonic happiness are most interested in whether individuals are using their capacities—both their general human capacities and their own peculiar individual strengths—to flourish in life. As we will see, both the eudaimonic and the hedonic approaches to happiness have much to offer; however, I would first like to explore the eudaimonic view of happiness. Most positive psychologists follow Aristotle in their understanding of eudaimonia; nevertheless, it is important to acknowledge that Aristotle was one of several different ancient Greek philosophers who took the eudaimonic approach to happiness. All of these approaches, however, emphasized the importance of fulfilling one's *true nature* (Haybron, 2008). In this sense, eudaimonic happiness is achieved when we fulfill our true human potential. We flourish when our life fulfills our human capacities. Aristotle tended to emphasize the importance of becoming a virtuous person. Importantly for Aristotle, it was the virtues that should be pursued, not happiness in and of itself (Haybron, 2008). Of course, the disagreement comes as to what really is our true nature. What are the virtues that humans should pursue? This question is the focus of Chapter 2.

There are several advantages to the eudaimonic tradition of happiness. Perhaps most importantly, this approach does not divorce morality and virtue from the study of happiness. Most of us would agree with Aristotle in that a life simply filled with consumptive pleasure is not a happy life. Cows may have all the pleasure of eating grass and grain to their hearts' content, but are they really happy? No. Aristotle would claim that the authentically happy life is also the virtuous life.

The eudaimonic view of happiness is an important tradition that positive psychologists would be foolish to neglect. But there are a number of problems with this approach to defining happiness. First, it can come across as being overly prescriptive or even paternalistic. The eudaimonic definition of happiness basically tells people that they have to be doing certain things or they have to be developing certain qualities or they aren't happy, regardless of whether they think they are happy. For me, this is not a serious criticism of eudaimonia. If indeed this turns out to be the right definition of happiness, then it shouldn't really matter that this definition offends me because of its paternalism. If I don't like the fact that it prescribes certain virtues for me to pursue, that doesn't preclude the possibility that those virtues might really create happiness.

But the real rub involves the issue of human nature. What really are our capacities as humans? What is my personal potential? What are the human needs that need to be satisfied in order to flourish? On this issue, even among eudaimonic theorists, there is little agreement (Haybron, 2008; Jayawickreme, Forgeard, & Seligman, 2012). A related issue has to do with the measurement of this kind of happiness. Although measures have been developed for this construct (often referred to as measures of *psychological well-being*), are they really measuring eudaimonic happiness? A good measure of Aristotle's eudaimonia would accurately assess whether we really are fulfilling our human potential. As Alex Wood pointed out to me recently (personal communication, June 2014), all measures of psychological well-being do not really measure whether I am effectively using my strengths to flourish; they only measure whether I am *satisfied* with my pursuit of strengths and *satisfied* with the fulfillment of my psychological needs. This means that these measures essentially turn out to be hedonic measures of well-being. I can understand why researchers would develop self-report measures in this way; nonetheless, true eudaimonia takes more of an objective approach to happiness, rather than my subjective impression of whether or not I am meeting my potential. This may be why eudaimonic and hedonic measures of happiness are so highly correlated, and some have questioned whether they are really distinct forms of happiness (Biswas-Diener, Kashdan, & King, 2009; Kashdan, Biswas-Diener, & King, 2008).

Finally, and for me most importantly, I think that viewing eudaimonia as a distinct kind of happiness unnecessarily complicates the science of the good life. Not only are there a number of different approaches to eudaimonic happiness, but I am concerned that we might be dealing with a confusion of our dependent and independent variables, so to speak. It is one thing to say, "This is what happiness is." But it is quite another thing to claim, "This is what *causes* happiness." By identifying happiness as the fulfillment of our human capacities, it seems to me that we are including both the causes and the consequences in our definition of happiness. It may well be that pursuing certain virtues *causes* happiness; however, that is quite different from saying that this *is* happiness. Indeed, I believe that this is where Aristotle and the eudaimonic approach have much to offer: theories about what causes happiness. But for me, defining happiness as the pursuit of those virtues muddies the waters a bit. Thus, I must conclude with Biswas-Diener and associates that eudaimonic and hedonic approaches represent "two traditions of happiness research, but not two distinct types of happiness" (2009, p. 208). This is not to say, however, that the current emphasis on eudaimonia is not a valuable contribution to positive psychology. This approach provides needed theories that will continue to guide our research efforts to understand happiness and its antecedents.

I believe that the hedonic approach offers a more parsimonious account for defining happiness. A simple definition of *hedonic happiness* is the positive balance of one's emotional experiences. If you have more pleasant than unpleasant emotional experiences, then you are considered to be a happy person. But as stated earlier, most of us look at happiness as a more enduring state and not simply as the sum of our positive and negative experiences. Indeed, positive psychologists also prefer to view happiness in this way. Thus, the dominant hedonic happiness approach prefers to identify happiness with what they refer to as SWB: "People's evaluations of their lives" that "encompasses both cognitive judgments of satisfaction and affective appraisals of moods and emotions" (Kesebir & Diener, 2008, p. 118). From this perspective, the components of SWB are: life satisfaction, high positive emotion, and lack of negative emotion. Life satisfaction here involves two aspects: global satisfaction with one's life, as well as satisfaction with specific domains of life that are important to well-being (satisfaction with one's marriage, one's friends, one's job, one's leisure activities, etc.; Kesebir & Diener, 2008).

There are a number of advantages to the hedonic approach to happiness. Let's consider the happiness of someone we'll call Jerome. First, the hedonic approach leaves the decision about Jerome's happiness to Jerome. This implies a couple of notable benefits. First, there is the practical issue of accurately measuring happiness. If Jerome is the best judge of his own happiness, then all we have to do is to ask him. Second, it avoids the paternalistic problems discussed earlier. If Jerome says that he is truly happy, who am I to say that he's not, just because I'm a positive psychology expert? There are some problems with this, of course. Jerome could always be lying about his happiness. In other words, he might know that he really isn't happy, but he still reports to me that he is. But this is a problem with any psychological self-report instrument, and currently the eudaimonic measurement tools of happiness are just as vulnerable to this issue. But Jerome might be deceiving himself. He might truly believe that he is happy when in fact he is not. But is this really possible? If Jerome truly believes that he is happy, who am I to say that he is not? Most of us believe that, at bottom, people's happiness is indeed *their* happiness, and thus they are likely to be the best judge of their own SWB. Third, the hedonic approach to happiness seems to offer a more parsimonious account. Rather than having to argue about which strengths and virtues should be included in our definition of well-being, we simply define it as individuals' personal judgment as to how happy they are, and then we can investigate what factors (including personal strengths and virtues) contribute to that happiness.

Of course, there are several well-known problems with the hedonic happiness perspective. John Stuart Mill (1972) argued that the hedonic approach to happiness implies that a satisfied swine would be viewed as happier than a suffering Socrates. Similar to this argument is the famous "experience machine" example explained by Nozick (1974). He points out that the hedonic approach to happiness implies that if we could be connected to an "experience machine" that would give us continual pleasure,

9

this would be the happiest life. But as I think you would agree, not many of us would choose this life, and fewer still would view this as a good or happy life. But I think that the SWB approach to hedonic happiness effectively avoids these criticisms. For it is not simply the sum total of one's pleasurable experiences that amounts to happiness, rather it is one's *general emotional tone*, combined with one's *general satisfaction with one's personal life*. As Kristjansson and other philosophers have pointed out, pigs do not have the capacity for judging their satisfaction with life, and most of us would not view being hooked up to an "experience machine" as a satisfying life: "People—at least reflective people with faculties higher than those of common animals—do not only have pleasures, they evaluate them as good or bad for themselves" (2010, p. 300).

I would like to suggest a more subtle and nuanced hedonic approach to happiness that may allay many concerns about hedonistic happiness. First, let me point out that our usual understanding of hedonism is not synonymous with the hedonic approach to happiness. The popular understanding of hedonism is that the hedonistic lifestyle seeks continual and exciting pleasure. The hedonic approach to happiness, on the other hand, simply defines happiness as the general hedonic tone that an individual experiences in life, and thus does not necessarily prescribe seeking pleasure at all costs. Indeed, I shall argue that seeking high-intensity pleasure as one's preeminent life goal will actually inhibit the frequency of pleasant experiences and satisfaction with life.

First, it will probably be obvious to you that not all pleasures are all that pleasant. Surely you know of an individual who has engaged in a sexual pleasure that turned out to be unpleasant. Second, my approach to hedonic happiness emphasizes *all* pleasant experiences, no matter how subtle they may be. Indeed, research has found that in terms of SWB, it is the frequency of pleasant experiences that matters more than how much intense pleasure these experiences bring us (Diener, Sandvik, & Pavot, 1991). This is a significant finding for positive psychology, and I will explore the importance of *simple pleasures* to happiness throughout this volume. One of the criticisms of the dominant emotion measurement tool in psychology, the Positive and Negative Affect Schedule (the short PANAS; Watson, Clark, & Tellegen, 1988) scale, is that it only measures high-activation emotions. The positive affect scale on this measure includes emotion descriptors such as *excited, inspired,* and *enthusiastic,* but no emotions that might be indicated by adjectives such as *contented, tranquil,* and *calm* (to be fair, the long version of this measure—the PANAS-X—does contain terms like these). Research suggests that more subtle positive emotions such as contentment may be as important to your enduring happiness as spectacular raw pleasures. Indeed, studies have shown that there are important individual and cultural differences in what kind of pleasant experiences we value (e.g., Tsai, Knutson, & Fung, 2006), so it is essential that we not neglect the more subtle positive emotions. Some positive psychologists have tried to balance this neglect by developing measures of more subtle positive states like "peace of mind" (e.g., Lee, Lin, Huang, & Fredrickson, 2013). Because I believe that the consideration of more subtle positive emotions is vital to the study of happiness, I look forward to the development of more of these measures.

We have seen that a more nuanced approach to hedonic happiness will include the study of subtle and less intense positive emotional states, and this would not seem to be the focus of popular hedonism. Because a nuanced hedonic happiness approach emphasizes a more enduring positive emotional tone, we may see that, contrary to popular hedonism, individuals often undergo suffering in order to experience more pleasure in the future. Perhaps the most notable example of this in psychology is in *delay of gratification* research. The classic studies in this realm involved Walter Mischel's so-called marshmallow test with children (Mischel, Shoda, & Peake, 1988; Mischel, Shoda, & Rodriguez, 1989). In these studies researchers presented children with a marshmallow (or some other treat) and told them that they could have this treat now, or if they waited until the researcher returned they could have two treats. The obvious dependent variable was how long the children could wait before consuming the marshmallow. They found that "suffering" by not giving in to the temptation of eating the treat right away resulted in more pleasure later. Indeed, Mischel and colleagues were able to show an impressive array of long-term beneficial outcomes to the ability to delay gratification (Mischel et al., 1988, 1989).

Even in the Christian tradition, the encouragement to withstand temptation or to suffer was not because suffering was good in and of itself, but rather because it could bring more benefits in the future. Chesterton (1924/1990) argued that Saint Francis of Assisi intentionally devoted himself to experiences of deprivation, not so much because suffering and deprivation were inherently good, but rather because the deprivation enhanced enjoyment of those benefits later (a similar observation is made by Maslow, 1996). For example, if I give up wine for Lent, I am likely to enjoy my glass of red wine even more on Easter. In the Christian tradition, the prototypical suffering event was Christ's crucifixion. Even here, the writer of Hebrews informs us that Jesus "endured the cross" "for the joy set before him" (Hebrews 12:2, New American Standard Version). These examples illustrate how individuals may go through suffering because, in the big picture, this will improve the emotional tone of their lives. The best way to avoid all emotional pain and suffering is to avoid other people, and as we shall see in Chapter 5, this is a surefire path to an unhappy life. Therefore, we can see that a more nuanced hedonic happiness emphasizes that humans need to suffer at times in order to achieve greater levels of happiness. Surely this is not what a popular hedonism would recommend to us.

Relatedly, this approach to hedonic happiness would be quick to recognize that we can see many examples of a pleasure-seeking lifestyle that might actually inhibit pleasant emotional experiences, increase negative emotion, and decrease life satisfaction. For example, individuals who seek constant pleasure through inebriation will likely experience much more negative affect than if they moderate their drinking. The obvious example is with the next morning's hangover, but more than likely the enjoyment of relationships and pursuing fulfilling achievements will be inhibited as well. Moreover, excessive use of substances like alcohol might actually decrease one's enjoyment of a favorite beverage. Similarly, the man who seeks constant pleasure through sexual experiences is likely to enjoy his relationships less, enjoy sex less, and it may even result in him being constrained to a situation where sex is difficult (prison). These examples show how constant pleasure seeking is likely to result in less pleasure and lower life satisfaction, over the long run.

One criticism of the hedonic approach to happiness is that it divorces the study of happiness from the study of virtue. Whereas some might argue that this is an advantage of the hedonic approach, in philosophy, rarely is the study of happiness divorced from ethics, and this is certainly consistent with the rich tradition of classical philosophy offered to us by figures such as Aristotle (Haybron, 2008). Although it is certainly true that the hedonic definition of happiness tends to exclude virtue, emphasizing a hedonic definition of happiness and well-being need not divorce the study of happiness from the study of virtue. I submit that human strengths and virtues will indeed be important to the study of happiness because we will see how important virtue is to SWB. For example, research has begun to demonstrate how virtues like gratitude and hope are important to happiness (we will explore this in greater depth in Chapters 2 and 4).

So we have wandered through the minefield of defining happiness, but I have as yet to present a concise definition. If I may, I would like to go "back to the future" so to speak, for I still believe that David Myers's definition of happiness is most helpful, and this is the definition that I will rely on for this book. He defined happiness as: *"A pervasive sense that life is good"* (Myers, 1992, p. 23; italics added). First, note that the word *pervasive* implies that happiness is not a limited or fickle state. Myers goes on to explain that:

> Well-being outlasts yesterday's moment of elation, today's buoyant mood, and tomorrow's hard time; it is an ongoing perception that this time in one's life, or even life as a whole, is fulfilling, meaningful, and pleasant. (p. 24)

Two important concepts emerge from this understanding of happiness: (a) happiness is enduring (it's not just that I feel pleased in the moment), and (b) happiness is global (I'm satisfied with my life as a whole, not just with select domains in my life). For me, Myers's definition of happiness provides the most parsimonious and least problematic understanding of happiness, and this understanding is best approximated by the *SWB approach to happiness*: a high frequency of positive emotional experiences, low frequency of unpleasant experiences, combined with high life satisfaction. In short, "A pervasive sense that life is good" is best understood through the SWB tradition: "A subjective appreciation of life's rewards" (Snyder, Lopez, & Pedrotti, 2011, p. 119).

THE LEGACY OF HAPPINESS

A comprehensive survey of the history of happiness is far beyond the scope of this book; however, here I will try to give you a good synopsis of what I feel to be the important trends and events in this history. For a comprehensive and engaging explanation of the history of happiness, I would encourage you to consult McMahon's book (2006; for a briefer version see McMahon, 2008), and in this section I have relied heavily on his work.

The purpose of this segment is not only to help you understand how we have viewed happiness through the ages, but more importantly, what we can learn from the significant insights and mistakes of the past. As with most histories, I will proceed chronologically (with a few notable exceptions), and unfortunately my survey will be biased toward the Western tradition. But before we launch into the legacy of happiness, let me make one observation about happiness that seems to be consistent across the ages. Although people seem to be interested in happiness no matter the stage of history, it is interesting to me that sages and critics seem to be most prone to speculating about the nature of happiness when times are relatively good. My observation is that most of the discussion of happiness has taken place in times and locations of relative material prosperity and political stability. This seemed to be true of the ancient Greeks, and even now we seem to want to discuss happiness in the midst of our current prosperity. Is happiness only a concern when times are good enough that we can imagine being happy? Perhaps, but as we shall see, humans have concerned themselves with happiness in "the worst of times" as well.

Ancient Greek Ideas of Happiness

The rich Greek tradition of happiness involves much more than Aristotle and the eudaimonic approach described earlier. For example, many Greek philosophers followed a hedonistic approach to happiness. But even the most famous hedonists— the Epicureans—had a much more nuanced view of happiness than popular hedonism would suggest. Indeed, those of the Epicurean camp were much more likely to represent happiness as the "pleasures of tranquility" (Haybron, 2008, p. 28), rather than the accumulation of raw unadulterated pleasure. One thing that seemed to distinguish the Epicureans from the disciples of Aristotle, however, was that this tranquil, happy life could be an explicit goal, whereas for Aristotle any kind of psychic harmony was simply the result of the virtuous life. Even the Stoics—who strove to push pleasure and pain toward the margins of life—felt that inner psychological harmony was an important aspect of the virtuous life (Haybron, 2008). Thus, for virtually all philosophers, the good life was a pleasant life, although they would emphasize different paths to this end.

But as McMahon has emphasized (2006, 2008), there was always something of a tragic theme in the Greek approach to happiness for it seemed that happiness for the Greeks was never completely under one's control; for one never knew when luck, fate, or the capricious act of some god might completely derail one's journey to happiness. McMahon emphasizes that this theme seems to come through in early Judeo–Christian thought as well, albeit in a notably different form, but we will see that in the Enlightenment this refrain shifted markedly.

Before we move on to discuss happiness in the Jewish and Christian traditions, I would like to make an observation about Greek writings of happiness that probably applies to all historical periods before the modern era. Indeed, this insight applies not only to our understanding of the history of happiness, but to our understanding of the history of any area of thought. We must remember that in discussing the Greek view of happiness, I really am only presenting the view of happiness represented by literate Greeks, and then only by literate Greek scholars whose thoughts were written down in a record that survived the ravages of time. Surely there is a problem of external validity here; there must remain real questions as to whether these writings were representative of the common Greek woman or man. Thus, as we journey through the history of happiness, let us remember that the written history of happiness may not be the popular or dominant view of happiness through the ages.

Jewish and Christian Thought

It is somewhat curious to me that many treatments of the history of happiness spend little time on ancient Jewish contributions to our understanding of well-being. Perhaps this is because many feel that Jewish literature has much to say about virtue, but little to say about happiness. However, my reading of the ancient Jewish literature suggests otherwise. Many commentators would see "shalom" as an approximation of happiness, and there are several other Hebrew words that refer to well-being. Unfortunately the Hebrew word that most closely approximates happiness is often translated "blessed," even though another Hebrew word is also translated "blessed." Thus the opening verse of the Psalter may be read: "Truly happy are those who walk not in the counsel of the wicked." Seen in this way, ancient Jewish literature has much to offer about happiness.

First, in agreement with Aristotle and as Psalm 1 illustrates, happiness in Jewish wisdom literature seems to result from a virtuous (read "righteous") life. There are clearly exceptions to this rule where the psalmists and the writer of Job seem to complain about the well-being of ungodly people, but generally speaking one of the benefits of the righteous walk is psychic harmony and SWB. But here it is important to emphasize that it was not just following the rules that resulted in happiness, but rather the person's relationship with God that caused psychic harmony. Indeed, there is a common structure of propositions about happiness in the Psalms: "Happy are those who . . . ." And more often than not, the happy person is the one who takes refuge in their God.

Other themes of happiness emerge in Jewish literature. For me, happiness is one of the main themes of the book of Ecclesiastes. Often this book is seen as a work that highlights the futility of secular life, but I believe that this is a misreading of this text. Although

17

the writer sees that a perfect permanent happiness may never be attained in this life, clearly this work recommends the enjoyment of the blessings that God has given humanity. For example, in 9:7 the writer recommends to the reader "Go, eat your bread with joy, and drink your wine with a merry heart, for God has already approved what you do" (English Standard Version) and in verse 9, "Enjoy life with the wife whom you love, all the days of your vain life that he has given you under the sun, because that is your portion in life." Moreover, note the sage's conclusions in 3:12: "I perceived that there is nothing better for them than to be joyful and to do good as long as they live; also that everyone should eat and drink and take pleasure in all his toil—this is God's gift to man." While fully admitting the inconsistencies and the drudgery of the cyclical patterns in life ("A generation goes, and a generation comes," 1:4), the preacher encourages his readers to enjoy the blessings and their lot in life. The theme to enjoy God's gifts with gratitude clearly continues in early Christian writings as well.

Because of the Judeo–Christian view of the sovereignty of God, an interesting dilemma arises. In early Jewish thought, many believed that if a person was well off in life, this must be evidence that a person was approved of by God. Hence, if one is happy, does that mean that they must be virtuous? This is a kind of moral "just world" attitude that virtue must result in well-being and well-being must mean that one is virtuous. This thinking exists not only in Jewish thought, but in Christian and Islamic thought as well, and perhaps in every major religion of the world (e.g., karma in Eastern religions). Although the book of Job and the words of Jesus (Luke 13:1–2; John 9:1–3) seem to speak directly against this kind of "just world" approach to happiness, this attitude was prominent in biblical times, and seems to continue to be prevalent in religious thought today. Rodgers and Hammerstein immortalized this philosophy in their musical *The Sound of Music*. When Maria is finally in the arms of her beloved Georg, she sings that sometime in the distant past, she must have been good. Something very good is happening to me now; this must be because I've been good in the past. This may be why Jesus's disciples were shocked when Jesus said that the rich would have difficulty getting into heaven. They believed that a "rich young ruler" must be a person who is approved of by God (Mark 10:17–27), thus their surprise when Jesus said that a person like him would have more difficulty reaching heaven than "a camel going through the eye of a needle." Indeed, King and Napa found that people still believe that happy individuals are more likely to go to heaven. Although this seems to be a popular religious approach to happiness in the past and even to this day (hence the popularity of the so-called "prosperity gospel" movement), it should be pointed out that a number of Jewish and Christian writings would seem to repudiate this view.

Perhaps the most striking development in the early Christian approach to happiness is best illustrated by Jesus's iconic words: "Happy are those who mourn, for they shall be comforted" (Matthew 5:4; Luke 6:21). This paradox continues through early Christian thought, emphasizing the theme of the joy one may experience through suffering. It is apparent that this is not a masochistic theme—one does not obtain joy by inflicting pain on oneself—but rather an acknowledgment that through suffering, one may obtain even greater joy. This harkens back to my earlier discussion where I emphasized that the hedonic approach to happiness does not amount to popular hedonism. Enduring suffering may indeed result in greater future joy. The point is that by avoiding all pain, we may also end up denying ourselves considerable pleasure.

From the early Christian tradition, writers encouraged enduring suffering now in the light of future happiness in the afterlife. However, this does not appear to be an argument that suffering in this life earns one joy in heaven. Rather, focusing fellow believers on the perfect happiness of heaven is used as assistance for enduring suffering in the present. Thus, even here there is a hedonic quality to Christian happiness; although one cannot achieve permanent perfect happiness in this life, hope for perfected well-being in the afterlife was given for the purpose of encouraging joy in the present. As did their Jewish forebearers, Christian writers emphasized that happiness in this life would always be imperfect. Because of the pervasive influence of fallen creation, suffering would be inevitable—and people should not be surprised when they do suffer—but contentment and joy were possible now, in part because of the hope of the Eternal City.

But joy in the midst of suffering seems to be part of a broader theme in early Christian thought: the independence of happiness from one's circumstances. Early Christian writers taught that one's lot in life need not determine one's happiness. Thus St. James writes: "Count it all joy . . . when you meet trials of various kinds" (James 1:2). Likewise, St. Paul observes, "I have learned to be content whatever the circumstances" (Philippians 4:11). There is no suggestion here that what happens to a person in life doesn't matter, only that one can learn to be happy despite undesirable life circumstances.

Also like their Jewish antecedents, Christian writers emphasized the importance of enjoying the gifts of God, and most particularly God's gift of forgiveness. Happiness based on God's gift of grace was not unique to the Christian tradition because this blessing was enjoyed by earlier Jewish writers as well. For example, the psalmist writes in the opening of Psalm 32: "Happy are those whose transgression is forgiven, whose sin is covered. Happy are those to whom the LORD imputes no iniquity."

Finally, early Christian writers emphasized the importance of the presence of God for the believer's enduring happiness. Humans were created for a relationship with the Divine, they argued, and therefore true happiness was found in a relationship with him. Thus the famous words of Augustine, "Thou madest us for Thyself, and our hearts are restless, until it rests in Thee" (Book I, I:1). Christian writers emphasized that humans were created with a "God-shaped vacuum" that could only be filled with the Divine. Thus, true happiness for the Christian could not be found outside of a relationship with God. In sum, the Judeo–Christian writings have much to say about happiness. Contrary to popular belief, the Bible has many more references to positive than negative states (Watkins, 2014), and the encouragement of St. Paul to his discouraged Philippian readers appears to be typical of the Judeo–Christian approach to happiness: "Rejoice, and again I say rejoice" (Philippians 4:4).

The Christian view of happiness seemed to dominate the West until the Enlightenment, although to be fair, there does not appear to be extensive writing on the topic during the Middle Ages. In the so-called Enlightenment there appears to be a considerable shift in writings on happiness. First, it is apparent that happiness literature experiences a renaissance of sorts; there appears to be a great increase of interest in happiness in sages and philosophers of this era. Indeed, now common folks dared to think that they too could be happy (McMahon, 2006, 2008). In part, this may be attributed to a parallel development of the "sovereign self" (Haybron, 2008), which has become much more established in the modern era. Now, seemingly for the first time, people began to imagine that they were the masters of their own fate, rather than the puppets of luck, tragic events, minions of the Church, or victims of the capricious acts of the gods. Now, people began to believe that their happiness might actually be under their own control. Notably here, with the ascent of individualism in the West, one's own happiness was to gradually take precedence over the well-being of the community.

The Enlightenment and Modernity

With the dawn of a more individualistic mind-set, people in the West now believed that attaining happiness was something under their control. Indeed, some writers after the Enlightenment argued that people were entitled to happiness, and certainly we see this attitude of happiness entitlement today. Another gift that we have inherited from the Enlightenment is that people now feel guilty when they're not happy (McMahon, 2008). Because we believe that happiness is essentially up to us, when we're unhappy this must mean that we're doing something wrong or that we're not trying hard enough. Thus, ironically, our new-found responsibility for our own happiness can actually make us unhappy. Indeed, after the Enlightenment and through modern times, many governments have taken the right to happiness so seriously that they have launched human engineering attempts to force people to be happy (McMahon, 2008). These experiments may be seen as failures because a sure way to make people unhappy is to try to force them to do something.

But the American happiness experiment was somewhat different. Much has been made over the fact that the *Declaration of Independence* did not declare the right of happiness, only that people have the right to *pursue* their own happiness. Although this seems to have morphed into assuming that one is entitled to happiness for many modern Americans, the right to the pursuit of happiness may still be seen as an important development in the history of government.

This brings us finally to the current positive psychology movement. Although humanistic psychology had emphasized human strengths and well-being before, the current movement can be easily traced back to Martin Seligman's presidency of the American Psychological Association in 1998. Interestingly, this movement was not borne out of the predominant human concern for happiness in the modern era, but rather the opposite imbalance that was observed by Seligman. In looking for a theme to his presidency, he stumbled on the insight that in psychology, we are overly focused on what's wrong with life, to the extent that we have neglected what's good about life (Seligman & Csikszentmihalyi, 2000). This negativistic bias in psychology research has been demonstrated a number of times (e.g., Watkins, 2014), and it doesn't seem to be consistent with what we actually experience in life. Indeed, although psychologists study negative states far more than positive states, we actually experience positive emotions more frequently. Seligman had found a calling for his presidency, and this resulted in what was for many of us a historic call. In his presidential column in the *APA Monitor*, Seligman (1998, p. 2) observed:

> Sadly, while plumbing the depths of what is worst in life, psychology has lost its connection to the positive side of life—the knowledge about what makes human life most worth living, most fulfilling, most enjoyable and most productive.

And this has brought us to where we are today: in the middle of a thriving and flourishing science we call positive psychology.

Learning From the History of Happiness

Does the history of happiness have anything to offer us? Is there a legacy of happiness from which we can learn? As I conclude this section I would like to emphasize four takeaways from this account of happiness through time. First, although pure hedonists have always been around (those who seek pleasure and avoid pain at all costs), this has never been the dominant view of happiness. People have never really been all that concerned with an accumulation of momentary experiences of happiness. Rather, people have sought an overall positive hedonic tone, a more stable sense of SWB. Second, various traditions throughout history have emphasized that happiness need not be determined by one's circumstances. This is an important observation that we will see has largely been confirmed by research. Your circumstances do matter to your happiness, but only to a little bit of your happiness. The problem is that so many people take great cost and effort to change their station in life, only to find they have very little happiness to gain from it. Third, as McMahon (2006, 2008) rightly observed, governmental experiments that have tried to force human happiness have largely been failures. I believe this is an important observation because amid our current worldwide obsession with happiness, it seems that we may be returning to governmental engineering of happiness, and I am concerned that any attempt of this manner that limits people's choices as to how they may pursue happiness is doomed to fail. This is not to say that SWB research is irrelevant to public policy, only that I am wary of any governmental approach that attempts to engineer human happiness.

And this leads to my final concern, which has also been emphasized by McMahon (2008). Currently, it seems that happiness is all the rage. For many people, their direct pursuit of happiness has consumed their lives, and this worries me. As many wise people have observed throughout the ages (including Aristotle and J. S. Mill), happiness as an all-consuming goal in life is likely to backfire. The research that we will explore in this book demonstrates that happiness is mostly the result of pursuits other than obtaining happiness, such as helping others and developing character. As the late Chris Peterson (2006) said, the essence of positive psychology is "other people matter." Indeed, this is one of the most important themes of this book. When *my happiness* is all that matters, I'm not likely to end up being very happy. But when the happiness of others is my goal, I'm probably going to lead a very enjoyable and fulfilling life.

CRITICISMS OF POSITIVE PSYCHOLOGY

When I first learned of Seligman's goals for positive psychology, I thought: "Uh-oh, here we go." As much as I thought that the new direction of positive psychology was a needed correction, I could only imagine the barrage of criticism that was to come. To be honest, the criticism has not been as severe as I thought it might be; however, there are still some notable concerns that have been raised by scholars, and these need to be addressed.

The first criticism was that the new positive psychology movement wasn't really new. Many humanistic psychologists wondered why Seligman was calling psychology to a concern for human strengths and well-being when they had been doing that for more than 30 years. Indeed, it was not Seligman but Maslow (1954) who coined the very term *positive psychology*. Initially, it must be said that humanistic psychology did not invent positive psychology either; decades earlier William James introduced the concept of "healthy mindedness" (1902/1958). That being said, humanistic psychology had much to offer about optimal human functioning, and those with an interest in positive psychology would be foolish to neglect the important contributions of humanistic psychologists on these issues. But I must agree with Seligman: There was a real need for a new call and a new movement of positive psychology. Positive psychology is first and foremost the *science* of the good life. Because humanistic psychologists had always been suspicious of the dehumanizing potential of scientific inquiry, despite the concern of humanistic psychologists for human strengths and well-being, little progress was being made in the advance of knowledge about the good life. Seligman's call to a more positive psychology was an explicit call for scientific inquiry and, for me, this was needed. And by most accounts, the progression of knowledge regarding the good life has increased substantially since his call.

Another concern often mentioned by critics is that happiness is such an elusive state, why should we even pursue it? They argue that happiness is rare—hardly anyone is happy—and if happiness is so difficult to achieve, perhaps it is foolish to encourage people to pursue it. Undoubtedly, if only 1% of people were happy, then I think this argument would hold some water, but this is simply not the case. As some studies have concluded, "Most people are happy" (Diener & Diener, 1996), so happiness does not seem to be the elusive state that these critics would have us believe. By some accounts, fully 89% of people say that they are at least "pretty happy," so it does not appear that pursuing happiness is an unrealistic pursuit. I think there may be a point to this argument, however. It does seem to me that many people are pursuing an unrealistic happiness. Although most people are pretty happy, many people still seek a kind of happiness that may not be achievable, and their very pursuit of this state might make them unhappier. But in general, we may conclude that happiness is not an unrealistic pursuit because "most people are happy."

Another common complaint is that positive psychologists want us to neglect the negative. Negative emotions, human suffering, and human vice are real aspects of life, critics argue, and to neglect them would be to our harm. For me, this is an interesting criticism because I've never heard or read any positive psychologist say that we should stop investigating unpleasant emotions and human vice. Rather, the encouragement has been for us to shift our research energies more to the positive, but this has never entailed excluding the study of the negative. Clearly, it would be foolish to neglect the negative side of life. In fact, negative psychology is of utmost importance to positive psychology. In order to effectively understand happiness, we must comprehend how people deal with the heartbreaks of life, as well as how they handle the good things that come their way. Seligman's call (1998) was not an encouragement to ignore the negative. Rather, it was a call for more research effort to be spent on the positive.

Some have also been concerned that the positive psychology movement has suffered from a lack of theory. Why is theory important to any scientific endeavor? Theories are meaningful because they help us grasp what research results mean. If a psychologist finds that thinking about one's own death makes one more racist, well, that's kind of interesting, but if that finding is specifically predicted by a theory, then the finding becomes much more significant. If there is a theory that predicts this relationship, the finding provides more validity to the theory, and it becomes not just an isolated curiosity, but also a finding that relates to a whole network of research that helps us understand how we tend to deny our mortality. Thus, some have felt that positive psychology researchers have launched into a whole series of study questions without any guiding theory. This criticism is largely valid but, to be fair, any new scientific endeavor usually suffers from a lack of theory. Of course, this is no excuse for not developing good theories about what makes people happy, but positive psychology is beginning to see new and exciting theoretical developments (Jayawickreme et al., 2012), and we will explore some of these theories later.

A related criticism is that some have been concerned that positive psychologists have jumped too quickly to investigating treatments designed to improve happiness. Because we are all interested in ways to improve our happiness, positive psychology researchers have moved rapidly to develop happiness interventions. This is understandable because people naturally want to know what will make them feel better. When we develop treatments without the guidance of theory, however, our investigations can largely be a waste of time. For example, I could investigate the "rock-chewing treatment of happiness." I could randomly assign people to either chewing rocks, or chewing gum, and see which group is happier at the end of treatment. Even if I find that chewing rocks increases your happiness more than chewing gum, what have we gained from this research? Well, you might say, now we can just get people to go out and wash up some rocks and chew them, and they'd be happier. And after all, this is a pretty inexpensive treatment (not accounting for dental bills, of course). But even if chewing rocks increases your happiness, what do we know about happiness now that we didn't know before? Not much, because the idea that chewing rocks increases your happiness has no theory behind it. So, while I do not blame positive psychologists for actively researching ways to increase happiness, there is much more to be gained from treatment studies that are grounded in theory. Thus, I believe that positive psychology needs to engage in more theory building, and more studies that test specific treatment interventions designed to change particular psychological mechanisms are necessary (e.g., see Watkins, Cruz, Holben, & Kolts, 2008, for a study that attempted to do this).

Perhaps one of the most frequently heard criticisms of positive psychology asks the question of whether we really want people to be happier. This is the *contented cow criticism* of positive psychology. A number of years ago, I was asked to present my research at a local business club meeting. Generally speaking, the response to my talk was very positive, but one young, successful businessman asked me a very pointed question. "If you could make everyone grateful, that would make them all happy," he observed, "and wouldn't that make them lazy because they wouldn't be motivated to get anything done?" That's a good question. What if we were able to develop effective happiness treatments that could make a large proportion of the world happy? Would that really be a good thing? If you're content with life, then you won't be motivated to work hard and you'll just sit around feeling like there's nothing more to be done. Well, the simple answer to this criticism is that it simply isn't true. Whereas it might make logical sense to you that if people are happy they will be less motivated to get things done, it doesn't make empirical sense. In fact, the research findings are so consistent that these are a major theme of this book: Study after study has found that happy people are active people. So the picture of the happy person sitting around like a contented cow just has no basis in reality. But the question itself does bring up a significant issue in positive psychology: Is happiness really a good thing?

WHY HAPPINESS? THE BENEFITS OF HAPPINESS

Why is this topic of happiness important? Should there even be a science of positive psychology? Psychological disorders only seem to be increasing; so why should students and researchers be interested in positive psychology? First, as I have discussed previously, psychological science has been overly biased toward the negative. Indeed, some have estimated that the negative bias in publications is more than 17:1 (Myers & Diener, 1995). Because we know that people experience positive emotion more frequently than negative states, this extreme negative bias is not reflective of human experience (Watkins, 2014). "Bad is stronger than good" was the conclusion of a classic contemporary review (Baumeister, Bratslavsky, Finkenauer, & Vohs, 2001). In general, people let bad emotions, bad events, bad feedback, and bad interactions drown out the good. Apparently, researchers also let the bad overshadow the good in their research emphasis. By focusing our research efforts more on the positive side of life, this should increase our understanding of how people can enhance their SWB.

Second, the study of happiness is important simply because people want it. Multiple studies have shown that happiness is a preeminent life goal for most people, and people overwhelmingly prefer a happy life (e.g., Diener, Suh, Smith, & Shao, 1995; King & Broyles, 1997; King & Napa, 1998). As William James so famously remarked, "How to gain, how to keep, how to recover happiness is in fact for most men the secret motive of all they do" (1902/1958, p. 76). Consequently, an important reason for studying happiness is simply that people want it, and they're very motivated to get it. But simply because you want something, doesn't necessarily mean that thing is good. Many people would like to see rivals removed from their lives, but that doesn't mean that getting rid of them is a good thing. Hence we're still left with the question: Is the pursuit of happiness really a good thing?

In a nutshell, studies overwhelmingly support the conclusion that it's good to be happy. Research shows that happiness itself is consequential. Many have complained that happiness is not a worthwhile research endeavor because it is simply the consequence of success. Although there is a grain of truth to this criticism, studies now clearly show that happiness itself is consequential; happiness *results* in success. The article that clearly demonstrated the consequential nature of happiness was written by Lyubomirsky, King, and Diener (2005), and I rely heavily on their results and conclusions. An adequate discussion of their review and all the investigations behind their conclusions is beyond the scope of this chapter; however, I would encourage readers to consult this piece frequently because the information contained in this review is really a gold mine for positive psychology researchers. Let me highlight here their most important conclusions.

Lyubomirsky et al. (2005) divided up their review into three sections representing different research designs: cross-sectional correlational, longitudinal, and experimental studies. In each case, the evidence strongly supported their hypothesis that frequent positive affect leads to success; nevertheless, I focus on the longitudinal and experimental studies, since they represent a stronger test of their theory. The summary results of the longitudinal studies are represented in Figure 1.1, and Figure 1.2 summarizes the results from experimental designs. In the longitudinal studies illustrated in Figure 1.1, happiness was measured and this score was used to predict various variables months or years later. As can be seen, happiness favorably predicted higher levels of occupational, relational, and health variables. In other words, these results suggest that happiness made people more successful at work, in their relationships, and in health. Although many of these studies did not control for these indices at the

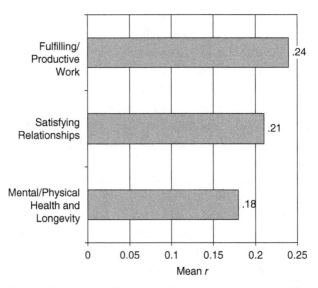

FIGURE 1.1 Summary effect sizes for impact of positive affect in longitudinal studies.

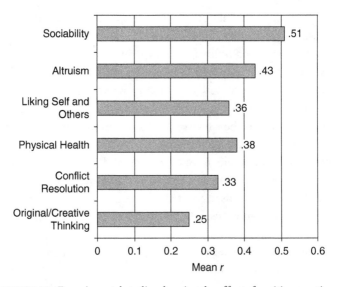

FIGURE 1.2 Experimental studies showing the effect of positive emotion.

initial assessment of happiness, this is strong evidence for the consequential nature of SWB.

It would be fun to explore all of these studies, but let me emphasize a few that I think are quite interesting. The so-called "yearbook study" has become a classic in positive psychology (Harker & Keltner, 2001). These researchers took the photographs of women from two college yearbooks (1958 and 1960), and coded each face as to how closely each woman was expressing a *Duchenne smile*. A Duchenne smile is a facial response that can be reliably coded by trained observers, and is indicative of genuine positive emotion. This smile is very difficult to fake, and so it's very likely that the women who showed Duchenne smiles were genuinely happy. Astonishingly, this exercise showed that women who appeared to be genuinely happy were more likely to be married by age 27, less likely to be single in middle adulthood, and demonstrated more marital stability and satisfaction some 30 years later.

Another longitudinal study suggests that experiencing positive emotion frequently (as happy people are prone to do) can actually help you live longer (Danner, Snowdon, & Friesen, 2001). This study is often referred to as "the nun study" because it followed the lives of a particular order of Roman Catholic nuns. Here the researchers had access to the spiritual autobiographies of the nuns (written in the 1930s), and they coded them for the proportion of positive emotion sentences. The positivity of the nuns' autobiographies predicted their longevity some six decades later. Figure 1.3 illustrates this amazing result. When the researchers divided up the autobiographies for positivity in quartiles, it can be seen that the more positive a nun was in the 1930s, the longer she lived. This graph shows that the most positive nuns lived almost 7 years longer than the least positive nuns. Interestingly, the negativity of the autobiographies did not predict longevity. Of course, one could complain that there's a problem with external validity here: The lifestyle of most nuns is not a typical

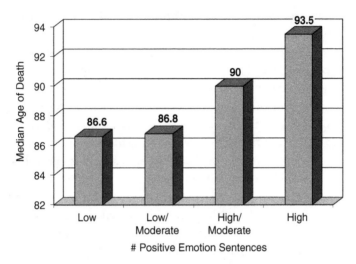

FIGURE 1.3 Longevity of nuns by the positivity of their spiritual autobiographies.

lifestyle. But this finding has been replicated in the writings of psychologists (Pressman & Cohen, 2012) and in the photographs of professional baseball players (Abel & Kruger, 2010), who can in no way be accused of living the lifestyle of nuns. There really do seem to be health advantages of happiness, supporting the biblical proverb: "A joyful heart is good medicine, but a crushed spirit dries up the bones" (Proverbs 17:22).

Now let us turn to the experimental studies that were reviewed by Lyubomirsky and colleagues (2005). Of course, we can't experimentally manipulate overall happiness levels in a laboratory, hence most of these experiments manipulated a person's immediate emotional state. Although this is not exactly happiness as I have defined it, it is a close analog to happiness because happiness is made up of frequent positive emotional experiences. Accordingly, I think that these experimental studies have a lot to say about how the frequent experience of positive emotions contributes to various forms of life success. Figure 1.2 summarizes these outcomes as reviewed by Lyubomirsky et al. (2005). Here again we see that the research strongly supports the idea that happiness results in a number of favorable characteristics.

Here I would like to highlight one of the studies that best represents experimental work in this area. Long before there was a positive psychology movement, Alice Isen started a research program investigating the effects of subtle positive affect. In a series of studies, she demonstrated that small inductions of positive emotion enhanced people's creative problem-solving ability (Isen, Daubman, & Nowicki, 1987). The results were particularly striking in one study. In Study 1 the researchers manipulated emotion using positive and neutral films. Then, participants were presented with Duncker's Candle Problem. This is a task that requires creative problem solving, where subjects are each given a box of tacks, a candle, and a book of matches. They are to attach the candle to the wall so that while it is burning, the candle won't drip wax on the floor. This problem can be solved by emptying the matchbox, tacking it to the corkboard (the wall), and then using the matchbox as a candleholder. How did positive emotion affect people's ability to solve this problem? The results of this study were striking, and can be seen in Figure 1.4. Those who were made to feel better were almost four times more likely to solve the problem correctly than those in the control conditions. Most experimental studies don't show such spectacular results; however, Figure 1.2 illustrates that experimental studies can demonstrate that happiness results in a number of desirable consequences. The advantage of these experimental designs is that we can make more confident assertions that happiness is indeed consequential; happiness causes a number of positive aspects of success.

We have seen that there is compelling evidence that happiness results in a number of beneficial consequences. But it is also true that there are beneficial circumstances that enhance happiness. Thus, along with Lyubomirsky and colleagues, I propose that happiness—or frequent positive affect—results in an *upward spiral*, a *cycle of virtue*, if you will. Figure 1.5 illustrates how this might work. As Lyubomirsky et al. (2005) clearly demonstrated, research shows that happiness results in beneficial consequences, namely that it encourages us to do things that build up our personal resources, and to engage in approach-oriented goals. In

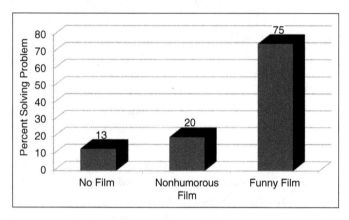

FIGURE 1.4 Positive emotion facilitates creative problem solving.

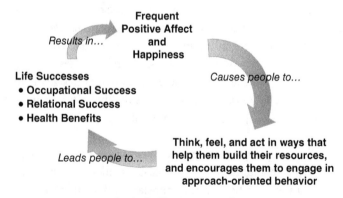

FIGURE 1.5 An upward spiral of happiness and success.

other words, when we're happy we approach things and people that are good for us (p. 804). This leads to various kinds of success: in our jobs, relationships, and mental and physical health. Successes like these result in more positive emotions and happiness, and so the spiral continues upward.

In sum, why should there be a positive psychology? Why should we study happiness? Very simply, because people want it and they want it for good reason. Research now provides compelling support for the idea that happiness has many beneficial consequences.

IMPORTANT THEORIES OF SUBJECTIVE WELL-BEING

He who loves practice without theory is like the sailor
who boards ship without a rudder and compass
and never knows where he may be cast.

Leonardo da Vinci

As explained earlier, one of the criticisms of positive psychology is that we have jumped too quickly to treatment, and where this criticism has been valid it is largely because we have failed to ground our treatments in theory. It is here where theory building becomes very important to positive psychology. There is something of a contradiction here because although some have complained about the lack of theory in positive psychology, others have criticized the multiplicity of theories. The truth probably lies somewhere between these two criticisms, but all would agree that good theories are important for any science to progress. Sometimes the word *theory* scares people off; however, a theory is simply a causal explanation of the relationship between two or more variables. Thus SWB theories essentially try to explain what *causes* SWB. What makes people happy is the primary concern for theories of SWB. Theories provide two critical functions. First, they provide an organizational framework for understanding research results on a particular topic. For example, there were numerous studies that had investigated *gratitude* prior to 2000, but nobody had bothered to try and make sense of those results. When McCullough, Kilpatrick, Emmons, and Larson presented their *moral affect theory of gratitude* (2001), much of this research became understandable and comprehensible. With this theory we could understand what the available research had to teach us about gratitude. But second, theories about SWB help direct future research. When we have a good theory about what causes SWB, then that theory should provide clear directions for our research, and meaningful predictions for how our explorations will turn out. In a nutshell, theories provide meaning to data, and that is why it is important to discuss notable theories of SWB. Data without theories are mere numbers. There are many useful theories of happiness, but rather than providing a comprehensive review, I am going to focus on two theories that I believe are both representative and helpful to the field of positive psychology: the Self-Determination Theory (SDT) and the Hedonic Adaptation Prevention (HAP) model.

Self-Determination Theory

Briefly, SDT (Niemiec & Ryan, 2013; Ryan & Deci, 2000) says that the more self-determined your life is, the happier and healthier you'll be. The Ryan and Deci concept of self-determination is closely related to their view of motivation. Why are you reading this book right now? What has motivated you to read this book? You might be reading it because your instructor required you to read it, and if you don't read it you'll flunk the test. But you just can't see how the information in this text relates to you and to what you really want in life (this is what Ryan and Deci call *externally regulated extrinsic motivation*). On the other hand, you could be reading this book because your instructor required it; however, you see how important it is to your education, and you see it as being important to what you really want in life (called *integrated regulation extrinsic motivation*). Finally, for some unknown reason you might be reading this book because you find the information *intrinsically interesting.* The information you are reading naturally seems to catch your interest, and you're reading the book because the reading itself is enjoyable (called *intrinsic motivation*). These examples highlight the different kinds of motivations posited by Ryan and Deci. The first example illustrates behavior that is really not very self-determined, the second example is somewhat more self-determined, and the intrinsically motivated reading is most self-determined. Essentially, *intrinsic motivation* is involved when we engage in activity because the activity is enjoyable in and of itself. On the other hand, *extrinsic motivation* is involved when we are doing something not because it is enjoyable in itself, but rather because it is instrumental to bringing us something else that we want. It would be nice if life was only filled with intrinsically motivated activities, but many activities that are needed in life require extrinsic motivation. Unless you're a very unusual student, not every course that you have taken in college has been enjoyable for you, but you probably realize that some courses need to be completed because you have a goal of attaining a college degree. Thus not all activities can be intrinsically motivated, but Ryan and Deci argue that extrinsically motivated activities can be more or less self-determined. The more self-determined an extrinsically motivated activity is, the more involved and interested we are in that activity, and this is more likely to lead to the successful completion of that activity. Accordingly, what promotes self-determination? Ryan and Deci argue that when three basic psychological needs are filled, we are more likely to be self-determined.

SDT proposes that there are three fundamental psychological needs that are "innate, essential, and universal" (Ryan & Deci, 2000, p. 74). Although there are a number of need-based theories of well-being that posit any number of psychological needs, I believe that SDT offers the most parsimonious account. SDT theorizes that there are three fundamental psychological needs: competence, autonomy, and relatedness. Ryan and Deci submit that all three basic needs must be satisfied or well-being will not be achieved. Just as individuals would not survive if they had enough water but no food, so eudaimonic well-being requires that all three basic needs be satisfied. To illustrate, research has shown that when feelings of *competence* are enhanced, this encourages intrinsic motivation. But the theory also argues that competence will not encourage intrinsic motivation unless it is accompanied by a sense of autonomy. By *autonomy* they mean that people think their engagement in the activity is self-determined; they don't feel forced to do the activity, rather they think the cause comes from within. Research has also shown that relatedness is a critical aspect of an extrinsically motivated activity becoming more self-determined. *Relatedness* refers to your feelings of acceptance of others, or how much you feel connected or belonging to others. If you feel accepted by those you're with, you are far more likely to participate in an activity that you don't find inherently enjoyable.

Simply stated, SDT argues that there are three fundamental needs that must be satisfied in order to be happy. When people feel competent in their life tasks, when they feel autonomous (that they're engaging in life activities because they want to, not because others are telling them what to do), and when they feel related to those they deem to be important in their lives, then they are likely to be happy. Research has provided considerable support for this theory, and SDT is important to understanding and explaining the many findings that we will explore in this book.

Hedonic Adaptation Prevention Model

Another theory important to understanding how SWB is
enhanced and maintained is called the HAP model, which grew
out of the authors' *Sustainable Happiness Model* (Lyubomirsky &
Layous, 2013; Lyubomirsky, Sheldon, & Schkade, 2005; Sheldon, Boehm, & Lyubomirsky, 2013). In creating their model,
these authors were primarily concerned with *sustained happiness*. These authors are not so concerned about what causes
your initial bump in happiness after moving into a new house.
Rather, they want to explain why most people have returned to
their initial state of happiness 2 years after the move. The theory
begins by creating a "happiness pie," so to speak, that is based
on past studies on happiness. First, research suggests that 50%
of this pie is probably determined by your genetics, which may
be reflected in certain stable personality traits. More about this
in Chapter 4, but for now it's important to see that what you
inherit from your parents does not produce a set point for your
happiness; rather, it is likely that genetics give us a set range
for happiness. Second, Lyubomirsky and colleagues (2005) and
Sheldon and associates (2013) point out that only about 10%
of your happiness is due to circumstances. Somewhat surprisingly, how much you earn, where you live, how old you are, and
your gender have little effect on your happiness (more about
this in Chapter 3). Why is this? Well, this is probably because
your circumstances are static, and are therefore prone to suffering from the psychological *law of hedonic adaptation*. It is a
well-founded principle in emotion research that we tend to
get used to—become adapted to—any static stimulus (Frijda,
1988, 2007). Anything that doesn't change over time, we tend
to get accustomed to and don't react to it the way we originally
did. Why doesn't my new house result in a permanent increase
in my happiness? Because for the most part, the house doesn't
change and I get used to it, which is why most people return

to their previous levels of happiness after the initial boost of excitement after a major purchase.

But this leaves about 40% of your happiness unexplained, and the HAP model argues that this proportion of your happiness is due to what they call *intentional activities*. According to this theory, intentional activities are less subject to hedonic adaptation, and thus are important in explaining an individual's sustained happiness. So if people want to increase their happiness, or live in the upper regions of their "happiness range," their best option is not to get a higher paying job, or to buy a new house, but to participate in *positive activities*. Positive activities are "simple, intentional, and regular practices" that are basically the activities that happy people engage in (Lyubomirsky & Layous, 2013, p. 57). Obviously this has real implications for designing treatments to increase happiness.

So after something happens that makes us happy, what maintains that boost of happiness, or what causes us to return to our previous level of happiness? The HAP model argues that hedonic adaptation has a critical role to play here. The HAP model posits there are two explanatory routes that help explain whether or not the happiness boost is maintained after a positive event. First, if something good happens to us, this might (or might not) increase the number of positive events in our lives; hence this should increase the positive emotions we experience as well, which would maintain (or even increase) our levels of SWB. There are some things, the HAP model asserts, that might encourage or discourage this route to maintaining our happiness boost, and engaging in surprise and variety are critical moderators. Positive activities that result from the original positive event may serve to enhance the variety that sustains happiness. Marriage is a positive event for most people, and for many it increases the number of positive events and emotions in their lives. Positive experiences of intimacy, shared leisure, and newfound companionship increase for many people, and thus the postmarital boost in well-being is sustained. If the marriage results in more arguments, more heartache, and more hostility, then obviously the individuals' marital bliss will not be maintained, and their happiness may even go down.

The other route to explaining whether or not happiness is sustained after a positive event involves increased aspirations. Often, when something good happens to us we increase our aspirations or expectations. If I get an article published, instead of simply enjoying the accomplishment, I may start increasing my expectations about my career ("I should get a raise now," "I should get a lot more publications," "I should become a famous psychologist"). Increasing expectations in the wake of a positive event greases the skids of adaptation, and makes it more likely that the boost in well-being that I experienced will not be maintained. But if I intentionally engage in appreciation of the positive event (a positive activity), then I won't tend to take it for granted, I won't believe that I am entitled to it, and more than likely my aspirations will not increase, thus preventing hedonic adaptation and encouraging sustained happiness.

In my view, the HAP model is an important development in positive psychology because, as we will see in Chapter 3, hedonic adaptation is one of the main enemies of happiness. Because positive emotions are critical to the positive psychology endeavor, I also describe Fredrickson's (1998, 2001) Broaden-and-Build Theory of positive emotions, but first let's examine just exactly what positive emotions are.

POSITIVE EMOTIONS AND THE BROADEN-AND-BUILD THEORY

One of the pillars of positive psychology is the study of positive states. Enduring happiness, of course, is one of the most important positive states that we study; nevertheless, the positive emotions that make up happiness are an important research endeavor for positive psychologists too. But first, before we discuss positive emotion, let's define emotion itself. I could spend a whole book discussing the issues and debates surrounding the definition of emotion; however, let me offer a brief definition so that this book doesn't end up being as long as *War and Peace*. You experience an emotion when you appraise an activating event, which then results in a psychophysiological response, which prepares us for certain modes of acting and thinking (called *thought/action readiness modes*). The feelings that we experience during an emotional response reflect the thought/action readiness mode that we are in. Appraisal refers to how we think about an activating event, and there are two levels at which this thinking takes place. First, we must appraise that the event is relevant to our goals or preferred states. Unless we deem that an event either furthers or frustrates our goals, an emotional response will not ensue. Second, if we think the event is important to us, then how we appraise the event determines the specific emotion that we experience. If I see a bear while hiking in Glacier National Park, I'm likely to think that this animal is dangerous to me (and just might frustrate my goal of staying alive), and I'll probably experience fear. If, on the other hand, I observe a bear in the Portland Zoo, I may instead think that I am safe in this situation. And because the sight of bears is fairly novel for me and I find the bear's behavior somewhat humorous, I may experience interest and amusement. It is important to note that appraisals may take place at various levels of consciousness and intentionality. An emotion may ensue after conscious deliberation about some event, but more than likely our emotions result from appraisals that are quick, automatic, and perhaps even unconscious.

So what makes an emotion positive or negative? Briefly, events that you think might satisfy or further your goals result in *positive emotions*, but events that you think signify frustrating or harming your goals result in *negative emotions*. In general, positive emotions feel pleasant whereas negative emotions feel unpleasant (although there is some debate about anger here). Research now suggests that positive and negative emotions may be mediated by two different brain systems (Gray, 1990, 1991). Although these brain systems tend to inhibit each other, because emotions are relatively short lived, how I'm feeling right now may tell me little if anything about how I'll be feeling tomorrow at this time. Indeed, research has shown that although positive and negative emotions are strongly and negatively correlated in the moment, over time the frequency of positive and negative emotions shows little relationship. In other words, if you're feeling good right now, it's very unlikely you're feeling bad too. But if I know that you have had a lot of positive experiences over the course of last month, that tells me very little about how many negative emotional experiences you have had. This is because the brain system that mediates your positive emotions is probably functionally independent from the brain system that mediates your negative emotions.

So we have seen that if you appraise an event as being conducive to your goals, you'll experience a positive emotion, but which one? Well, according to the appraisal approach, this depends on *how* you think this event is conducive to your goals. If you think that the event signifies that you are in a safe, familiar place, and are progressing well toward your goals, then you'll experience *joy*. When I was a junior professor I remember experiencing great joy when I found out that I had been awarded a National Institutes of Health (NIH) grant for my research. Now I experienced other positive emotions as well (notably pride and gratitude); however, finding out about this meant to me that I was likely to get tenure, I was likely to gain more respect from my colleagues, and I would have full financial support for two summers. Clearly, this event meant to me that I was progressing well toward my goals. If I think that my situation means that I am in a safe and *certain* place that doesn't require much activity, then I'm probably experiencing *contentment*. Often, when I sit on my front porch with a glass of good red wine after a fulfilling day of work, I feel contented. If I feel that I am in a safe place, but I think that there's something new about this situation that might be important to me, I'm experiencing the emotion of *interest*.

Hope is a very interesting positive emotion, because it arises in the context of a negative event. When I'm aware that something bad could result from an event but I believe that things could get better, I will experience the emotion of *hope*. This often happens when a loved one is suffering from a serious disease. We know that there might be a very bad outcome from the disease, but something about the situation suggests to us that things might get better for that person, and we experience hope. When I believe that I have achieved something that affirms my value, I'm likely to experience the emotion of *pride*. This emotion is probably intimately related to the basic psychological need of competence. If I encounter a situation where I feel that someone else has done something important for me, I will experience *gratitude*. You can see where this emotion is experienced in the context of satisfying the basic need of relatedness. When I received the good news about my NIH grant submission, I experienced both pride and gratitude: pride because I felt that I had achieved something important, but gratitude as well because I was very aware of all the people who contributed to the success of receiving this grant. Because we have gained a great deal in our understanding of gratitude, and research has shown its importance to the good life, a fair amount of space in this book is devoted to evaluating this emotion and virtue.

What about love? Is love a distinct emotional state? Whereas there is some debate about this question, I take the position that "love is a many splendored thing"; *love* actually comprises a constellation of positive emotions such as joy, interest, contentment, and gratitude—all focused on a particular person. One emotion that is often included in this list is compassion, and there is some

45

debate as to whether this should be viewed as a distinct emotion and if it is, if it should be included in the list of positive emotions. We experience *compassion* when we think someone is in need, and we want to help that person. Is this actually a pleasant experience? Well, I think this is a complex question that deserves much discussion. Since compassion is one of the emotions that positive psychologists have endeavored to study, I think it is important that we include it in our list here. Clearly, it is an emotion important to love. Moreover, just because I take the position that love is not a distinct positive emotion does not mean that it should be off limits for positive psychologists. As we'll see, love is very important to well-being, and has been identified as one of the six primary categories of human strengths (Peterson & Seligman, 2004).

The functionality of negative emotions is pretty obvious; if I experience fear in the context of real danger, it motivates and prepares me to escape the danger, thus enhancing the likelihood of my gene pool continuing. But it is not so obvious as to how positive emotions help us survive, and this is where Barbara Fredrickson's Broaden-and-Build Theory of positive emotions becomes important (Fredrickson, 1998, 2001). For me, her theory was crucial to the development of positive psychology, and now many of the basic tenets of her model have garnered empirical support (for a review, see Conway, Tugade, Catalino, & Fredrickson, 2013).

In this theory, Fredrickson explains clearly how positive emotions help us live well. According to this approach, positive emotions are functional in two basic ways: They *broaden* our momentary thought/action readiness, and they *build* personal resources that are important for living well in the future. Essentially, she is arguing that positive emotions benefit us in the present and for the future.

First, let's explore how positive emotions broaden our thought/action repertoire in the present. Whereas negative emotions tend to be focused (e.g., on the perceived threat in the environment), and motivate us to fix what is wrong, positive emotions tend to broaden our thought/action readiness. Fredrickson argues that positive emotions broaden our thought/action readiness in at least three ways: They broaden our scope of attention, of cognition, and of action. First, when we experience a positive emotion it tends to broaden our scope of attention because research shows that we are more likely to attend to many aspects of the situation and look more at the big picture rather than the details of a circumstance (e.g., Fredrickson & Branigan, 2005; Isaacowitz, 2005; Johnson, Waugh, & Fredrickson, 2010; Wadlinger & Isaacowitz, 2006). Whereas negative emotions focus our attention on what is wrong with a situation, in positive emotional states we are more likely to attentionally explore the many aspects of a situation.

Second, positive emotions broaden our scope of cognition. By this, Fredrickson means that positive emotions tend to help us think outside of the box, so to speak. Isen (1987, p. 222) explains this effect well, "Positive affect gives rise to an enlarged cognitive context." Research has shown that when we are encouraged to be in a positive mood, we tend to be more creative, we use more flexible cognitive categories, and we are better able to process information in an integrated but flexible manner (Isen, 1987; for a review of this research, see Conway et al., 2013).

Third, positive emotions help us in the moment because they broaden our scope of action. In other words, when we're in a positive emotional state, we're more likely to want to think and act in a number of different ways, compared to when we're in a negative state. Fredrickson (2004) used the example of gratitude and indebtedness to illustrate this point (gratitude being a positive and indebtedness a negative emotion). When we are grateful for what someone has done for us, we want to do something for them. But there is a whole array of things that we might think about to enhance our benefactor's well-being. On the other hand, when we feel indebted (or obligated to repay), more than

47

likely we're in a tit-for-tat mode of thinking, and we'll probably attempt to repay our benefactor in exactly the same way that we were benefited. Indeed, we found that this is one thing that distinguishes gratitude and indebtedness (Watkins, Scheer, Ovnicek, & Kolts, 2006).

Not only are positive emotions adaptive in that they broaden our momentary thought/action readiness, they also build important personal resources for the future. Fredrickson (1998, 2001) proposes that positive emotions build three important personal resources: physical, intellectual, and social. Positive emotions build our physical resources because they often motivate activity (e.g., play) that then should improve coordination and physical fitness. Positive emotions also may have the ability to undo the adverse physical effects of negative emotions, and research like the "nun study" that we examined earlier suggests that positive emotions may provide other benefits for our physical health (Danner et al., 2001). Next, because positive emotions can broaden one's scope of cognition, this might build intellectual resources in such a way that improves problem solving and coping for the future. Finally, positive emotions may build social resources. Research across a variety of areas in psychology has shown that people enjoy spending time with happy people, and tend to avoid those who are depressed. As Myers (1992, p. 20) summed up the data, "Misery may love company, but company doesn't love misery." Thus, if people enjoy being with happy people, it is likely that people who experience and express positive emotions frequently will have more stable and supportive relationships and, in fact, research shows that this is the case (see Chapter 5). Research has now provided promising evidence that experiencing positive emotions does indeed build resources such as resilience, and traits like resilience create more positive emotions, thus resulting in an upward spiral (Fredrickson, Cohn, Coffey, Pek, & Finkel, 2008; Fredrickson, Tugade, Waugh, & Larkin, 2003).

In short, positive emotions are a crucial element in positive psychology and, indeed, they are an important area of study in psychology as a whole. Positive emotions are not simply the by-product of success in life; research now shows that they have important consequences for living well. Fredrickson's Broaden-and-Build theory has provided a useful framework and explanation for how positive emotions are adaptive. She argues that positive emotions broaden our momentary thought/action readiness, and this builds personal resources that are important for living well.

RESEARCH IN POSITIVE PSYCHOLOGY

Because positive psychology is committed to the scientific study of the good life, it is important that we investigate what the scientific enterprise in this area is like. In this brief overview, I will try to give you a snapshot of research in positive psychology from a methodological point of view. Because most of the empirical work has been in some way related to SWB, my focus is on characterizing this research. Prior to Diener, Suh, Lucas, and Smith's benchmark review of SWB in 1999, research in SWB was understandably dominated by correlational designs. Happiness—at least in terms of a more stable positive hedonic tone—cannot be reasonably manipulated in the laboratory, and so studies relied on measuring SWB along with other variables to investigate how they might be related. Most of these designs have used a cross-sectional format, measuring all the variables at one point in time. Whereas this research was very helpful as we began to explore well-being, there are of course many well-known problems with this approach. For instance, personal goals have often been found to correlate positively with happiness, with the natural implication that if one develops meaningful goals in life, this could improve happiness. But of course, the finding that goals and well-being are related can just as easily be interpreted as supporting the theory that happy people tend to create more goals for themselves. Or it could even be a third variable that is producing the association. To illustrate, it could be that optimism creates both happiness and the creation of goals somewhat independently, rendering the relationship between goals and happiness somewhat uninteresting. Although correlational designs will continue to be used in positive psychology, in my judgment most areas of research should move beyond this methodology.

Prospective designs, although still essentially correlational, offer a more informative approach to understanding what factors might enhance well-being. In this method, researchers measure variables at two points in time. The goal is to see what variables might predict changes in well-being over time. The length of these studies varies somewhat, but is often constrained to the length of the semester or the quarter that the student subjects are in. Usually some predictor variable is measured at Time 1 along with the relevant well-being variable, and then these measures are administered again at Time 2 sometime later. The Time 1 predictor variable is then associated with the Time 2 well-being measure while controlling for Time 1 assessments of well-being. This allows us to see how the predictor variable at Time 1 predicts changes in well-being at Time 2. For example, recently we measured variables we thought might inhibit gratitude along with gratitude at two time points 2 months apart. We found that cynicism and narcissism inhibited the growth of gratitude over time (Watkins, Solom, McCurrach, & Hutchison, 2014). These designs are very useful for investigating factors that might enhance or inhibit SWB but because of their correlational nature, questions regarding causation will remain.

The research design that most clearly demonstrates causation is the *true experimental design*, and in the last decade positive psychology researchers have increasingly turned to this approach.

Typically in these designs, research participants are randomly assigned to one of several conditions, and then some well-being measure is assessed. Often, because happiness as defined here is more stable and traitlike in nature, some analog of happiness or the well-being construct at issue is assessed. So for example, when we first began using experimental paradigms to investigate whether gratitude enhanced happiness, we would randomly assign some participants to a gratitude condition (e.g., thinking about someone you are grateful for), and others to some control condition, and then measure changes in positive emotion (see, e.g., studies 3 and 4 of Watkins, Woodward, Stone, & Kolts, 2003). If the predicted increases in positive emotions are seen in the gratitude conditions compared to the control conditions, this is then seen as an analog for happiness because happiness is made up of frequent experiences of positive emotions.

Other studies, however, have used more rigorous experimental designs to actually test whether certain variables can enhance SWB over time. These studies often use the gold standard in medical and clinical psychology, randomized controlled trials (RCTs). In RCTs participants are first assessed with the well-being outcome measure of interest, then they are randomly assigned to one of several treatment conditions. At least one of these treatment conditions contains the specific positive psychology intervention of interest, and another treatment condition consists of a placebo. After the treatment phase, well-being is measured again, and in some studies well-being is measured at several follow-up assessments later. Perhaps the best example of such a study was conducted by Seligman, Steen, Park, and Peterson (2005). In this online study participants were randomly assigned to either the placebo condition (recalling early memories), or one of several positive psychology interventions. In studies such as these, it is important that the placebo condition actually reveals a placebo effect—an increase in well-being over the treatment phase—so that we can demonstrate that the positive psychology intervention actually outperforms placebo effects. Indeed, Selgman et al. demonstrated a significant increase in SWB over the treatment phase in the placebo group, but several of the positive psychology interventions outperformed the placebo group. Notably, some of the positive psychology treatments continued to show increases in SWB after the treatment had ended, and we have found this in some of our studies as well (Watkins et al., 2008; Watkins, Uhder, & Pichinevskiy, 2015). Thus it would seem prudent for positive psychology researchers using RCTs or other treatment outcome designs to assess outcome not just at the end of treatment, but at one or more follow-up assessments as well. I predict that the use of experimental designs will continue to increase in positive psychology research, and at present I believe that these are the designs of choice. Of course, the design one chooses must ultimately depend on the investigator's research question, so one cannot indiscriminately apply the experimental method to any research issue.

For any research endeavor to progress, one must be able to accurately measure the variable of interest, and this is no exception in research pertaining to SWB. Hence the issue of accurately measuring SWB is paramount in positive psychology research. There are now entire books devoted to the measurement of positive psychology variables (e.g., Lopez & Snyder, 2003), so clearly it is beyond the scope of this chapter to cover all of these issues. Here, I limit my brief discussion of this topic to the measurement of SWB.

Any discussion of the measurement of happiness or SWB must be guided by two questions: First, what is the definition of SWB? Second, what is the research question about SWB that one is pursuing? We have explored the first question previously, and I have argued for Diener and colleagues' (1999) approach: High SWB is the frequent experience of positive affect, infrequent negative affect, and judgments about life satisfaction. Whereas other approaches to hedonic well-being have made interesting contributions (e.g., Cummins, 2013), the arguments for these alternatives are not compelling and in general do not seem to result in any pragmatic changes as to how SWB should be measured. Although there are many happiness measures to choose from (an excellent selection can be found at the website for the Australian Centre on Quality of Life: www.deakin.edu.au/research/acqol/instruments/instrument.php), following the suggestion of Diener and colleagues (1999), one can use a measure of positive and negative affect, along with the Satisfaction with Life Scale (SWLS) to effectively measure SWB. In our research, we often use the PANAS (Watson et al., 1988), along with the SWLS (Diener, Emmons, Larsen, & Griffin, 1985). The negative affect scale of the PANAS is reverse-scored; we create Z-scores of each scale, and then add them to form a composite measure. One advantage of using the PANAS is that different time frames can be used. For one researcher, assessing momentary emotions may be more important; for others, inquiring about affect experienced during the last week may be more appropriate to their research question. One criticism of the PANAS is that it tends to assess only high-activation positive and negative emotions; thus some may choose to use the PANAS-X, which also includes subscales for more subtle emotions.

Of course, to this point I have begged the question about self-reporting one's own happiness. Although many of the well-known problems with self-report certainly apply to measures of happiness as well, it appears that the large majority of adults would have the capacity to report their own happiness. The problem with self-report measures usually comes when we ask our subjects to report on psychological processes that they do not have the ability to report on (such as nonconscious processes or traits like humility). But with happiness, who is best able to report on one's happiness but oneself? Thus, if any one mode of measurement is used, I would recommend self-report (Cummins, 2013). But if a thorough assessment of SWB is desired,

Diener and colleagues (1999) suggest multimodal assessment including informant measures and indirect measures of well-being such as life-event recall. As I close this section, remember there are several principles in the final analysis that must guide one's choice of SWB measures: one's view of SWB, the research question being investigated, and the practical limitations of the research setting.

SUMMARIZING THE FOUNDATIONS OF POSITIVE PSYCHOLOGY

In this chapter I have attempted to explain the foundations of positive psychology. We have looked at basic conceptions of happiness and SWB including all the debates therein, we have explored the history of happiness along with the lessons it has taught us, we have debated the criticisms of positive psychology, we have examined important theories of SWB and positive emotion, and finally I have attempted to give you a taste of research in positive psychology. Hopefully, now I have provided you with a solid foundation of positive psychology. However, the most significant goal of this chapter is to demonstrate the importance of the study of happiness and SWB. We have seen that SWB is not simply the result of success in life, indeed happiness is consequential: It results in important outcomes for living well. In general, happy people appear to be more successful in many areas of life, and happiness may even result in a longer life. Moreover, as Fredrickson's theory has shown us (1998, 2001), positive emotions are crucial, in that they broaden our momentary thought/action readiness and build essential personal resources for the future. Happiness and joy are consequential, as Helen Keller affirmed, "Joy is the holy fire that keeps our purpose warm and our intelligence aglow."

REFERENCES

Abel, E. K., & Kruger, M. L. (2010). Smile intensity in photographs predicts longevity. *Psychological Science, 21*, 542–544.

Baumeister, R. F., Bratslavsky, E., Finkenauer, C., & Vohs, K. D. (2001). Bad is stronger than good. *Review of General Psychology, 5*, 323–370.

Biswas-Diener, R., Kashdan, T. B., & King, L. A. (2009). Two traditions of happiness research, not two distinct types of happiness. *Journal of Positive Psychology, 4*, 208–211.

Chesterton, G. K. (1990). *Saint Francis of Assisi.* New York, NY: Doubleday. (Original work published 1924)

Compton, W. C., & Hoffman, E. (2013). *Positive psychology: The science of happiness and flourishing* (2nd ed.). Belmont, CA: Wadsworth.

Conway, A. M., Tugade, M., Catalino, L. I., & Fredrickson, B. L. (2013). The broaden-and-build theory of positive emotions: Form, function, and mechanisms. In S. A. David, I. Boniwell, & A. Conley Ayers (Eds.), *The Oxford handbook of happiness* (pp. 17–34). Oxford, England: Oxford University Press.

Cummins, R. A. (2013). Measuring happiness and subjective well-being. In S. A. David, I. Boniwell, & A. Conley Ayers (Eds.), *The Oxford handbook of happiness* (pp. 185–200). Oxford, England: Oxford University Press.

Danner, D., Snowdon, D. A., & Friesen, W. V. (2001). Positive emotions in early life and longevity: Findings from the nun study. *Journal of Personality and Social Psychology, 80*, 804–813.

Diener, E., & Diener, C. (1996). Most people are happy. *Psychological Science, 7*, 181–185.

Diener, E., Emmons, R. A., Larsen, R. J., & Griffin, S. (1985). The Satisfaction with Life Scale. *Journal of Personality and Social Psychology, 49*, 71–75.

Diener, E., Sandvik, E., & Pavot, W. (1991). Happiness is the frequency, not the intensity, of positive versus negative affect. In F. Strack, M. Argyle, & N. Schwarz (Eds.), *Subjective well-being: An interdisciplinary perspective.* Elmsford, NY: Pergamon Press.

Diener, E., Suh, E. M., Lucas, R. E., & Smith, H. L. (1999). Subjective well-being: Three decades of progress. *Psychological Bulletin, 125*, 276–302.

Diener, E., Suh, E. M., Smith, H. L., & Shao, L. (1995). National differences in reported well-being: Why do they occur? *Social Indicators Research, 34,* 7–32.

Fredrickson, B. L. (1998). What good are positive emotions [Special issue]? *Review of General Psychology: New Directions in Research on Emotion, 2*(3), 300–319.

Fredrickson, B. L. (2001). The role of positive emotions in positive psychology: The broaden-and-build theory of positive emotions. *American Psychologist, 56,* 218–226.

Fredrickson, B. L. (2004). Gratitude, like other positive emotions, broadens and builds. In R. A. Emmons & M. E. McCullough (Eds.), *The psychology of gratitude* (pp. 145–166). New York, NY: Oxford University Press.

Fredrickson, B. L., & Branigan, C. (2005). Positive emotions broaden the scope of attention and thought-action repertoires. *Cognition and Emotion, 19,* 313–332. doi:10.1080/02699930441000238

Fredrickson, B. L., Cohn, M. A., Coffey, K. A., Pek, J., & Finkel, S. M. (2008). Open hearts build lives: Positive emotions, induced through loving-kindness meditation, build consequential personal resources. *Journal of Personality and Social Psychology, 95,* 1045–1062.

Fredrickson, B. L., Tugade, M. M., Waugh, C. E., & Larkin, G. (2003). What good are positive emotions in crises? A prospective study of resilience and emotions following the terrorist attacks on the United States on September 11, 2001. *Journal of Personality and Social Psychology, 84,* 365–376.

Frijda, N. H. (1988). The laws of emotion. *American Psychologist, 43,* 349–358.

Frijda, N. H. (2007). *The laws of emotion.* Mahwah, NJ: Lawrence Erlbaum.

Gray, J. A. (1990). Brain systems that mediate both emotion and cognition. *Cognition and Emotion, 4,* 269–288.

Gray, J. A. (1991). The neuropsychology of temperament. In J. Strelau & A. Angleitner (Eds.), *Explorations in temperament: International perspectives on theory and measurement.* New York, NY: Plenum Press.

Harker, L., & Keltner, D. (2001). Expressions of positive emotions in women's college yearbook pictures and their relationship to personality and life outcomes across adulthood. *Journal of Personality and Social Psychology, 80*, 112–124.

Haybron, D. M. (2008). Philosophy and the science of subjective well-being. In M. Eid & R. J. Larson (Eds.), *The science of subjective well-being* (pp. 17–43). New York, NY: Guilford Press.

Honderich, T. (Ed.). (1995). *The Oxford companion to philosophy.* New York, NY: Oxford University Press.

Isaacowitz, D. M. (2005). The gaze of the optimist. *Personality and Social Psychology Bulletin, 31*, 407–415.

Isen, A. M. (1987). Positive affect, cognitive processes, and social behavior. *Advances in Experimental Social Psychology, 20*, 203–253.

Isen, A. M., Daubman, K. A., & Nowicki, G. P. (1987). Positive affect facilitates creative problem solving. *Journal of Personality and Social Psychology, 52*, 1122–1131.

James, W. (1958). *Varieties of religious experience.* New York, NY: Mentor Books. (Original work published 1902)

Jayawickreme, E., Forgeard, M. J. C., & Seligman, M. E. P. (2012). The engine of well-being. *Review of General Psychology, 16*, 327–342.

Johnson, K. J., Waugh, C. E., & Fredrickson, B. L. (2010). Smile to see the forest: Facially expressed emotions broaden cognition. *Cognition and Emotion, 24*, 299–321.

Kashdan, T. B., Biswas-Diener, R., & King, L. A. (2008). Reconsidering happiness: The costs of distinguishing between hedonics and eudaimonia. *Journal of Positive Psychology, 3*, 219–233.

Kesebir, P., & Diener, E. (2008). The pursuit of happiness: Empirical answers to philosophical questions. *Perspectives on Psychological Science, 3*, 117–125.

King, L. A., & Broyles, S. J. (1997). Wishes, gender, personality, and well-being. *Journal of Personality, 65*, 49–76.

King, L. A., & Napa, C. N. (1998). What makes a life good? *Journal of Personality and Social Psychology, 75*, 156–165.

Kristjansson, K. (2010). Positive psychology, happiness, and virtue: The troublesome conceptual issues. *Review of General Psychology, 14*, 296–310.

Lee, Y., Lin, Y., Huang, C., & Fredrickson, B. L. (2013). The construct and measurement of peace of mind. *Journal of Happiness Studies, 14*, 571–590.

Lopez, S. J., & Snyder, C. R. (2003). *Positive psychological assessment: A handbook of models and measures.* Washington, DC: American Psychological Association.

Lyubomirsky, S., King, L., & Diener, E. (2005). The benefits of frequent positive affect: Does happiness lead to success? *Psychological Bulletin, 131,* 803–855.

Lyubomirsky, S., & Layous, K. (2013). How do simple activities increase well-being? *Current Directions in Psychological Science, 22,* 57–62.

Lyubomirsky, S., Sheldon, K. M., & Schkade, D. (2005). Pursuing happiness: The architecture of sustainable change. *Review of General Psychology, 9,* 111–131.

Maslow, A. (1954). *Motivation and personality.* New York, NY: Harper & Row.

Maslow, A. (1996). The psychology of happiness. In E. Hoffman (Ed.), *Future visions: The unpublished papers of Abraham Maslow* (pp. 21–25). Thousand Oaks, CA: Sage.

McCullough, M. E., Kilpatrick, S. D., Emmons, R. A., & Larson, D. B. (2001). Gratitude as moral affect. *Psychological Bulletin, 127,* 249–266.

McMahon, D. M. (2006). *Happiness: A history.* New York, NY: Grove Press.

McMahon, D. M. (2008). The pursuit of happiness in history. In M. Eid & R. J. Larson (Eds.), *The science of subjective well-being* (pp. 80–96). New York, NY: Guilford Press.

Mill, J. S. (1972). *Utilitarianism, liberty, representative government.* New York, NY: E. P. Dutton.

Mischel, W., Shoda, Y., & Peake, P. K. (1988). The nature of adolescent competencies predicted by preschool delay of gratification. *Journal of Personality and Social Psychology, 54,* 687–696.

Mischel, W., Shoda, Y., & Rodriguez, M. L. (1989). Delay of gratification in children. *Science, 244,* 933–938.

Myers, D. G. (1992). *The pursuit of happiness: Discovering the pathway to fulfillment, well-being, and enduring personal joy.* New York, NY: Avon Books.

Myers, D. G., & Diener, E. (1995). Who is happy? *Psychological Science, 6,* 10–18.

Niemiec, C. P., & Ryan, R. M. (2013). What makes a life well lived? Autonomy and its relation to full functioning and organismic wellness. In S. A. David, I. Boniwell, & A. C. Aters (Eds.), *The Oxford handbook of happiness* (pp. 214–226). Oxford, England: Oxford University Press.

Nozick, R. (1974). *Anarchy, state, and utopia*. New York, NY: Basic Books.

Peterson, C. (2006). *A primer in positive psychology*. New York, NY: Oxford University Press.

Peterson, C., & Seligman, M. E. P. (2004). *Character strengths and virtues: A handbook and classification*. Washington, DC: American Psychological Association, and New York, NY: Oxford University Press.

Pressman, S. D., & Cohen, S. (2012). Positive emotion word use and longevity in famous deceased psychologists. *Health Psychology, 31*, 297–305. doi:10.1037/a0025339

Ryan, R. M., & Deci, E. L. (2000). Self-determination theory and the facilitations of intrinsic motivation, social development, and well-being. *American Psychologist, 55*, 68–78.

Seligman, M. E. P. (1998). Positive social science. *APA Monitor, 29*(4), 2, 5.

Seligman, M. E. P. (2002). *Authentic happiness*. New York, NY: Free Press.

Seligman, M. E. P., & Csikszentmihalyi, M. (2000). Positive psychology: An introduction. *American Psychologist, 55*, 5–14.

Seligman, M. E. P., Steen, T. A., Park, N., & Peterson, C. (2005). Positive psychology progress: Empirical validation of interventions. *American Psychologist, 60*, 410–421.

Sheldon, K. M., Boehm, J. K., & Lyubomirsky, S. (2013). Variety is the spice of happiness: The hedonic adaptation prevention (HAP) model. In S. A. David, I. Boniwell, & A. C. Aters (Eds.), *The Oxford handbook of happiness* (pp. 901–914). Oxford, England: Oxford University Press.

Snyder, C. R., Lopez, S. J., & Pedrotti, J. T. (2011). *Positive psychology: The scientific and practical explorations of human strengths* (2nd ed.). Los Angeles, CA: Sage.

Tsai, J. L., Knutson, B., & Fung, H. H. (2006). Cultural variation in affect valuation. *Journal of Personality and Social Psychology, 90*, 288–307.

Wadlinger, H. A., & Isaacowitz, D. M. (2006). Positive mood broadens visual attention to positive stimuli. *Motivation and Emotion, 30*, 87–99.

Watkins, P. C. (2002). Implicit memory bias in depression. *Cognition and Emotion, 16*, 381–402.

Watkins, P. C. (2014). *Gratitude and the good life: Toward a psychology of appreciation*. Dordrecht, The Netherlands: Springer.

Watkins, P. C., Cruz, L., Holben, H., & Kolts, R. L. (2008). Taking care of business? Grateful processing of unpleasant memories. *Journal of Positive Psychology, 3,* 87–99.

Watkins, P. C., Martin, C. K., & Stern, L. D. (2000). Unconscious memory bias in depression: Perceptual and conceptual processes. *Journal of Abnormal Psychology, 109,* 282–289.

Watkins, P. C., Scheer, J., Ovnicek, M., & Kolts, R. (2006). The debt of gratitude: Dissociating gratitude from indebtedness. *Cognition and Emotion, 20,* 217–241.

Watkins, P. C., Solom, R., McCurrach, D., & Hutchison, D. E. (2014, May). *Narcissism and cynicism inhibit gratitude: A prospective study*. Poster presented at the meeting of the Annual Convention of the Association for Psychological Science, San Francisco, CA.

Watkins, P. C., Uhder, J., & Pichinevskiy, S. (2015). Grateful recounting enhances subjective well-being: The importance of grateful processing. *Journal of Positive Psychology, 2,* 91–98.

Watkins, P. C., Woodward, K., Stone, T., & Kolts, R. (2003). Gratitude and happiness: Development of a measure of gratitude, and relationships with subjective well-being. *Social Behavior and Personality, 31,* 431–452.

Watson, D., Clark, L. A., & Tellegen, A. (1988). Development and validation of brief measures of positive and negative affect: The PANAS scales. *Journal of Personality and Social Psychology, 54,* 1063–1070.

Cataloging the Good Life: The Strengths of Happiness

erhaps one of the most notorious classification systems in science is the *Diagnostic and Statistical Manual of Mental Disorders* (*DSM*). Published by the American Psychiatric Association (APA), the *DSM* is now in its fifth iteration (APA, 2013), and each new edition seems to agitate more controversy. The *DSM* is essentially a catalog of human vice and psychic suffering. Of course, something like this is needed if we are to treat the specific needs of those suffering from psychological illness, but if we have a catalog of human vice, why not one of human virtue? The *DSM* has assisted us in understanding human suffering and how to treat it. Wouldn't an un-*DSM*—a classification system for human strengths—provide the impetus and structure for understanding what is good about human character? Wouldn't an un-*DSM* help us focus on the character that helps us thrive? An un-*DSM* would be no replacement for the *DSM*; however, it might provide the means for systematically developing our comprehension of the strengths of human character. Thus the development of a useful classification system of human strengths became one of the primary tasks of the fledgling positive psychology movement. In this chapter we explore positive psychology's attempt to identify significant human virtues.

Early in the positive psychology movement it was recognized that in order to advance research on human excellence, there was a need to develop a classification system complete with measurable strengths that would be meaningful to the good life (Peterson, 2006). The late Chris Peterson was charged with leading this mission, and it was soon called the Values in Action (VIA) project. In Peterson's words, "Among the most critical tools for positive psychologists are a vocabulary for speaking about the good life and assessment strategies for investigating its components" (2006, p. 137).

The first step was to investigate whether all virtues were culture-bound—socially constructed moral characteristics that are culture-specific—or to see if some virtues transcend culture (Dahlsgaard, Peterson, & Seligman, 2005). These scholars conducted extensive reviews of primary sources related to Confucian, Taoist, Buddhist, Hindu, Platonic and Aristotelian, Christian, Jewish, and Islamic virtues. The result of this literature review was that "Particular core virtues recurred with a sort of pleasant tenacity" (p. 210). Although different traditions emphasized different virtues, nearly all of these writings endorsed six core virtues: courage, justice, humanity/love, temperance, wisdom, and transcendence. In order for this research team to recognize a human strength, the strength or virtue had to meet 12 criteria: ubiquitous (cross-cultural), fulfilling (contribute to the life well lived), morally valued (the strength is valued in and of itself, not as a means to some other goal), not diminishing to others, possess a nonfelicitous opposite (each virtue has an opposite vice; Peterson, 2006, p. 141), traitlike (is fairly stable over time), measurable, distinct, has paragons (certain people are excellent examples of each strength), has prodigies (is shown by some youth early), can be absent in some people, and has enabling institutions. In my view, the four most crucial criteria are ubiquity, fulfilling, morally valued, and traitlike. Furthermore, this team of notable scholars also identified examples or paths to each of the six virtues, which they referred to as human strengths (Dahlsgaard et al., 2005; Peterson, 2006). It is important to note that Peterson viewed these strengths as dimensions. In other words, it's not that people either have or don't have a strength, but rather we all fall somewhere on the dimension of this strength. This is in contrast to the general approach of the *DSM* that follows a more categorical model; you either have a disorder or you don't. This work finally led to the publishing of the un-*DSM*, called *Character Strengths and Virtues: A Handbook and Classification* (Peterson & Seligman, 2004). Finally, the VIA project developed an assessment tool for the human strengths, the VIA Inventory of Strengths (VIA-IS), which I discuss in more detail later. In the remainder of this chapter, I describe and define the six core virtues, and also explore some of the more specific human strengths thought to be clustered with each virtue. After this discussion we explore how these human strengths are related to subjective well-being (SWB), in part answering the question: "Are these strengths indeed fulfilling?"

VIRTUES OF THE GOOD LIFE

In the following paragraphs I describe the six core virtues identified by the VIA project, along with the human strengths that are deemed to be examples of these virtues. Although space constraints prohibit a thorough review of the research related to each of these strengths, for each virtue I present some representative findings.

Wisdom

The strengths of wisdom are commonly referred to as *cognitive strengths* because they involve the good use of reason and thinking. These are positive traits that involve the effective use of knowledge to live a more fulfilling life. Not only are people who measure high in the virtue of wisdom able to acquire information important to the good life, they can also *use* this information to enhance their well-being. We all know people who possess a great deal of knowledge but can't seem to use it to solve life's critical dilemmas. These individuals probably rank low in the virtue of wisdom. In many traditions—most notably the Athenian tradition of Plato and Aristotle—wisdom was viewed as the preeminent virtue. The example strengths of the virtue of wisdom are:

- *Creativity*—thinking outside the box in new ways to solve problems and accomplish things in life
- *Curiosity*—finding interest in most of the things and topics encountered in life
- *Love of learning*—those with this strength love to learn new things, including new skills
- *Open-mindedness*—these people tend to resist drawing conclusions too quickly; rather they try to look at an issue from all sides and are able to change their minds if they think they were wrong
- *Perspective*—people with perspective are able to see the big picture; they're able to observe how different aspects of a situation relate to each other in a way that helps them accurately view the complete picture of a situation

I think you can see how these strengths relate to each other and are likely to overlap. For example, a curious person is also likely to be someone who loves to learn. Similarly, individuals may tend to be open-minded because they have a good sense of perspective. Probably the strength that most closely relates to what we think of as a wise person is perspective, and my guess is that this strength will prove to be more and more essential in the coming years as we are continually overwhelmed with information. People with perspective should be able to clearly see what information is important—and what is not. Wisdom is clearly a virtue that has been venerated cross-culturally and across the ages, and thus we would expect it to be related to SWB. Indeed, cross-sectional studies have found that wisdom positively correlates with happiness (e.g., Ardelt, 1997), and one longitudinal study found that it predicted increased well-being over a period of 10 years (Hartman, 2000). But to be fair, evidence that wisdom actually *causes* increased SWB is admittedly weak. This may be due in part to the difficulty in measuring wisdom (Peterson & Seligman, 2004); nevertheless, I look forward to new studies investigating whether wisdom can be trained, and whether it actually enhances one's happiness.

Courage

Although courage has always been venerated because of the importance of this virtue for those who protect the community, the surprise comes when we see that there are strengths beyond the warrior-mentality strengths that we might typically think of as falling under the virtue of courage. As we will see, strengths of courage are not limited to bravery in battle. Peterson (2006, p. 143) captures the essence of courage well: Courage is the ability ". . . to accomplish goals in the face of opposition." The VIA project has identified the strengths of courage as:

- *Bravery*—"The ability to do what needs to be done despite fear" (Peterson & Seligman, 2004, p. 199)
- *Persistence* (or perseverance)—the capacity to finish what you start, despite whatever adversity or obstacles might be encountered
- *Integrity* (authenticity or honesty)—the skill to be true to yourself and true to others, presenting yourself to others in a genuine way that is not pretentious
- *Vitality* (or zest)—adeptness at being able to approach life tasks and activities with vigor and excitement

I want to highlight how courage is a virtue that can be displayed—and is still valuable today—in nonbattle situations. With the strength of bravery, where courageousness in battle is the prototype of this strength, speaking out against a prevailing attitude or protecting another from a bully can be seen as a clear act of bravery. Some might wonder how persistence and integrity are strengths of courage. Nonetheless, I think that Michael Jordan—persisting in his pursuit of basketball despite being cut from his high school basketball team—can be seen as an example of courage. It takes courage to keep going even when confronted with failure, and with all successful pursuits we are going to encounter some failure and disappointments along the way. Similarly, with integrity it takes courage to present yourself in a way that is authentic (i.e., true to yourself), although you know that what you're standing for may not be approved of by others. In this context, I believe it's important to point out that going against public opinion may not be so courageous if it doesn't cost you something in your immediate social circle. I have several colleagues who believe that they are taking a courageous stance on a particular social issue. And although they may be running against the tide of general public opinion in the United States, their viewpoints fit in quite nicely with the general atmosphere of my university. For me, this is not a good example of integrity. The authors of the VIA emphasize that integrity entails owning and taking responsibility for one's presentation of oneself. Although "just sayin'" may be an accurate presentation of one's feelings, in my view it is an attempt to disown the consequences of the statement, hence failing to be a good example of integrity.

A good modern example of bravery is the act of whistle-blowing (identifying unethical behavior in an organization, even when costly consequences result). Interestingly, much like the Milgram (1963) obedience experiments, demographics such as gender, marital status, and religiosity had no impact on whether or not one was willing to whistle-blow (Rothschild & Miethe, 1999). These researchers did find that the older you tend to be, the more willing you might be to whistle-blow. As with other strengths (and vices), there seems to be a social facilitation effect with bravery. The more your social group engages in courageous behavior, the more it seems to inspire you to act likewise (Haidt, 2000; Rachman, 1990). Students and researchers interested in pursuing bravery research (which might be a courageous endeavor itself) should also consult the classic work of Rachman (1990).

Interesting research has also revealed the benefits of persistence that may indicate how this is a fulfilling strength. Following cognitive dissonance theory (Festinger, 1957), classic studies like those of Aronson and Mills (1959) have shown that the more you endure hardships and difficulties with a task, the more you'll appreciate the task (and particularly the outcome). Of course, the important caveat here is that you actually complete the task, and this is where the strength of persistence becomes crucial. The more you can persist with difficult tasks, the more you'll end up completing and enjoying them, which bodes well for a fulfilling life.

There are of course questions about the structure of this virtue. For instance, if authenticity and persistence are indeed strengths of courage, some studies suggest that the strengths of hope and kindness also have components of courage (Pury & Lopez, 2009). More questions arise about the strength of vitality. Although this strength typically shows the strongest correlations with SWB of any of the VIA strengths, one has to wonder if this isn't simply another way to measure happiness. Indeed, in the un-*DSM* recommendations for the measurement of vitality and zest, most of the suggested instruments are approximations of SWB. At best, one might wonder if zest is more a consequence of happiness rather than a cause. On the other hand, I can see how approaching difficult tasks with enthusiasm can be seen as virtuous in its own right; nevertheless, I wonder if this is something rather distinct from the more general trait of vitality. Peterson and Seligman (2004) suggest that vitality may end up being the virtuous way in which human strengths are employed, and this idea seems to have some traction. For example, one who is persistent in a virtuous way does so with a kind of enthusiastic vitality, not with extrinsic drudgery.

As one might imagine, research on the virtue of courage is sorely lacking, and my brief review of studies does not come close to doing these strengths justice. Those interested in pursuing research in this area would be wise to consult the work of Peterson and Seligman (2004) and Pury and Lopez (2009) for a much more comprehensive introduction into this critical area of investigation.

Humanity

Also referred to as the strengths of *love*, the qualities included under this virtue can be described as *interpersonal strengths*. As Peterson (2006) emphasized, "other people matter," and the strengths of love pick up this theme. The strengths of humanity are:

- *Love*—the ability to live well in reciprocal one-to-one relationships
- *Kindness* (compassion, altruism)—the disposition to be concerned with and to act in ways to enhance others' welfare
- *Social intelligence*—the capacity to process emotional and social information accurately and efficiently

Much of the research about love has followed the attachment tradition, showing that *securely attached individuals* have significant advantages in their relationships and in life (Mikulincer & Shaver, 2013). There is also a rich tradition of research showing that happy people tend to engage in more altruistic behavior, and *giving* in turn appears to enhance happiness. The emotional intelligence aspect of social intelligence also appears to have a number of advantages for well-being (Crum & Salovey, 2013). In sum, interpersonal strengths appear to be vital to well-being. They are so vital, in fact, that an entire chapter is spent on the importance of relationships to happiness (Chapter 5).

Justice

Whereas the strengths of humanity are other-oriented abilities in one-to-one relationships, the strengths of justice relate to interpersonal skills in larger social settings (one-to-many relationships). The VIA project has identified the following as the strengths of justice:

- *Leadership*—the ability to encourage a group to accomplish its task(s) while fostering good working relationships among group members

- *Fairness*—the skill to treat others in a similar manner, despite personal likes and biases
- *Loyalty* (citizenship or teamwork)—being loyal to a group or team in such a way that helps you work effectively in the group

Although there is some question as to whether these strengths are distinct from the strengths of humanity, there is no question that these traits have been valued across time and culture. For me, some of the most intriguing research results come from the leadership literature. A number of studies show the powerful effects that effective leadership can have on an organization (Peterson & Seligman, 2004). It appears that the strengths of justice may be more distinct than those of the other virtues, in that they are not as highly correlated with each other. To illustrate, it is easy to see how the strengths of love and kindness would mutually support each other, and it is hard to see how someone who is loving cannot be kind. Alternatively, it is much easier to imagine someone who is an effective leader but may not be particularly strong in fairness.

Temperance

The strengths of temperance are essentially strengths of *moderation*. We all know people who have ruined their lives because they have overindulged in the pleasures of the moment. People with strengths of temperance understand that short-term gain may result in long-term pain and, conversely, they are willing to endure some short-term pain to achieve long-term gain. In a way, temperance protects us from giving in to temptations that might harm us. The VIA strengths of temperance are:

- *Self-regulation* (self-control)—the ability to regulate your emotional and behavioral responses

- *Prudence*—being careful and smart about your choices in a way that enhances the likelihood of obtaining long-term goals
- *Forgiveness* (mercy)—not holding the wrongs from others against them and refraining from revenge
- *Humility and modesty*—the capacity to acknowledge and accept your weaknesses and limitations, as well as your strengths

Perhaps the master strength of the temperance traits is self-regulation. If you can't regulate your emotions and behaviors, it's unlikely you'll be able to forgive, be humble, or be prudent. All of these strengths may be seen as protectors against some rather unsavory characteristics. For example, forgiveness protects us against hatred; prudence protects us from thoughtlessness; self-regulation protects us from emotional excess and indulgence; and humility protects us against arrogance. Humility has proven to be one of the most difficult strengths to investigate, and that is largely because of the difficulty in measuring this construct. You can't just ask people how humble they think they are. One is reminded of the joke where the man was given a ribbon for humility at the church picnic. Sadly, the ribbon was taken away when he wore it. Recently, however, there has been some progress in the development of self-report humility measures (Davis et al., 2011; Exline & Hill, 2012; Powers, Nam, Rowatt, & Hill, 2007). In fact, humility was found to be a trait perhaps worthy of an addition to the Big Five personality traits (Ashton & Lee, 2005), and research has found that humility is positively correlated with measures of SWB (e.g., Uhder, Watkins, & Hammamoto, 2010).

Whereas research into humility seems to be just getting under way, forgiveness has been the focus of several intensive research programs. Although this research shows promising evidence that forgiveness is a highly adaptive trait (Enright,

2012; McCullough, 2000; McCullough, Root, Tabak, & Witvliet, 2009), most of the findings are cross-sectional and correlational in nature, and thus more prospective and experimental studies are needed (Peterson & Seligman, 2004). Whereas several experimental treatment outcome studies have shown that forgiveness treatments enhance well-being, they used no-treatment controls. Thus, it is difficult to conclude from these studies that the outcome was specifically due to the forgiveness treatment or to nonspecific treatment effects. Research in this area has flourished, however, and I expect to see more exciting results regarding forgiveness in the future.

It is easy to conclude that the strengths of temperance are somewhat dated and old-fashioned. But I propose quite the contrary: I believe that as technology continues to invade our lives, these virtues will become more and more essential to well-being. One of the main functions of technology is to shorten the time between felt needs or wants, and the satisfaction of these needs and desires. For instance, whereas in the past families often spent two or more hours preparing dinner, now, with the help of the microwave, most dinners can be ready in less than five minutes. As technology continues to shorten the time between the activation and the satisfaction of desires, it seems that we have become less able to delay gratification. In short, we are much less patient than we used to be. However, as Walter Mischel's research clearly shows (Mischel, Shoda, & Peake, 1988; Mischel, Shoda, & Rodriguez, 1989), the ability to delay gratification is important to a number of different areas of life success. In the future, individuals who have the capacity to delay gratification may be particularly able to achieve their long-term goals and greater success in life. The virtues of temperance are essentially strengths of patience—traits that help us delay gratification. Thus the strengths of temperance may be particularly important in modern life.

Transcendence

The strengths of transcendence help individuals develop connections to something above and beyond themselves. All of these traits help you to see and reach for realities greater than yourself. The VIA strengths of transcendence are:

- *Religiousness/spirituality*—the ability to see a higher purpose and meaning in your life; being able to see the sacred in the universe
- *Hope*—the skill to see a positive future for your life and develop a way to achieve that future
- *Gratitude*—the capability to see and affirm the good that others contribute to your life, and making sure that you express your thanks
- *Appreciation of beauty and excellence*—the trait of noticing and appreciating beauty and excellence
- *Humor*—the capacity to see the funny side of life (both in oneself and in others); enjoying laughter and the ability to make others laugh as well

This might appear to be a kind of "garbage can" category—a group of strengths put together because we can't quite figure out how to categorize them—but I believe that this virtue has some coherence. All of these strengths help us get beyond ourselves; they help us get beyond the self-preoccupation that can so easily drag us down. Whereas this might seem to be a virtue that is somewhat of an afterthought, there is actually quite a bit of research on these strengths. The least amount of research appears to be devoted to the appreciation of beauty and excellence, although even here new measures and research programs have been developed (e.g., Diessner, Iyer, Smith, & Haidt, 2013; Diessner, Solom, Frost, Parsons, & Davidson, 2008). Much more research has been devoted to the other strengths. The *psychology of religion* has a long and rich history in psychology, and I devote considerable space to describing the relationship between religiosity and well-being in Chapter 4. One of the interesting stories in positive psychology is the development of a research program in the *psychology of hope* by the late Rick Snyder (Snyder, 2000; for a more recent review of hope literature, see Rand & Cheavens, 2009), and the significance of hope and optimism to SWB is covered in some depth in Chapter 4.

Many have identified the strength of gratitude as one of the success stories of the positive psychology movement (Watkins, 2014). Before 2000, there was scant research on this state and trait, but now research on gratitude is flourishing and it has been identified as one of the critical components of the good life (Watkins, van Gelder, & Frias, 2009). The trait of gratitude is strongly correlated with measures of SWB, and experimental studies have shown that gratitude interventions enhance happiness (for reviews, see Watkins, 2014; Watkins et al., 2009). Although concerns have been raised about early investigations using control conditions that might have decreased well-being (Wood, Froh, & Geraghty, 2010), a recent study showed that a gratitude intervention outperformed a placebo condition that also enhanced SWB (Watkins, Uhder, & Pichinevskiy; 2015). Furthermore, this study showed the significance of grateful processing of positive events. In other words, it wasn't simply the recollection of positive events that was increasing SWB; this research demonstrated that *grateful thinking* about those events was crucial. Research in this area has now turned to the mechanisms of the gratitude/SWB relationship, attempting to answer the question: *How* does gratitude enhance well-being? I have argued that gratitude encourages happiness by amplifying the good in one's life (Watkins, 2008, 2014) and, indeed, gratitude does seem to amplify the good in your social world (Algoe, 2012), in your coping ability (Watkins, Cruz, Holben, & Kolts, 2008), and in your thinking (Watkins et al., 2015). In my view, however, the success of gratitude interventions has led to an overestimation of the potential of gratitude. Particularly in the popular press, gratitude has been promoted as something of a panacea—an elixir for all that ails you. Because of my own work in this area and the surprising number of benefits that seem to result from gratitude, I would be the first to argue for the good of gratitude. But when any trait or practice—whether it be mindfulness or gratitude—is promoted as *the* treatment for permanent happiness and well-being, we ought to be skeptical. What I have observed is that people start arguing that gratitude results in every benefit that you might want and then, in order to support this argument, gratitude starts becoming everything that is good. When this happens, gratitude loses its meaning and essential character, and paradoxically we end up depriving gratitude of its real power. Although this should serve as a warning to gratitude and positive psychology researchers alike, I should be quick to emphasize that gratitude is still an exciting area of research and I look forward to further development of the science of gratitude (for more information about gratitude, see Chapters 4 and 7).

Perhaps the most curious member of the strengths of transcendence is *humor*. Why should humor be something that helps us get beyond ourselves? But that is just what effective humor does: It breaks us out of our usual way of thinking about things, and may help us see larger, different realities (Earleywine, 2011). Whereas humor has somewhat of a complicated relationship with SWB—clearly there are healthy and unhealthy types of humor—I submit that healthy forms of humor should prove to be more fulfilling. I would like to propose that one of the healthiest forms of humor might be the ability to laugh at oneself. If I can laugh at my frailties and missteps, this should help me to acknowledge and accept my weaknesses, and in turn this should help me break out of my self-preoccupation. The capacity to be able to laugh at oneself may be a critical component of humility, and I look forward to more research on healthy expressions of humor.

VIRTUES, STRENGTHS, AND HAPPINESS

One of the critical prerequisites for the VIA strengths and virtues is that they should be fulfilling. In other words, if they are indeed virtues of the good life, they should contribute to a happy and flourishing life. In short, using your strengths effectively should make you a happier person. How are the VIA strengths and virtues related to well-being? In this section I review research that has investigated this question. The research that I consider here is largely limited by the fact that fairly straightforward self-report measures in cross-sectional studies were used. But I still believe these studies are informative as to the relative contribution of the different strengths to the good life.

Research shows that two dimensions or factors tend to characterize the VIA strengths: head versus heart strengths, and self versus other strengths (Peterson & Park, 2009). Thus all strengths fall somewhere in this two-dimensional space. For example, gratitude, kindness, and love fall in the heart and other-oriented quadrant, whereas the strengths of perspective and open-mindedness fall in the mind and self-oriented quadrant. In general, studies have confirmed that strengths of the heart are more predictive of SWB, and of these, hope, gratitude, love, and zest show the most robust correlations with happiness (e.g., Buschor, Proyer, & Ruch, 2013; Park, Peterson, & Seligman, 2004; Proyer, Gander, Wellenzohn, & Ruch, 2013; Toner, Haslam, Robinson, & Williams, 2012; for reviews, see Niemiec, 2013; Peterson & Park, 2009). Interestingly, the strength of curiosity often shows strong correlations with SWB. Whereas one might think of this as a strength of the mind rather than heart, studies show that curiosity is slightly more a strength of the heart than mind. This is an interesting finding and although it does not fit well with the VIA structure of strengths, the relationship between curiosity and other strengths deserves more research attention. Curiosity (perhaps like zest) may be more of a consequence than a cause of happiness.

The notion of strengths and virtues as proposed by the authors of the VIA project states that all strengths are fulfilling. Thus one might reasonably predict that all strengths should show some positive association with measures of happiness. Although generally speaking this prediction has borne out, there are several strengths that show low or even no correlations with happiness. To illustrate, several studies have shown that creativity, open-mindedness, and the appreciation of beauty show low and inconsistent relationships with SWB (Park & Peterson, 2008; Park et al., 2004). These findings bring interesting challenges to the VIA model, but one could argue that these strengths result in forms of flourishing that may not be reflected in SWB. Alternatively, all of these efforts tend to suffer from the possibility of inflated correlations due to method invariance. In other words, self-report measures of the virtues may simply reflect the same positivity bias that is seen in self-report measures of SWB.

Another criticism of these studies is that they are all cross-sectional and correlational. Thus, correlations between gratitude and SWB, for example, might mean that gratitude enhances happiness; it might mean that happiness promotes gratitude; it might be a reciprocal relationship between gratitude and happiness (gratitude causes happiness but happiness in turn creates more gratitude); and it could be that a third variable has created a spurious relationship between gratitude and happiness. The state of affairs in this regard calls for more prospective studies: studies that investigate whether the strengths can predict future increases in happiness. One study accomplished this aim in an adolescent population (Gillham et al., 2011) and found that other-oriented strengths (e.g., kindness and teamwork) predicted decreases in depression, and transcendence strengths (meaning, love, zest, and gratitude) predicted the greatest increases in life satisfaction over time. With the exception of their leadership strengths, the other virtue factors also predicted increases in life satisfaction. This provides some support for the VIA model of strengths and virtues; nevertheless, we need many more longitudinal studies of this kind to confirm that strengths actually promote future well-being.

The eudaimonic approach to happiness emphasizes that it is not simply having virtues that enhances happiness. More importantly, this approach argues that happy persons effectively use their strengths in their lives, and this produces happiness. One study investigated this theory with a 6-month prospective design (Wood, Linley, Maltby, Kashdan, & Hurling, 2011). They found that self-reports of the use of strengths predicted increases in SWB at both 3- and 6-month assessments. These findings provide promising evidence that understanding and using your strengths can encourage your happiness. Stronger evidence comes from a major randomized controlled trial (RCT) where participants in the active treatment condition were encouraged to find a new way each day for using their strengths (Seligman, Steen, Park, & Peterson, 2005). This was a daily treatment that was accomplished for 1 week. The treatment showed greater increases in SWB than the placebo condition even 6 months after treatment. The one major issue with this study is that we cannot really be sure that these individuals were actually using their strengths; nonetheless, these are impressive findings and more treatment outcome studies on the use of strengths are needed.

VICES OF THE VIRTUES: CRITICISMS OF THE VALUES IN ACTION PROJECT

It is perhaps no surprise that a secular approach to identifying culturally transcendent virtues has come under considerable criticism. The concerns largely fall into two categories: structural/

conceptual and measurement criticisms. First, does the original structure and conception of the virtues of the VIA project hold up to empirical examination? Second, are the current measurement instruments used to measure the VIA strengths adequate? Both of these issues are explored in this section.

Although the authors of the VIA project stated that the structure of strengths and virtues was intended to be a conceptual rather than an empirical organization, if particular strengths are indeed related to a particular virtue, one would think that those strengths would cluster together empirically. Of the many studies that have attempted to evaluate this structure with the VIA-IS and similar instruments, the original VIA organization has not been replicated and no two studies have found the same structure of strengths. Even the number—let alone the content—of the factors varies from study to study, with most studies finding four or five clusters (factors), but one finding only three (Shryack, Steger, Krueger, & Kallie, 2010). Because of the apparent inconsistency of results it is difficult to draw any general conclusions, but a few regularities in the results stand out. First, most studies reveal some factors that appear to be similar to the proposed VIA structure. Cognitive strengths tend to cluster together in a factor that appears to be like the wisdom virtue; strengths of self-restraint cluster as the temperance virtue; and usually something similar to the transcendence factor emerges. A second conclusion is that the humanity and justice strengths tend to cluster as one factor, a pattern of results that was predicted by Peterson (2006). Remember that the humanity and love strengths were characterized as one-to-one or one-to-few social abilities, whereas the justice strengths are better characterized as one-to-many social traits. Thus both are virtues related to your ability to connect to others, so it is not surprising that empirically these strengths cluster into one interpersonal factor. In short, although much research and conceptual development went into the original VIA structure, this organization has only partly been supported (Gillham et al.,

2011; McGrath, 2014; Peterson & Park, 2009; Shyrack et al., 2010; Toner et al., 2012). Nonetheless, the original organization of the un-*DSM* has provided a very helpful starting point for the field.

The structure of the VIA strengths has taken something of a beating by the data but virtually all of these studies used the VIA-IS, which is a self-report measure of strengths. Perhaps there is a more fundamental issue here that is producing problems in our results. Maybe the problem is in self-report—after all, how reasonable is it to ask people to report on their strengths? Surely we all want to believe that we are good people full of virtue, so wouldn't we be biased to reporting ourselves to be abundantly virtuous? Indeed, research has found that the VIA-IS is nega- tively skewed, meaning that most people report that they are on the upper end of the scales. Peterson (2006) argues that we rely on people's self-reports on their pathology, why not on their strengths? Speaking from a clinical point of view, I believe there is something qualitatively different about reporting your strug- gles versus your strengths. It is precisely because we would rather not admit that we're struggling, that when people say that they are depressed or stressed out, we tend to believe them. None- theless, there isn't a great deal of empirical support behind my suspicions. And, undoubtedly, it is easier for individuals to self- report about some strengths as opposed to others. For example, it is probably a lot easier for individuals to make judgments about their self-control than their humility. Would you trust a person who claims to be humble?

In this regard there may be problems with specific items of the VIA-IS. For instance, one of the items on the forgiveness scale reads: "I always allow others to leave their mistakes in the past and make a fresh start." Is anyone really like that? Those familiar with the Minnesota Multiphasic Personality Inventory (MMPI) might say that would make a good lie-scale item—anyone endorsing that statement is probably not telling the truth (or at best is quite defensive). There may also be problems with the reliability of the scales. Although for the most part the scales that tap the 24 strengths seem to have adequate internal consistency, at times the internal consistency is unacceptable (e.g., .48; Toner et al., 2012), and reliability seems to vary quite a bit from study to study. Moreover, adequate internal consistency may not be enough when it comes to what these scales are trying to accomplish. The purpose of these scales is for each scale to tap only one strength (i.e., they're unidimensional), but some studies have questioned whether some of the scales really are tapping just one strength. Indeed, some scales seem to show quite an overlap with other scales (e.g., McGrath, 2014). One of the problems with the VIA-IS is that each strength has 10 items to measure this strength. Surely, certain strengths (such as modesty and humility) are more difficult to measure than others, so one wonders about the wisdom of this limitation. Specific strengths may require more (or fewer) items than other strengths.

That being said, there is much to be said in support of the VIA-IS, and I believe that this is still the most efficient assessment of human strengths available. It is probably the best instrument to use if you are trying to measure the full breadth of human strengths, and particularly if you are interested in looking at how the strengths compare against each other. If, however, you are interested in a particular strength such as gratitude or humility, I would recommend the more specific instruments that have been designed to measure these traits.

CONCLUSIONS: THE FUTURE OF THE VIRTUES

It is perhaps an unfortunate scholarly tradition that we tend to end our articles and chapters with the downside of our topic: criticisms and limitations of our conclusions. I have followed this tradition in this chapter and my fear is that it might overshadow the significant accomplishments of positive psychology's attempt to study virtue. I believe that the most significant achievement of the VIA project was to identify virtues and strengths that appear to transcend time and culture. This was a significant endeavor because, in it, psychology as a discipline needed to be transcended as well. As I conclude this chapter I would like to emphasize and recommend two other attempts to identify transcendent virtues that come from outside of psychology. The works of C. S. Lewis (1944/2001) and André Comte-Sponville (2001) are notable in that they show good conceptual agreement with the VIA project (Park et al., 2004). These books are substantive but delightful reads, and the agreement is worthy of note in that one author was a theist and the other an atheist—more affirmation from very divergent worldviews that there are common morals and virtues that humanity has extolled across time and culture. Lewis referred to these emergent virtues as the "Tao" and in the appendix of this work he provides ample examples of these moral laws from diverse sources. As we conclude this rather incomplete primer of the qualities of the good life, I would like to emphasize one other aspect of Lewis's approach that I believe deserves more research attention in psychology. Not only did Lewis argue that there were certain ubiquitous moral principles to the life well lived, he also argued that these virtues need to be kept in balance. In other words, it is not enough to just be compassionate; one must also respect the other principles of the Tao. To emphasize one virtue without the others is bound to result in an imbalanced life. Particular virtues often become trendy and popular, at the risk of ignoring other key virtues. As I now write, gratitude and compassion seem to be all the rage, and my concern is that by overly focusing on these virtues we may end up with a very unbalanced picture of the good life. By emphasizing a balanced approach to the strengths of the good life, we can counteract problems that may result from exclusively emphasizing one virtue (cf. Peterson & Park, 2009). For example, when compassion is lifted up as *the* transcendent virtue, self-control may suffer. When gratitude is touted as *the* way to happiness, we may lose perspective. Gratitude and compassion are very important to the good life; however, when we also emphasize strengths such as prudence, humility, self-control, and integrity, we are much more likely to flourish.

REFERENCES

Algoe, S. B. (2012). Find, remind, and bind: The functions of gratitude in everyday relationships. *Social and Personality Psychology Compass, 6*, 455–469.

American Psychiatric Association. (2013). *Diagnostic and statistical manual of mental disorders* (5th ed.). Washington, DC: American Psychiatric Publishing.

Ardelt, M. (1997). Wisdom and life satisfaction in old age. *Journal of Gerontology: Psychological Sciences, 52B*, 15–27.

Aronson, E., & Mills, J. (1959). The effect of severity of initiation on liking for a group. *Journal of Abnormal and Social Psychology, 59*, 177–181.

Ashton, M. C., & Lee, K. (2005). Honesty-humility, the big five, and the five-factor model. *Journal of Personality, 73*, 1321–1354.

Buschor, C., Proyer, R. T., & Ruch, W. (2013). Self- and peer-rated character strengths: How do they relate to satisfaction with life and orientations to happiness? *Journal of Positive Psychology, 8*, 116–127.

Comte-Sponville, A. (2001). *A small treatise on the great virtues.* New York, NY: Henry Holt.

Crum, A. J., & Salovey, P. (2013). Emotionally intelligent happiness. In S. A. David, I. Boniwell, & A. C. Aters (Eds.), *The Oxford handbook of happiness* (pp. 73–87). Oxford, England: Oxford University Press.

Dahlsgaard, K., Peterson, C., & Seligman, M. E. P. (2005). Shared virtue: The convergence of valued human strengths across culture and history. *Review of General Psychology, 9*, 203–213.

Davis, D. E., Hook, J. N., Worthington, E. L., Van Tongeren, D. R., Gartner, A. L., Jennings, D. J., & Emmons, R. A. (2011). Relational humility: Conceptualizing and measuring humility as a personality judgment. *Journal of Personality Assessment, 93,* 225–234.

Diessner, R., Iyer, R., Smith, M. M., & Haidt, J. M. (2013). Who engages with moral beauty? *Journal of Moral Education, 42,* 139–163.

Diessner, R., Solom, R. C., Frost, N. K., Parsons, L., & Davidson, J. (2008). Engagement with beauty: Appreciating natural, artistic, and moral beauty. *Journal of Psychology: Interdisciplinary and Applied, 142,* 303–329.

Earleywine, M. (2011). *Humor 101.* New York, NY: Springer Publishing Company.

Enright, R. D. (2012). *The forgiving life: A pathway to overcoming resentment and creating a legacy of love.* Washington, DC: American Psychological Association.

Exline, J. J., & Hill, P. C. (2012). Humility: A consistent and robust predictor of generosity. *Journal of Positive Psychology, 7,* 208–218.

Festinger, L. (1957). *A theory of cognitive dissonance.* Evanston, IL: Rowe & Peterson.

Gillham, J., Adams-Deutsch, Z., Werner, J., Reivich, K., Coulter-Heindl, V., Linkins, M., . . . Seligman, M. E. P. (2011). Character strengths predict subjective well-being during adolescence. *Journal of Positive Psychology, 6,* 31–44.

Haidt, J. (2000). The positive emotion of elevation. *Prevention and Treatment, 3*(3). Retrieved from http://journals.apa.org/prevention/volume3/pre0030003c.html

Lewis, C. S. (2001). *The abolition of man.* New York, NY: HarperCollins. (Original work published 1944)

McCullough, M. E. (2000). Forgiveness as human strength: Theory, measurement, and links to well-being. *Journal of Social and Clinical Psychology, 19,* 43–55.

McCullough, M. E., Root, L. M., Tabak, B. A. & Witvliet, C. (2009). Forgiveness. In S. J. Lopez & C. R. Snyder (Eds.), *Oxford handbook of positive psychology* (pp. 427–436). New York, NY: Oxford University Press.

McGrath, R. E. (2014). Scale- and item-level factor analysis of the VIA inventory of strengths. *Assessment, 21,* 4–14.

Mikulincer, M., & Shaver, P. R. (2013). Adult attachment and happiness: Individual differences in the experience and consequences of positive emotions. In S. A. David, I. Boniwell, & A. C. Aters (Eds.), *The Oxford handbook of happiness* (pp. 834–846). Oxford, England: Oxford University Press.

Milgram, S. (1963). Behavioral study of obedience. *Journal of Abnormal and Social Psychology, 67*, 371–378.

Mischel, W., Shoda, Y., & Peake, P. K. (1988). The nature of adolescent competencies predicted by preschool delay of gratification. *Journal of Personality and Social Psychology, 54*, 687–696.

Mischel, W., Shoda, Y., & Rodriguez, M. L. (1989). Delay of gratification in children. *Science, 244*, 933–938.

Park, N., & Peterson, C. (2008). The cultivation of character strengths. In M. Ferrari & G. Poworowski (Eds.), *Teaching for wisdom* (pp. 57–75). Mahwah, NJ: Erlbaum.

Park, N., Peterson, C., & Seligman, M. E. P. (2004). Strengths of character and well-being. *Journal of Social and Clinical Psychology, 23*, 603–619.

Peterson, C. (2006). *A primer in positive psychology.* New York, NY: Oxford University Press.

Peterson, C., & Park, N. (2009). Classifying and measuring strengths of character. In R. Snyder & S. Lopez (Eds.), *Oxford handbook of positive psychology* (2nd ed., pp. 25–33). New York, NY: Oxford University Press.

Peterson, C., & Seligman, M. E. P. (2004). *Character strengths and virtues: A handbook and classification.* Washington, DC: American Psychological Association, and New York, NY: Oxford University Press.

Powers, C., Nam, R. K., Rowatt, W. C., & Hill, P. C. (2007). Associations between humility, spiritual transcendence, and forgiveness. *Research in the Social Scientific Study of Religion, 18*, 75–94.

Proyer, R. T., Gander, F., Wellenzohn, S., & Ruch, W. (2013). What good are character strengths beyond subjective well-being? The contribution of the good character on self-reported health-oriented behavior, physical fitness, and the subjective health status. *Journal of Positive Psychology, 8*, 222–232.

Pury, C. L. S., & Lopez, S. J. (2009). Courage. In S. J. Lopez & C. R. Snyder (Eds.), *Oxford handbook of positive psychology* (2nd ed., pp. 375–382). New York, NY: Oxford University Press.

Rachman, S. J. (1990). *Fear and courage* (2nd ed.). New York, NY: W. H. Freeman.

Rand, K. L., & Cheavens, J. S. (2009). Hope theory. In S. J. Lopez & C. R. Snyder (Eds.), *Oxford handbook of positive psychology* (2nd ed., pp. 323–334). New York, NY: Oxford University Press.

Rothschild, J., & Miethe, T. D. (1999). Whistle-blower disclosures and management retaliation: The battle to control information about organization corruption. *Work and Occupation, 26,* 107–128.

Seligman, M. E. P., Steen, T. A., Park, N., & Peterson, C. (2005). Positive psychology progress: Empirical validation of interventions. *American Psychologist, 60,* 410–421.

Shryack, J., Steger, M. F., Krueger, R. F., & Kallie, C. S. (2010). The structure of virtue: An empirical investigation of the dimensions of the virtues in action inventory of strengths. *Personality and Individual Differences, 48,* 714–719.

Snyder, C. R. (2000). *Handbook of hope: Theory, measures, and applications.* San Diego, CA: Academic Press.

Toner, E., Haslam, N., Robinson, J., & Williams, P. (2012). Character strengths and well-being in adolescence: Structure and correlates of the Values in Action Inventory of Strengths for Children. *Personality and Individual Differences, 52,* 637–642.

Uhder, J., Watkins, P. C., & Hammamoto, D. (2010, August). *Would the humble please stand: Can self-reported humility be valid?* Paper presented at the Annual Convention of the American Psychological Association, San Diego, CA.

Watkins, P. C. (2008). Gratitude: The amplifier of blessing. In A. Przepiorka (Ed.), *Closer to emotions II* (pp. 49–62). Lublin, Poland: Publishing House of Catholic University of Lublin.

Watkins, P. C. (2014). *Gratitude and the good life: Toward a psychology of appreciation.* Dordrecht, The Netherlands: Springer.

Watkins, P. C., Cruz, L., Holben, H., & Kolts, R. L. (2008). Taking care of business? Grateful processing of unpleasant memories. *Journal of Positive Psychology, 3,* 87–99.

Watkins, P. C., Uhder, J., & Pichinevskiy, S. (2015). Grateful recounting enhances subjective well-being: The importance of grateful processing. *Journal of Positive Psychology, 2,* 91–98.

Watkins, P. C., van Gelder, M., & Frias, A. (2009). Furthering the science of gratitude. In R. Snyder & S. Lopez (Eds.), *Oxford handbook of positive psychology* (2nd ed., pp. 437–446). New York, NY: Oxford University Press.

Wood, A. M., Froh, J. J., & Geraghty, A. W. A. (2010). Gratitude and well-being: A review and theoretical integration. *Clinical Psychology Review, 30,* 890–905.

Wood, A. M., Linley, P. A., Maltby, J., Kashdan, T. B., & Hurling, R. (2011). Using personal and psychological strengths leads to increases in well-being over time: A longitudinal study and the development of the strengths use questionnaire. *Personality and Individual Differences, 50,* 15–19.

How Do One's Circumstances Impact Happiness?

Many people seem to take the "if only . . ." approach to happiness. "If only I had _____," they say, "then I'd be happy." "If only I were rich; if only I were younger; if only I were smarter; if only I were beautiful—then I'd be happy." This chapter explores many of these circumstances, and whether they actually impact your happiness. Here we will look at the demographics of happiness and ask the question: "Do your circumstances matter to your happiness?"

GENDER AND HAPPINESS

The first circumstance we examine is whether one's gender has any impact on one's happiness. Are men happier than women? Are women happier than men? These are important questions because, generally speaking, men and women have somewhat different circumstances in life, and if men indeed are happier than women this might tell us a lot about happiness. In brief, the research shows that there are no gender differences in subjective well-being (SWB). Stated differently, knowing whether a person is a man or a woman tells us almost nothing about his or her happiness. Although an early study concluded that women are slightly happier than men (Wood, Rhodes, & Whelan, 1989), more recent reviews and large multinational surveys show no gender differences (e.g., Diener, Suh, Lucas, & Smith, 1999; Inglehart, 1990; Pavot & Diener, 2013). This should not imply, however, that the structure of happiness is identical in men and women. For example, women are more likely than men to say they have more extreme levels of happiness (either high or low; Fujita, Diener, & Sandvik, 1991). Thus there are still important gender issues in the science of happiness that have yet to be explored but, in general, we may conclude that there are no meaningful gender differences in SWB.

The fact that there are no substantial gender differences in happiness brings up a few interesting conundrums. For example, it is well known that there are important gender differences in clinical depression; women suffer from depression about three times more frequently than men (American Psychiatric Association, 2013). Moreover, it could be reasonably argued that in peaceful societies women encounter more barriers to well-being than do men (e.g., lower income). So then why are women just as happy as men? It is possible that women engage in certain thinking patterns more so than men, and this explains why—despite encountering more difficulties—they show similar levels of SWB. For instance, a number of studies have demonstrated that the disposition of gratitude is higher in women than in men (Watkins, 2014), and dispositional gratitude is very predictive of happiness. If women naturally engage in grateful thinking more so than men, it is easy to see how they might overcome obstacles to their happiness.

So, more than likely, if you are saying to yourself "if only I were a man," or "if only I were a woman, then I'd be happier," this conclusion is going to distract you from more successful pursuits of happiness. I'm guessing that not many of you are thinking this, however. People are much more likely to say: "If only I were more beautiful or handsome, then I'd be happy." Even here though, studies show that objective beauty (i.e., beauty judged by independent observers) has virtually no relationship with your happiness. Indeed, some investigations suggest that what little relationship there is between objective attractiveness and happiness is because happy people actually make themselves more beautiful than most (Diener, Wolsic, & Fujita, 1995). In short, changing your attractiveness is not likely to change your happiness.

INTELLIGENCE, EDUCATION, AND HAPPINESS

Are smarter people happier or is ignorance bliss? Overall, it appears there's little or no relationship between your cognitive intelligence and your happiness (Veenhoven & Choi, 2012). Although there is some evidence that education and intelligence at a national level matter (more educated nations tend to be happier; Veenhoven & Choi, 2012), simply being smart doesn't guarantee your happiness. Whereas happy people think they're smarter than others, objectively measured intelligence doesn't show much of a relationship with happiness at all. Because of how much we value intelligence in the West, this finding surprises me. Apparently, even though intelligent people may know more than those less intellectually gifted, this might not translate into knowledge about happiness. To illustrate, people of high intelligence tend to value knowledge and critical thinking and in so doing may tend to de-emphasize their relationships with others. It turns out that this isn't the smartest thing to do when it comes to your own happiness, and this might be one reason why intelligence isn't related to happiness.

I should be quick to emphasize that there is one type of intelligence that is strongly related to happiness: *emotional intelligence* (Crum & Salovey, 2013). I submit that wisdom—as distinct from cognitive intelligence—would also be related to SWB. For me, this all points to the possibility of a different type of intelligence that might be important for our purposes here: *happiness intelligence*, and of course one of the primary goals of this book is to increase your happiness intelligence.

Like cognitive intelligence, education shows little if any relationship with SWB. Clearly, when occupational status is controlled, any relationship between education and SWB seems to all but disappear. In short, intelligence doesn't help or hurt your happiness.

GEOGRAPHY AND HAPPINESS

"If I could live in Hawaii, then I'd be happier." Surely you've said something like this to yourself at one time or another (I certainly have). "If I could only live in a sunnier climate, in a big city, in the mountains, at the beach, then I'd be happy." Often we fantasize about living somewhere else because we're sure it would improve our well-being. In this section we examine whether geography is related to happiness. As we delve into this subject, a few clarifications are in order. In this discussion, by geography I am referring to place, not necessarily to culture. Although it is virtually impossible to separate place from culture, in general I want to evaluate the question of whether living in a particular type of place influences happiness—not whether some cultures are more conducive to well-being than others. I touch on the latter issue in detailing the relationship of wealth to SWB. As we will see, where you live doesn't seem to impact your happiness much, although most of us believe it does. Whereas research shows that the weather does impact your daily mood (but there are some important nuances here; e.g., Keller et al., 2005), moving to a new place probably won't impact your satisfaction with life. Let's now address some of the particulars of this relationship.

First, a quick warning: Beware of overinterpreting ranking studies. These are the studies that ask such questions as: "What's the happiest state?" "What's the most livable city?" "What's the country with the happiest people?" Although these studies are interesting and the popular media loves to report these findings, often the states, cities, and countries at the top of the list are so close statistically that the rank they finally fall in is really somewhat trivial. The top 10 or 20 countries may be so close on the variable of interest that the poor country that fell from first to fifth in the last 2 years really hasn't changed all that much. There's usually something to be said about the differences between the top and bottom countries, cities, and states but be careful about comparing those places that cluster in the top of the ranking.

Schkade and Kahneman (1998) conducted one of the most interesting and illustrative studies showing the impact of place on happiness. These authors polled a large number of college students in the Midwest and in Southern California. Both midwestern and Californian students thought that the Californians would be happier but, in fact, the students from the two regions were almost identical in their life satisfaction. Moreover, students from both regions thought that Californians would be happier for the same reasons: because of the better weather and cultural and recreational opportunities that California has to offer. The authors thought this was an example of the *focusing illusion:* The reason we think people are happier in California even when they're not is because we tend to focus on the most salient aspects of California (the fun and sun), and forget about all the hassles of living down there (crowds, traffic, expense, etc.). This offers some explanation as to why we might think that moving some-where else would make us happier: We tend to focus on the good aspects of the location we would like to move to, while forgetting about some of the drawbacks. My wife and I love to vacation in Hawaii. Often, people ask us what our favorite island is and my wife invariably responds, "the one we were just on." When we're in Hawaii, at some point my mind almost always drifts to the question: "Wouldn't it be great to retire over here?" At that point, what I'm usually focusing on is the wonderful weather, sunning on the beach, swimming in the warm ocean, and bodyboarding at my favorite break. Rarely am I concentrating on how expensive it is or how far we would be from our children and friends.

In general, not only does geography matter little in terms of one's happiness, it also appears that ethnicity tells us very little about one's happiness, particularly after income is controlled for. However, there's one group of people who every year seem to be happier than their European peers: the Danish. Year after year the Danes rank highest in contentment. Why are the Danes so happy? In a wonderful but somewhat tongue-in-cheek article, Chris-tensen, Herskind, and Vaupel (2006) explored this question. Are Danes happier because blondes have more fun? No, because their Scandinavian neighbors are blonder than they, but are less happy as well. Is it because the Danes drink and smoke less? It appears not, because the Danish have the highest cigarette and alcohol consumption in Europe. Is it because they have happier marriages?

Nope. Although the Danes have one of the highest marriage rates in Europe, they also have the second highest divorce rate in the European Union (EU). Is it because the Danes are healthier? Again the answer seems to be "no" because the Danes have one of the shortest average life spans in the EU. Is it because Denmark won the World Cup in 1992? Well, maybe, because it was at that point that Denmark showed a significant increase in happiness. The authors finally decided that the most likely reason the Danes are consistently happier than their peers is that they have such low expectations. When asked, Danish people have relatively low expectations for the coming year. The authors concluded: "Year after year they are pleasantly surprised to find that not everything is getting more rotten in the state of Denmark" (Christensen et al., 2006, p. 1290). There may be some drawbacks to having expectations for the future that are too high.

In sum, moving to a new place is not likely to change your happiness. Big city or small town, rainy Seattle or sunny Los Angeles, city or country living, people seem to be similarly happy (Inglehart, 1990). So more than likely, moving somewhere else to improve your happiness is probably not going to be an effective move. Why is it that geography matters little when it comes to happiness? When you move, you take you with you, and as shall be seen: Who you are, what you do, and what you choose are the most important determinants of your happiness. Perhaps happiness really is to be found in your own backyard.

AGE AND HAPPINESS

Much like intelligence, gender, and geography, it appears that your age has little to do with your happiness. Typically, over your adult years of life your SWB is not likely to change. Although early work predicted that twentysomethings would be happiest (e.g., Wilson, 1967), more recent reviews have shown that, if anything, your happiness increases slightly along with your age (Horley & Lavery, 1995). A bit like gender, however, the structure of SWB varies somewhat with increasing age. For example, the intensity of both positive and negative affect seems to decrease with age (Charles, Reynolds, & Gatz, 2001).

I find this information somewhat surprising. We appear to have a culture that worships youth. People in their 20s and 30s are at the peak of their abilities, their lives are before them with all of their potential, and those of us at the other end of the spectrum are consistently confronted with our declining abilities and the ever-approaching specter of death. So why doesn't age reliably predict SWB? Some research suggests that some of the aforementioned barriers to SWB in later life may be counteracted by positive cognitive biases. Studies have found, for example, that older adults attend to and remember positive information more than their younger counterparts (e.g., Gallo, Korthauer, McDonough, Teshale, & Johnson, 2011; Mather & Carstensen, 2005). The important point here is that individuals' ages tell us very little about their happiness.

FORTUNE AND FELICITY

When we have provided against cold, hunger, and thirst,
all the rest is but vanity and excess.

Seneca

Perhaps economic wealth is the life circumstance that has received most of the research attention in the study of happiness. After all, people have long been asking the question: "Can you buy your happiness?" So now we explore the question: Is one's wealth predictive of one's SWB? As shall be seen, the answer to this question appears to be "not much." But this response washes over some important nuances in the research, so now let's explore the relationship between wealth and happiness.

Wealth Predicts Increased Happiness

A simple summary of the research regarding wealth and well-being is that wealth is positively associated with SWB; the more wealth people have, the happier they tend to be (Biswas-Diener, 2008; Diener & Biswas-Diener, 2002). This would seem to suggest that you can buy your happiness. However, this simple summary hides a great deal of significant information and caveats. First, it obscures the level of analysis in these studies and, as it turns out, this is a crucial issue. Thus, in this section we explore this relationship at the level of analysis of nations, followed by discussing the relationship within nations at the individual level.

Generally speaking, cross-sectional studies that have compared gross domestic product (GDP) per capita to a nation's SWB have found a strong association between national wealth and happiness (Diener & Biswas-Diener, 2002). In other words, rich nations tend to be much happier than poorer nations. This appears to suggest that the more money you have, the happier you will be; nevertheless, there are several confounds that complicate any simple interpretation of this correlation. For example, we know that people are happier in stable democracies, and the longer a nation has been a democracy the higher its GDP tends to be. Hence the apparent relationship between a country's riches and its happiness may simply be an artifact of richer nations being happier because people are happier in stable democracies. There is much more to be said about this phenomenon. For instance, multiple studies have found that individualist nations tend to be happier than collectivist countries (Suh & Koo, 2008), and this doesn't appear to simply be the result of self-report biases in the different cultures. Here too, political structure is somewhat confounded with this variable (individualistic nations tend to be democratic), but it now appears clear that this relationship is not just because individualistic countries tend to be richer (Suh & Koo, 2008). A full discussion of this critical cultural issue is beyond the scope of this chapter. The point to be made here is that the positive correlation between a nation's wealth and its SWB is confounded by a number of issues, and no simple interpretation of this association can be made now.

Another interesting issue emerges with a casual glance at the scatterplot of the relationship between national wealth and SWB. Here one finds that nations seem to fall into one of two clusters: developed and undeveloped. Although the developed nations tend to be toward the top of the happiness index and the undeveloped nations are much lower, within these two groups there does not appear to be a very strong relationship between wealth and well-being. Accordingly, the strength of the correlation seems to be the result of the two clusters of nations.

Whereas the cross-sectional relationship between a nation's riches and its happiness appears to be strong, longitudinal studies paint a very different picture. Various reviews have shown that as a nation's wealth has increased over the years, there has been little or no increase in its happiness (Blanchflower & Oswald, 1999; Diener & Biswas-Diener, 2002; Diener & Oishi, 2000; Easterlin, 1974). Consequently, we are presented with a conundrum: Although in cross-sectional studies there is a strong relationship between a nation's wealth and its happiness, in longitudinal evaluations there seem to be little if any relationship at all. This apparent contradiction is so well known in economics and psychology it is called the *Easterlin Paradox*, named after the individual who first demonstrated this pattern of results (Easterlin, 1974). There is a more recent caveat that has emerged, however: As underdeveloped nations become more developed economically, there is a tendency for their SWB to improve with their wealth (Howell & Howell, 2008). Summing up, as a developed nation's riches increase, there is little corresponding increase in its happiness; however, in underdeveloped countries we do see a tendency for their SWB to increase along with their prosperity. Although this might seem to complicate matters, as shall soon be seen, this pattern of data actually fits quite well with a fairly simple conclusion.

We now move from the national unit of analysis to the individual. Whereas studies have shown a strong correlation between wealth and well-being at the national level, the association at the individual level within nations is much weaker. Indeed, although correlations at the national level reach as high as .70, at the individual level correlations range between –.02 to .45 (average .19; Diener & Biswas-Diener, 2002). This is a large range of correlations but clearly most of these relationships are in the small to trivial range (accounting for less than 4% of the variance). Whereas virtually all of these relationships were statistically significant (due to large samples), clearly they are much lower than the relationship at the national level. Moreover, some sense can be made about the large variance between studies. Correlations between individual wealth and happiness in underdeveloped nations are relatively high (e.g., .35 in villages in northern India; Brinkerhoff, Fredell, & Frideres, 1997) compared to correlations in the United States (e.g., .12; Diener, Sandvik, Seidlitz, & Diener, 1993).

In short, the relationship between fortune and felicity at the individual level is small but even here there is an observation to highlight: People's subjective perceptions of their wealth are much more strongly correlated with their happiness than is their objective wealth. Studies have shown that your satisfaction with your income is much more predictive of your happiness than your actual income (Campbell, 1981). Perhaps this finding should not be surprising; we have already seen that your perceived attractiveness is much more predictive of your happiness than your objective appearance. But this finding highlights an important principle. As Myers concludes: "Satisfaction isn't so much getting what you want as wanting what you have" (1992, p. 39). It is here where gratitude may come into play. As seen in Chapter 2, dispositional gratitude is one of the most reliable predictors of happiness. The extent of your possessions may not be so important to your happiness. Rather, the critical variable might be how grateful you are for your possessions.

Thus far, we have seen that the correlation between individuals' income and their happiness is somewhat small, but the relationship does vary depending on whether or not individuals live in an economically developed country. Research has also found that the relationship varies according to the person's economic level: the correlation between income levels and SWB is stronger for those at the lower end of the economic spectrum (Biaswas-Diener, 2008; Diener & Biswas-Diener, 2002). In other words, your income is much more predictive of your happiness if you are poor than if you are rich. Although there is still evidence that wealth benefits well-being in individuals above the poverty level (Biswas-Diener, 2008), the contribution drops substantially. In one of the most interesting studies of the very rich, Diener, Horwitz, and Emmons (1985) surveyed 49 of the richest Americans as listed by *Forbes* magazine. All of these people had a net worth greater than $125 million in 1983. These individuals were only slightly happier than the average American, and although they were obviously very rich, an overwhelming majority (about 80%) knew that money couldn't buy their happiness—it all depended on how the money was spent. Indeed, none of these well-off respondents believed that money was a major source of happiness. Moreover, 37% of these very wealthy participants showed happiness levels lower than the average person who was not rich, demonstrating that money is no guaranteed path to happiness.

Up to now, we have explored studies at the individual level of analysis that have been cross-sectional in nature. What about longitudinal studies? If you became wealthy, wouldn't you be happier than before? Fortunately, we have a few studies that speak to this issue. Perhaps the most famous study—and one that certainly rates as a classic in positive psychology—compared lottery winners to nonwinners and victims of accidents (Brickman, Coates, & Janoff-Bulman, 1978). These researchers compared 20 lottery winners to 20 matched controls. The lottery winners had won large sums of money (averaging almost $500,000, with the most frequent winnings being $1 million), and although they considered winning the lottery to be a very positive event, their happiness was not significantly greater than the controls. Whereas one might complain that this failure to find significant differences was the result of low statistical power, the F score in this case was quite low (.27), so the fact that these groups were not significantly different is notable. None of the lottery winners was interviewed immediately after getting the good news of the jackpots, and so more than likely the happiness that they initially experienced with their good fortune had worn off. The two groups were significantly different, however, in their enjoyment of *simple pleasures* (called "mundane pleasures" by the authors). Simple pleasures are everyday activities that can be enjoyed relatively frequently, like hearing a joke, talking with a friend, drinking a latte, or watching television. Lottery winners actually enjoyed these simple pleasures less than their counterparts. In part, this might explain why the lottery winners were no happier than the controls. I believe this is an important issue, and it is an ongoing theme throughout this book. As we will see, simple pleasures are important to happiness because they are much more frequent than spectacular pleasures and, as it turns out, frequency of positive experiences is more important than intensity when it comes to your happiness. To be fair, other studies have shown that receiving a windfall of money does increase SWB; however, the effect appears to be temporary (see Diener & Biswas-Diener, 2002, for a review), so the question remains as to why finding your fortune doesn't equate with finding your happiness.

As we look at the relationship between income and happiness, there is one important interpretation to consider: It is possible that happiness actually creates more income (Diener & Biswas-Diener, 2002). The natural interpretation of the positive relationship between wealth and well-being is to assume that prosperity produces SWB, but it is important to consider the reverse direction of causation. Indeed, some evidence supports the idea that happiness might improve your earning potential. For example, Marks and Fleming (1999) conducted a study in Australia showing that happiness predicted increased income. These researchers also found that happy people were less likely to become unemployed. Similarly, Diener, Nickerson, Lucas, and Sandvik (2002) found that a student's cheerfulness in 1976 predicted greater income in 1993. The caveat here was that for those who were raised in poor households, cheerfulness didn't matter. Thus, as shown by Lyubomirsky, King, and Diener (2005), happiness appears to produce success in a number of areas of life, including one's financial success. Undoubtedly, this possibility does not completely explain the relationship between wealth and well-being, and more than likely there is a reciprocal relationship between one's happiness and one's financial status.

Clearly, the association between wealth and well-being is not a simple relationship. So what can we conclude about the relationship between happiness and financial prosperity? Any conclusions that we make must be able to account for the apparent paradoxes in the literature. Why at the national level is wealth strongly correlated with SWB, when within nations the correlation between individual wealth and well-being is weak? Why is individual wealth correlated much more strongly with SWB in poor than in rich nations? Why does money seem to produce more happiness in the poor than in those more well off? Why is it that, most often, economic growth in a country does not seem to produce increases in national SWB, but in less developed nations it does? The conclusion that seems to resolve these questions is that finances do contribute to your happiness when they help you fulfill basic biological needs such as adequate food and shelter. When money helps prevent hunger and protects you from the elements, then it does indeed contribute to your happiness. But once these basic needs have been satisfied, having more money does little to enhance your SWB. Or in the words of Myers (1992, p. 37), "Having more than enough provides little additional boost to well-being." Why is individual wealth more strongly correlated with happiness in poor than in rich countries? Because in economically deprived nations your income tells us a lot about whether your basic biological needs are being met, but in wealthy nations even those at the lower end of the financial spectrum typically have these needs fulfilled. Why is the correlation between wealth and well-being stronger for poor than for rich people? Because, once again, the poor persons' incomes may well determine whether or not their basic needs are being met, whereas with wealthier individuals there is no relationship between their income and the fulfillment of basic biological needs. It doesn't matter whether you earn $100,000 a year or $100 million a year, in either case your basic biological needs are going to be more than satisfied. Usually, a country's economic growth does not predict increases in happiness because the growth does not put many more people into the category of having their biological needs met. In less developed nations, however, economic growth significantly increases the proportion of the population whose biological needs are fulfilled; thus economic growth does predict increased SWB. What general conclusion can we draw from the wealth and well-being data? In short, after the necessities in life have been purchased, there's not much happiness left to be bought.

Why Doesn't Wealth Bring More Happiness?

The question of whether money increases your happiness has been examined, and the simple answer appears to be: not much. Why doesn't fortune bring felicity? If you had more money there's a great deal you could do with it that would seem to improve your happiness. You could go on better, longer vacations. You could buy a bigger, better house. You could eat at better restaurants with better food. You could buy a better, *cooler* car. You could have better clothes, a better television, and a more powerful computer. And I'm sure that right now you can think of many other things that you could buy with more money that would make you happier. So why is it that after the essentials of life have been purchased, there's not much happiness left to be bought? Perhaps the primary reason that riches don't equate to happiness is because of the principle of adaptation, or what emotion researcher Frijda calls the *law of habituation* (1988, 2007). Basically, this principle of adaptation states that we adapt to or cease to react to any stimulus that is consistently presented to us over time. You might say—to paraphrase a famous line from *My Fair Lady*—"you grow accustomed to your place." Whether it's something bad or something good, if you're constantly exposed to it, over time you tend to get used to it. This is good news when it comes to bad things in our lives; research shows that humans are amazingly adept at adapting to very harsh circumstances. But when it comes to the good things in our lives, the law of adaptation isn't so great. Recently, we moved from an old bungalow to a very new home and almost doubled our living space. After recovering from the stress of moving, we sincerely enjoyed our new home and the many modern advantages it afforded us. But over time, we grew accustomed to these advantages and no longer noticed them, and our happiness level became pretty much what it had been before the move. This is a good example of what Brickman and Campbell (1971) refer to as the *hedonic treadmill*. We purchase something because we think it will improve our happiness. Often it does—for a time. But over time we adapt to our new house, our new car, our new television, and our happiness returns to where it was before the purchase. But we go ahead and buy something new, that latest-and-greatest thing that we need to improve our happiness, and the whole process starts over again. So we get more but then we think we need even more to improve our happiness. C. S. Lewis's fictional demon Screwtape wrote about how to decrease human happiness: "An ever increasing craving for an ever diminishing pleasure is the formula" (1961/1982, p. 42). One reason that we can't buy much of our happiness is that the hedonic treadmill wields its sharp blade, cutting back our boosts of happiness.

Another reason why having more money doesn't necessarily equate with more happiness is because of *upward social comparison*. We are social animals, and thus we are prone to comparing ourselves with others (i.e., social comparison; Festinger, 1954). *Downward social comparison* is when you compare yourself with others who have less of something than you have; whereas in upward social comparison, individuals compare themselves with people who have more of something than they have. In general, research has shown that downward social comparisons make you feel better but upward social comparisons make you feel worse (Guimond, 2006; Suls, Martin, & Wheeler, 2002). For example, if you get 95% on a test you'll probably feel pretty good about your grade. If, however, you happen to see that the person next to you earned a 99% on the test this might kill the joy of your performance. Interestingly, happy people seem to be somewhat immune to the emotional impact of upward social comparisons (Lyubomirsky & Ross, 1997), but that's another story for another chapter (see Chapter 6). The point here is that if there are a great many people around you who have more money than you have, this creates multiple upward social comparisons and you aren't so likely to feel happy with what you've got. When we get richer, we don't get much happier. Why is that so? If my income is increasing, more than likely the economy is doing well, and that means that a great many other people are earning more money as well. Thus, even though I may have more money to spend, I've also got a great many more people to compare myself with who are making a lot more than me. There's an old-fashioned word for this: envy. And we know that envy prevents happiness. "Napoleon envied Caesar, Caesar envied Alexander, and Alexander, I daresay, envied Hercules, who never existed," observed Bertrand Russell (1930, p. 89). "You cannot, therefore, get away from envy by means of success alone, for there will always be in history or legend some person even more successful than you are" (p. 89). If I'm doing well financially, more than likely others around me are doing well too. So one reason you can't buy very much of your happiness is that there are always a great many folks who are wealthier than you are, which means there are numerous opportunities for upward social comparisons to dampen your happiness.

A third reason it's difficult to fund your felicity is that pursuing more income often distracts us from spending time in pursuits that really do produce happiness. As we shall see, well-spent leisure and social time are important to your happiness. Unfortunately, many times people take jobs because these positions offer more money; nevertheless, this often results in less leisure time and less time spent with friends and family. A number of years ago, I got the delusion that I might like to get into academic administration. The primary reason I started pursuing this career route—a reason I was not really willing to consciously accept—was because administrators made significantly more money than I. Fortunately, I did not get this position and, in the long run, I think this was a great boon to my happiness. If I had gotten the administrative position my life would not have been my own; I would have been at the beck and call of the administrators above me. And this would have made a serious dent in the amount of time I could have spent with my family and friends; undoubtedly, those relationships would have suffered. Moreover, it would have been much more difficult to spend significant time at my in-laws' cabin on the Oregon coast—a wonderful benefit for me early in my family life. So sometimes pursuing more money can distract us from the pursuits that really do contribute to our happiness.

One final reason there are limits to the ability of wealth to influence your happiness is because of unmet expectations. Often when we pursue more money it's because we expect that it will make us happier. But as has been demonstrated, making more money isn't very likely to result in much more happiness. So when we spend considerable effort in making more money to enhance our happiness but we don't see much in the way of results, this can be very disappointing. In this sense, the quest for more money might even make you less happy. I explore this possibility in greater depth in the following section.

Trying to Buy Your Happiness Might Make You Unhappy—Problems With Materialism

Although there is a small positive correlation between wealth and well-being, there is now compelling evidence to suggest that actively chasing your happiness through increased riches can make you *less* happy. *Materialism* is basically the belief that the primary path to happiness is through material possessions. It's the ultimate "He who dies with the most toys wins" philosophy and, paradoxically, research suggests that materialism is likely to inhibit your happiness (for a review, see Diener & Biswas-Diner, 2002). Several studies illustrate this relationship clearly. For example, Diener and Oishi (2000) conducted a study that included more than 7,000 students in more than 41 countries. They found that the more students put a high value on love, the more satisfaction increased in their lives. But the more these students valued money, the unhappier they were. Similarly, across three studies Kasser and Ryan (1993) found that the more financial aspirations were of central importance for individuals, the less happy they were. In addition to materialists being less happy than those not so inclined toward riches, research has identified a number of other problems with materialism that may help explain this relationship. Materialists have also been found to be more depressed, to be more narcissistic, and to have more financial problems (see Kasser, 2002, for an engaging explanation of the problems with materialism). The latter problem is likely because materialists are more inclined to spend beyond their means in order to gain happiness. Thus, in an attempt to gain their happiness now, they end up mortgaging their future happiness. This is another example of the old "short-term gain, long-term pain" principle, but the evidence seems to suggest that materialists are not even all that happy right now. Why are materialists less happy? There are probably several reasons, but a recent study points to a lack of gratitude as a major culprit (Tsang, Carpenter, Roberts, Frisch, & Carlisle, 2014). Research has found that it's pretty difficult to be happy if you're not grateful (Watkins, 2014), and materialism appears to degrade gratitude. Why do materialists have so much difficulty being grateful? It's probably because when your life orientation is to seek more possessions to enhance your happiness, you're always looking at what you don't have, and as long as you're focused on what you lack, it's difficult to be grateful for what you have. Indeed, Tsang and colleagues found that a major reason that materialists are less happy is that they are also less grateful. Although there are probably additional factors that help explain how materialism prevents happiness, the take-home message here is that pursuing your happiness through purchasing more possessions is likely to make you *less* happy.

How You Spend Your Happiness Money Matters

An anonymous quipster once said: "People who claim that money can't buy happiness just don't know where to shop" (cited in Diener & Biswas-Diener, 2002, p. 119). We have seen that after one's biological necessities have been purchased, there's very little happiness left to be bought. However, the relationship between wealth and well-being is a complex one; any one-sentence summary of the data is likely to be incomplete. Indeed, as it turns out, how you spend your money for enhancing your happiness matters.

If you had $1,500 to spend on improving your happiness, how would you use it? Would you buy a new television, a new computer, or a new stereo? Or would you use the money for a vacation, or a concert series? You might think that the money would be better spent on a *material purchase* (a television, computer, or stereo) because these items should last longer than the *experience purchase* (the vacation or concert series), and thus you should be able to derive more pleasure from these things over time. An enlightening research program conducted by Gilovich and collaborators has shown that, in fact, you're better off spending your money on experiences than on things (e.g., Carter & Gilovich, 2012; Van Boven & Gilovich, 2003; for a review, see Van Boven, 2005). Even though "stuff" like a television should last a lot longer than a 2-week vacation, studies show that people derive more happiness from the vacation.

Why is it that experiential purchases are better for one's happiness than material purchases? First, our memories of positive experiences seem to improve over time. Whereas the joy of the purchase of that new computer quickly wears off, the joy of that wonderful meal at that French restaurant in New Orleans only seems to grow in our memories (Van Boven & Gilovich, 2003). Second, Gilovich has found that our experiential purchases are more resistant to upward social comparisons (Carter & Gilovich, 2010). If I buy a 48-inch television but you show me your newly purchased 62-inch screen, this will likely pour cold water on the joy of my material purchase. But if I'm having a great vacation in Maui, I probably won't care how much more fun you're having in Tahiti. Relatedly, recent research also demonstrates that we're less likely to have buyer's remorse with experiential purchases (Rosenzweig & Gilovich, 2012). A third reason that we derive more happiness from experiential than material purchases is that they have more social value. Investigations show that I get more joy out of telling you about my backpack trip in the Grand Tetons than telling you about my new BMW, and perhaps more importantly, you enjoy hearing about my backpack trip more than about my fancy new car. Finally, experiential purchases may be more advantageous to your happiness because they are more important to your identity than material purchases. Experiential purchases tend to be more self-defining than material purchases; they tell both ourselves and others more about who we really are (Carter & Gilovich, 2012). More recently, Gilovich has suggested that experiences have a happiness advantage over "things" because they produce more gratitude, and his initial evidence supports this idea (Gilovich, 2014).

Recently, my wife called me out of the blue and said she'd found a great package for a week's vacation for the family on Maui. For me, it was a lot of money but we decided to go for it. In retrospect, this was money very well spent, and I still derive joy with my wife and kids telling stories and looking at photos from that vacation. In short, you're better off spending your happiness money on experiences rather than on stuff. One of the real advantages of experiential purchases is that they don't have to involve a lot of money. For example, camping at a national park may provide great benefits for your happiness without a great deal of expense and, as Gilovich (2014) has rightly argued, this has important policy implications as we consider what to do about the funding of our parks.

There are other important considerations when making decisions about how to spend your happiness dollars. To illustrate, research has found that you might be better off spending your extra cash on others rather than on yourself, if you want to improve your happiness. The importance to your happiness of giving to others is explored in greater depth in Chapter 5; however, for an engaging and informative read on smart spending for your happiness, see Dunn and Norton (2013). In short, although your wealth doesn't determine much of your happiness, how you spend your happiness money counts.

FINDING HAPPINESS AT WORK: WELL-BEING AND WORK

Employment and Happiness

In this chapter we have explored the demographics of happiness. We have looked at how several external circumstances might contribute to your happiness and, in general, the conclusion seems to be: not much. In terms of gender, intelligence, geography, age, and income, how these variables affect your happiness appears to be: not much. In contrast to these "not much" circumstances, however, your work and your play have more significant consequences for your happiness, and we now explore these issues.

It is perhaps no surprise that your employment status significantly impacts your happiness, but *why* employment impacts happiness is somewhat surprising. Numerous studies have shown that unemployed individuals are less happy than those with jobs. For instance, various surveys show that only about 10% to 12% of unemployed Americans say they're "very happy," in contrast with about 30% of the general population (Argyle, 2001). And it's not just that unhappy people are less likely to get a job; longitudinal studies show that people become significantly less happy after becoming unemployed (e.g., Warr, 1978). Moreover, after becoming unemployed, people don't tend to return to their previous happiness levels, even after they get a new job (Lucas, Clark, Georgellis, & Diener, 2004). Here is a good example of where adaptation theory is incomplete; there are some events that many people never completely adapt to, and unemployment appears to be one of those circumstances. Research now shows that this relationship is not a simple one-way street. Although it's clear that unemployment tends to degrade one's happiness, there is also evidence that unhappy people are more likely to lose their jobs (Luhmann, Lucas, Eid, & Diener, 2013). Thus the findings support the possibility of a *vicious cycle* or a *downward spiral:* Unhappy people are more likely to get fired, which is likely to make them unhappier, which might prevent them from being able to obtain more work. On the other hand, an *upward spiral* is also implied by this evidence: Happy people are more likely to be gainfully employed, having a job supports their happiness, which makes them more likely to stay employed. Either way, this suggests that happiness interventions might have an important impact on people's employment status.

Perhaps more surprising is why employment is important to your happiness. Of course, having some type of income is important for life's essentials and this is crucial to your happiness; nevertheless, there are other benefits of employment that may even be more important in modern societies. Indeed, in surveys about two thirds of people said that they would keep working even if it were financially unnecessary to work, and another 11% said they would stop working now but would consider working in the future. Only about 16% of the participants said that they would permanently stop working if they had enough money so that they wouldn't have to work (Warr, 1982). Clearly, employment offers people something much more than financial remuneration.

What are the nonfinancial benefits of having a job? Researchers have identified several additional benefits of work (Diener & Seligman, 2004; Jahoda, 1982; Warr, 1984, 2013). First, employment provides some type of structure to life. Often the lives of depressed individuals prove to be extremely unstructured. Thus, the goal for a number of successful treatment approaches is to provide more structure for the day-to-day activities of these individuals. To illustrate, for most employed people their work provides them with regular sleep/wake schedules—an important facet of SWB. If my job requires me to be there at 8:30 a.m. every morning, this would probably demand that I wake up at a consistent time, which likely means I'll be getting to sleep at roughly the same time each night. This would imply that jobs with irregular schedules might have a detrimental effect on worker happiness. Relatedly, jobs also provide consistent activity for people. As we will see, happy people tend to lead active lives (see Chapter 4). In fact, one of the main problems with unemployment is boredom (Winefield, Tiggermann, & Winefield, 1992). A third benefit of employment is that it provides built-in social contact for people. As shall be detailed in our examination of job satisfaction, on-the-job social contact can be for better or for worse but, generally speaking, this is seen as a benefit of consistent employment. As more and more people choose to work at home, it will be interesting to see if worker happiness declines somewhat because they are deprived of the social benefits of work. Fourth, our occupations provide us with a sense of identity. Years ago I went on a retreat with other men, and one of the rules was that we could not reveal our professions. For most of us this proved to be very difficult because "what we do" (i.e., our occupations) is a very important part of how we define ourselves. There are studies indicating that there are drawbacks to only defining ourselves by our professions; nonetheless, for many of us our professions are an important aspect of who we are. Relatedly, work also provides meaning and purpose. My profession is psychology professor. As such, my primary roles are to teach the subject matter and to write about psychological issues. These different roles provide purpose and meaning for me. My goals in writing this book were to complete it in a reasonable amount of time and, hopefully, to make it helpful for those who wish to get acquainted with positive psychology. One of the reasons that I enjoyed the writing of this volume was that it gave me some meaning and purpose in my life, above and beyond the activity it provided for me. Here, we can see that employment provides a number of benefits to your happiness beyond your finances.

Job Satisfaction and Happiness

We have seen that your employment status matters to your happiness but what about your satisfaction on the job? Is being satisfied at work important to being satisfied in life? Or is it that being happy in general makes you happy at work? Prospective research shows that indeed your *job satisfaction* impacts your life satisfaction but if you're satisfied with life, this seems to help your satisfaction at work as well. Interestingly, the stronger causal link appears to be from life satisfaction to job satisfaction (Heady & Wearing, 1992; Judge & Watanabe, 1993) but, clearly, your job satisfaction is one of the most important satisfaction domains for your happiness. Reviews have shown that, on average, job satisfaction correlates with life satisfaction around .44—a strong association (Tait, Padgett, & Baldwin, 1989).

If job satisfaction is important to happiness, it makes sense to ask: What makes a job satisfying? This has been the subject of entire books (and even book series); hence I only attempt to highlight a few important findings from the literature. Strikingly, how much people are paid predicts a very small amount of their job satisfaction (correlations range from between .15–.17; Argyle, 2001). Here again, we see that the financial aspect of having a job makes a very small contribution to your happiness. Job status seems to be more meaningful than pay, but even here it's only slightly more significant (Haring, Okun, & Stock, 1984). Other factors appear to be much more central to your happiness at work. One of the themes of this book is that when it comes to your happiness, "others matter" (Peterson, 2006) and, as it turns out, "others matter" for your job satisfaction as well. For example, in one study having good working relationships was the strongest predictor of job satisfaction (Argyle, 2001). Particularly when individuals work on cooperative and cohesive teams, they appear to be happy with their jobs (West, Borrill, & Unsworth, 1998). Although I have nearly always been pretty happy with my job, the most satisfying times of my career have been when I was working well with my colleagues.

Somewhat paradoxically, another predictor of job satisfaction is *autonomy*. When you feel you have some control of how you do your tasks at work, and you have control and responsibility for the outcome, research shows that you tend to be happier on the job (van der Doef & Maes, 1999). Although this might seem to be contradictory to the importance of working well with others, even when you're working on a team you can feel as though you have authority and accountability for the outcome of a task. So autonomy at work seems to matter, and studies have determined that when control is low and task demands are high, this is a formula for an unhappy worker (van der Doef & Maes, 1999).

Research also demonstrates that meaningful work is happy work, and this probably relates to some extent with your autonomy on the job. If you believe that what you do matters—it impacts others or the organization in a meaningful way—you're more likely to be satisfied with your work (e.g., Hackman & Oldham, 1976). More than likely, when you feel you have power over a project, you're likely to feel as though it's meaningful as well.

Not only is it crucial that tasks and projects are meaningful for them to be satisfying, it is also essential that one's skills fit well with the demands of the tasks. If the task is beneath your ability, or the job demands are too much for your skills, you're not likely to be happy in your work. For example, Caplan, Cobb, French, van Harrison, and Pinneau (1975) found that depression rates among workers were highest when there was either too little or too much complexity in their jobs. Depression was at its lowest, however, when there was a good fit between job complexity and worker skills. Similarly, research has shown that when there was a good match between people's needs and the rewards offered by their jobs, they tended to be more satisfied in their work (Furham & Schaeffer, 1984). I love to learn new things about people and I love to communicate that knowledge to others. Because these are exactly the rewards my job offers me, I am very happy in my work. In short, one of the characteristics of satisfying work is that the needs and abilities of the worker match up well with the demands of the job.

This leads to another important characteristic of satisfying work: Fulfilling work tends to be work that *flows*. Undoubtedly one of the more notable research programs in positive psychology is Csikszentmihalyi's (1975, 1988, 1990) work on the *flow experience*. According to Csikszentmihalyi, flow is an experience of intense, focused attention, where individuals are completely immersed in what they're doing. In this state, people are self-forgetful in that they have no self-consciousness. They are so involved with the activity that they have no sense of passing time because they are fully absorbed in the present. Although flow is an intrinsically enjoyable experience, these individuals are not really reflecting on how much they are enjoying the activity, for this would interrupt the flow. Csikszentmihalyi uses the term *flow* because when people describe this experience they talk about how they were just taken along with the flow of the activity, much as a stream would carry them along with the current. Tasks that are challenging, but for which the individual has the skills and interest to meet the challenge, tend to produce the flow experience. Projects that produce flow are also meaningful for the person. Obviously, work that produces flow experiences is advantageous in that these enhance job satisfaction and performance.

Up to this point, I have focused on the circumstances of work that predict job satisfaction but, clearly, there are factors within the person that are at least as important. Perhaps one of the most interesting internal factors identified by recent reviews involves how individuals experience their work. Research shows that people can be classified as experiencing their occupations in one of three different ways. People tend to experience their work either as a job, as a career, or as a calling (Bellah, Madsen, Sullivan, Swidler, & Tipton, 1985; Wrzesniewski, McCauley, Rozin, & Schwartz, 1997). People with a *job orientation* toward their work tend to view their positions as an instrument for other goals, for example, supplying finances and making enough money to support their lifestyles. This is basically the "working-for-the-weekend" approach to your job. People with a *career orientation* primarily work to advance their careers. Their orientation is to advance as much as they can within their company or organization. Finally, people with a *calling orientation* toward their occupations feel called to their profession; they believe that they have been made for this work and this is the work intended for them. As one might expect, having a calling orientation toward work predicts greater job satisfaction and happiness (e.g., Wrzesniewski et al., 1997), and also predicts a number of other positive outcomes (for a review, see Caza & Wrzesniewski, 2013). This research highlights the importance of intrapersonal variables in job satisfaction, and it is likely that these are stronger predictors of happiness on the job than objective job circumstances such as pay. Moreover, the circumstances of your workplace are always interacting with who you are as an individual. To illustrate, your working relationships are not just determined by the people you are working with, how you interact with them matters too.

In sum, we have seen that there are several notable characteristics of happy work. When we have good working relationships, our jobs tend to be more satisfying. When we have a sense of autonomy about our tasks at work, and when we feel that these tasks are meaningful, we experience more satisfaction on the job. We tend to be happier in our vocation when our needs and our skills fit well with our occupation, and work that flows is happy work. Finally, we have also seen that intrapersonal variables are important too: If you feel called to your work, you're much more likely to enjoy it. Myers (1992, p. 130) sums up the studies on job satisfaction well: "Happiness is loving what you do, and knowing it matters." These are the qualities of the workplace and the worker that tend to produce more job satisfaction; however, are there any advantages to having a happy worker?

There is now a great deal of research on workplace features that can enhance worker satisfaction. But why should a company be concerned about having happy workers? After all, we could argue that if a company were filled with happy people who turn out to be "contented cows," they wouldn't get anything done. Although the advantages of having a satisfied employee have probably been overblown, investigations have found some clear benefits to job satisfaction (Diener & Seligman, 2004; Wright, 2013). For instance, although the correlation is small, there is a positive relationship between one's job satisfaction and one's productivity (Iaffaldano & Muchinsky, 1985; Wright, 2013). More importantly, when people are happy in their work, they're more likely to be good citizens of the organization in terms of being helpful to others and complying with the company's goals (Spector, 1997). Indeed, when employees are satisfied in their jobs, customers are more satisfied as well (Fleming, 2000; Harter, Schmidt, & Hayes, 2002). Of course, these relationships are only correlational, so it is possible that being a good citizen of your organization makes you more satisfied with your work. Research suggests, however, that this is a reciprocal relationship: If you're happy with your job, this makes you a better citizen of your company, but being a helpful and supportive employee also makes you happier with your work (Bateman & Organ, 1983).

One of the most significant benefits of having happy employees is that they're less likely to miss work (Scott & Taylor, 1985). Of course, how people feel about their jobs is only one of many reasons that people miss work, but it makes sense that if you're happy with your job, you're more likely to decide to come to work in situations where attendance is a real question. If you'd rather be somewhere other than your workplace, you're probably going to choose that option. Perhaps the biggest advantage of having happy employees is that they're less likely to quit (Carsten & Spector, 1987). Employee turnover costs companies a great deal of money in terms of training and experience, and one would think, for this reason alone, that companies might want to create an environment that fosters job satisfaction. Finally, there is suggestive evidence that happy employees are healthier than those unsatisfied with their jobs (Wright, 2013). Research recommends that it is clearly to an organization's advantage to enhance their employees' happiness on the job; nevertheless, it appears that most companies pay little attention to promoting employee job satisfaction (Luthans & Youssef, 2004).

In short, we have seen that one's occupation is an important component of one's happiness. Employed people are happier than the unemployed, and the more satisfied you are with your job the more you tend to be satisfied with your life. Having an occupation provides people with a number of benefits that are critical to happiness, such as structure, regular social contact, identity, and meaning. But if the only way you define yourself is in your occupation, some studies indicate that your happiness is vulnerable. And although work dominates most of our waking hours before retirement, we still spend a significant amount of our lives in the pursuit of leisure. Now let's turn to the importance of leisure to SWB.

FINDING HAPPINESS AT PLAY: LEISURE AND WELL-BEING

Of course, there is one category of individuals who are not employed who are actually happier than those working: the retired. As you might guess, satisfaction with leisure is very important to the happiness of those who have retired, but research shows that it is vital to the happiness of working folks as well (Caldwell, 2005). Indeed, some observations show that leisure satisfaction is the strongest predictor of SWB when compared with other satisfaction domains (e.g., Balatsky & Diener, 1993). Engagement with leisure activities is positively associated with SWB, and this relationship is largely mediated by one's satisfaction with one's leisure activities (Kuykendall, Tay, & Ng, 2015). Moreover, increased frequency and satisfaction with leisure activities is associated with more happiness (Lloyd & Auld, 2002). In their landmark review, Diener and colleagues (1999) predicted that leisure satisfaction would become even more important to happiness in the coming years. Research has yet to confirm this hypothesis but, clearly, your satisfaction with your leisure activities is important to your SWB. When it comes to your happiness, how you spend your leisure hours matters.

Leisure Activities and Happiness

Knowing that people who are satisfied with leisure are also satisfied with life really doesn't tell us much. Why are some people satisfied with their leisure, while others are not? Obviously, *how* you spend your leisure time matters. Some leisure activities are more fulfilling than others. One of the more vital distinctions is *active versus passive leisure activities.* Generally speaking, active leisure activities—walking, sports, gardening, hobbies—are more conducive to your happiness than more passive activities such as watching television and playing on your computer. Interestingly, research with adolescents has found that although they enjoyed active more than passive leisure activities, they spent almost 10 times as much time in these passive pursuits (Csikszentmihalyi, Larson, & Prescott, 1977).

Perhaps because of the importance of the health implications of this activity, *exercise* is one of the active leisure activities garnering much of the research attention. Indeed, physical activities appear to enhance happiness (Argyle, 2001). Research has found that an activity as simple as a brisk, 10-minute walk produces improved emotion, less tension, and more energy, as long as 2 hours after the walk (Thayer, 1989). Moreover, regular exercise over a period of time appears to produce enduring increases in positive affect (Argyle, 2001). In fact, aerobic activity has shown such reliable mood effects that some have effectively used exercise to treat depression (e.g., Klein, Greist, & Gurtman, 1985).

As you might have guessed, all exercise is not created equal when it comes to happiness; the context of your physical activity matters. Some exercise environments produce more positive emotion than others. One of the most interesting happiness-enhancing environments for exercise is, well—the environment. Studies have found that when you're walking outside you're happier than when taking an indoor stroll (Shin et al., 2013). And it doesn't appear that it's simply getting outside that helps; walking in the forest makes you feel better than walking in the city. Indeed, it's not just walking that benefits from being outside; research findings indicate that simply spending your leisure hours out of doors is beneficial to your happiness and it might improve your mental skills as well (Berman, Jonides, & Kaplan, 2008; Nisbet & Zelenski, 2011). Moreover, in the Nisbet and Zelenski (2011) study, they determined that we significantly underestimate the happy advantages of interacting with nature. This suggests that spending time interacting with nature might be an important avenue for improving our use of leisure time.

Thus far we have seen that how you spend your leisure hours matters to your happiness. Passive leisure activities seem to produce less enjoyment than active leisure activities. Perhaps one of the best studies demonstrating this pattern was an experiencing sampling study conducted by Massimini and Carli (1988). In this study, participants were randomly cued to report their experiences during their leisure time. The remarkable results of this research can be seen in Figure 3.1. If they were beeped while they were watching television, well over one third of the people reported being apathetic, while only 3% said they were in a state of flow. Almost the opposite results were found when people were engaged with their hobbies. While doing their hobbies, only 4% of the participants said they were apathetic but almost half said they were in a flow state. This is significant because just as at work, flow is important when people are at play. Regardless of whether people are at work or leisure, they most enjoy their activities when they're in a flow state (Csikszentmihalyi & LeFevre, 1989). Therefore, if we want to enhance the enjoyment of our leisure hours, it seems prudent to pursue activities that flow, and active leisure pursuits such as hobbies produce more flow experiences than passive activities such as watching television. These results beg the question: If active leisure activities are

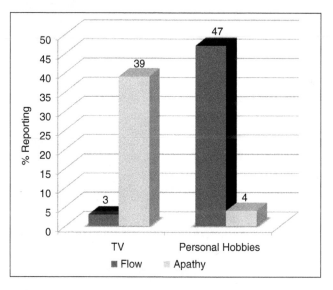

FIGURE 3.1 Percentage of individuals reporting apathy or flow.
Source: Massimini and Carli (1988).

more conducive to happiness, why do we spend more of our free time in passive activities? Perhaps it is that passive leisure activities are easier but not more enjoyable pursuits. Whatever the case, more research needs to be devoted to this significant question.

Leisure research has also investigated the impact of weekends and holidays on our happiness. First, how do weekends impact our happiness? Is there a TGIF (thank God it's Friday) effect? Is there a blue Monday effect? A study that utilized daily data during a 6-month period with more than 500,000 respondents examined the impact of weekends and public holidays on happiness (Helliwell & Wang, 2014). As seen in Figure 3.2, clearly there is a positive impact of weekends on our happiness. Starting with Friday, our happiness tends to go up and our anxiety goes

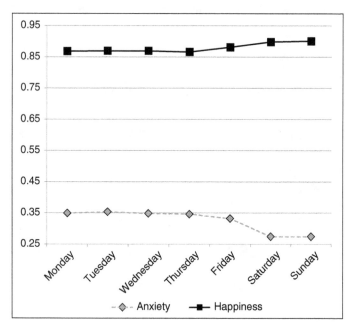

FIGURE 3.2 Reported moods by day of week.
Source: Helliwell and Wang (2014).

down (the emotions of sadness and anger followed the pattern of anxiety). Indeed, there is a TGIF effect. Second, note that there is no noticeable blue Monday effect. Our happiness and anxiety on Monday are pretty much what they are on Tuesday through Thursday. One implication of these findings is that we shouldn't waste our happiness on Sunday worrying about the upcoming Monday because it seems that Monday is pretty much the same as any other day of the week. So weekends do seem to boost our happiness, and Mondays are pretty much the same as any other day of the week. As shall be seen, however, what we do on our weekends does matter.

What about vacations? Can a vacation boost our happiness? Generally speaking, taking vacations can boost our SWB but the effect is largely temporary (e.g., Nawjin, 2011). Overall, the less stressful our vacations are, the more they benefit our happiness, but even with nonstressful breaks we still return to our pre-vacation happiness rather quickly. Interestingly, Nawjin found that one of the greatest happiness benefits of vacationing was the anticipation of the holiday. People were happier in the days before their vacations (see also Gilbert & Abdullah, 2002). He also found that the length of the vacation didn't seem to matter for the vacationers' happiness. Taken together, this implies that we might be better off taking several shorter vacations rather than one long break. This is because the more vacations we have to look forward to, the more frequently we will experience a boost in our happiness.

But since vacations don't seem to result in a permanent increase in our happiness, doesn't that imply that we shouldn't waste our money on vacations? I think not. As with many happiness-boosting activities, we shouldn't expect one trip to Maui to make us happier ever after. However, regularly taking these pleasant breaks from our normal routine is likely to be an important experience for happy people. Moreover, it's likely that how we spend our vacations is significant too. Vacations that encourage family bonds and trips that establish pleasant memories for us to reminisce about are likely to be important to our happiness.

Throughout this section on leisure and happiness I have emphasized that how you spend your leisure time matters. We have seen that, usually, active leisure activities support happiness more than passive activities. Research also shows that social leisure activities are more important to your happiness. For example, in the weekends and SWB study discussed earlier (Helliwell & Wang, 2014), they found that one of the most crucial reasons that weekends boost our happiness is because that's when we spend a lot more time with friends and family. In this, we find another important principle that can help us guide our decisions about leisure activities: Spending our time off with those who are important to us is more likely to enhance our SWB.

How Does Leisure Enhance Happiness? Bringing Some DRAMMA Into Your Life

We have seen that satisfaction with your leisure time is vital to your satisfaction with life. *How* does leisure enhance happiness? What are the psychological mechanisms that can help us understand why leisure activities encourage SWB? It is one thing to understand that leisure enhances your SWB; it is another to grasp *why* leisure is important to your happiness. This is critical because if we know *how* leisure enhances happiness, then we can make more informed decisions about our leisure activities. Recently, Newman, Tay, and Diener (2014) introduced their DRAMMA model, which I have found to be helpful for understanding how leisure impacts well-being. In this theory, the authors propose that leisure may promote well-being by activating core psychological mechanisms that are essential to happiness. These mechanisms are captured by their acronym DRAMMA:

- D–R, *Detachment–Recovery*—One function of leisure activities is to detach ourselves from our work life; this then allows us to engage in the recovery processes that are required to keep on functioning effectively in life.
- A, *Autonomy*—Leisure may encourage SWB because it enhances our sense of autonomy; when we engage in leisure, we often feel that we have independently chosen the activity and are participating in it because we want to, not because we have to.
- M, *Mastery*—Many leisure activities such as learning to play a new instrument or mastering a new video game may encourage our sense of competence and thus encourage SWB.
- M, *Meaning*—When we engage in leisure activities that accomplish something that we value in life this enhances meaning in our lives, and meaning-making activities may enhance well-being because they help repair the bad and amplify the good in our lives (Baumeister & Vohs, 2002).
- A, *Affiliation*—Leisure activities also enhance our happiness because they often help us fulfill our need to commune with others.

Note how these psychological mechanisms dovetail nicely with Ryan and Deci's (2000) model of psychological needs and well-being that we reviewed in Chapter 1, and the literature provides considerable support for these pathways to well-being. Research shows that participation in leisure activities restores people's feelings of control and freedom in their lives, thus promoting their perceptions of autonomy (Hutchinson, Loy, Kleiber, & Dattilo, 2003). Recall that activities promoting a sense of mastery and meaning are more likely to produce flow states, which are likely to put us in a positive mood (e.g., Pinquart & Silbereisen, 2010).

And we have already seen that one of the reasons our leisure time is important to us is that it can provide opportunities to encourage bonds with those who are important to us.

Perhaps the one mechanism that might seem at odds with Ryan and Deci's (2000) theory of well-being is the detachment-relaxation leisure pathway to well-being. But one of the reasons we become burned out at work is that work starts to dominate our leisure hours as well because we are fatigued with our job or we may tend to ruminate on unresolved issues at work. When issues with work start to dominate our consciousness when we're away from work, this prevents us from pursuing the activities that enhance our sense of autonomy, competence, meaning, and relatedness to others. So when we step back, we can see that this theory is quite compatible with Ryan and Deci's need theory.

There are several important implications of this theory that can help us as we evaluate our leisure activities. First, one important implication of the DRAMMA theory of leisure well-being is that different leisure activities might provide different functions for our happiness. I have been somewhat disparaging of the more passive leisure activities such as watching television; nevertheless, there are occasions in our lives when we need to simply "veg out" and watch some television because we need an activity that helps us detach from work and relax. Of course, the problem comes because this is the leisure activity of the least resistance; thus we tend to overuse it and, therefore, avoid other leisure activities that provide for the other potential functions of meeting our psychological needs. Watching a lot of television isn't likely to provide for us much autonomy, mastery, meaning, or affiliation in our lives; however, there are times when we simply need to detach and relax.

Second, I believe that the DRAMMA model of leisure well-being can provide us some direction for how we might choose or change our leisure activities. In evaluating our leisure life, it is important to look at the DRAMMA mechanisms to see what needs are not being fulfilled in our leisure hours. I would encourage you to monitor your leisure time to see what activities you actually participate in during your time off. Then, carefully evaluate these activities in light of the DRAMMA mechanisms that we have explored. This should help you identify what psychological needs are not being met through your leisure activities. If you're like me, you'll see that your leisure time is probably spent too much with the detachment–relaxation mechanism, and not enough of your time away from work is devoted to fulfilling your other psychological needs. Recently, my wife told me about an Italian for Travelers class that was going to meet on Friday nights. At first, I was hesitant to give up my Friday nights for the fall because I normally like to have these evenings free to relax. But to be honest, I get plenty of relaxation, and what I really need is to engage in more leisure activities that fill the rest of my DRAMMA needs. Taking an Italian class with my wife should help fulfill many of the leisure needs that I often neglect, such as mastery, meaning, and affiliation. And because my wife isn't pressuring me to take the class, I feel that I am freely choosing to pursue this activity, which should enhance my sense of autonomy as well. Different leisure activities fulfill different leisure needs (and some activities may fulfill a number of needs), and it is crucial for us to look at our leisure lives in light of the diverse needs that these activities may fulfill.

In this section we have seen that satisfaction with leisure contributes meaningfully to our satisfaction with life. I conclude this part of the chapter by reviewing an intriguing study conducted by Argyle (1996). In this study, he compared the amount of joy that people experienced while participating in 11 different types of leisure groups. These leisure group activities ranged from religious to music to volunteer to political. All of these social leisure occasions produced some joy, but one activity produced much more joy than all the others: *group dancing*. As we evaluate this finding, it is important to highlight what type of dancing Argyle was investigating. This was not single's nightclub or bar dancing, where often the primary motive in such an activity is to secure some kind of sexual encounter. Rather, the dancing was more like organized folk dancing, like highland dancing, or square dancing. So, why did this type of dancing produce so much joy relative to the other social activities? I submit that organized social dancing fulfills many of the things that we need from leisure. Clearly, it is social (and therefore affiliative); it is both cognitively and behaviorally active (and thus likely provides for detachment and relaxation); and because it involves certain steps that are organized to music, it involves a sense of mastery. If we freely choose to participate in the dance (rather than feeling forced to dance by our spouses), it will probably enhance our autonomy as well. Moreover, because dancing is essentially expressive movement to music, it incorporates the benefits of music in an embodied form. We're not merely listening to the music; we are living it out, so to speak. So in conclusion, when you're trying to enhance your happiness by improving your leisure life, perhaps you should consider bringing a little DRAMMA into your life; one thing you might consider doing is making your leisure hours dance.

CONCLUSION: DOES THE "IF ONLY" APPROACH TO HAPPINESS WORK?

This chapter explored the circumstances of happiness. We have evaluated whether things such as gender, age, income, work, and leisure have an impact on happiness. In general, we have seen that the circumstances of your gender, where you live, your age, and your income don't contribute much to your SWB. In this sense, I have called them the "not muches" of happiness. Do your gender, your geography, your age, and your income predict much of your happiness? The answer appears to be: not much. Although your income does predict a bit of your happiness, for the most part it appears that once the essentials of life have been purchased, there's not much happiness left to be bought. And people who believe that having more income will produce more happiness (materialists) are actually less happy than the rest of us. The only exceptions to the circumstances of happiness appear to be your work and leisure status. Here, we have seen that having a job and being satisfied with your work and your leisure time do matter to your happiness. But if you think about it, your work and your leisure are not so much circumstances of your life as they are chosen activities.

So in conclusion, does the "if only" approach to happiness work? Is it true that "if only I had more money, I would be happier"? "If only I were younger (or older), then I'd be happy." "If only I had a 62-inch smart television, then I'd be happy." "If only I had a PhD, then I'd be happy." In general, the research indicates rather clearly that the "if only" approach to happiness is not an effective route. If you think that your happiness resides in more money, growing older, more education, or a different spouse, you're likely to be greatly disappointed. Indeed, research suggests that happy people don't wait for their circumstances to change in order to be happy—rather, they actively engage in the intentional activities that life has to offer them now.

REFERENCES

American Psychiatric Association. (2013). *Diagnostic and statistical manual of mental disorders* (5th ed.). Washington, DC: American Psychiatric Publishing.

Argyle, M. (1996). *The social psychology of leisure.* London, England: Routledge.

Argyle, M. (2001). *The psychology of happiness.* New York, NY: Taylor & Francis.

Balatsky, G., & Diener, E. (1993). Subjective well-being among Russian students. *Social Indicators Research, 28,* 225–243.

Bateman, T. S., & Organ, D. W. (1983). Job satisfaction and the good soldier: The relationship between affect and employee "citizenship." *Academy of Management Journal, 26,* 587–595.

Baumeister, R. F., & Vohs, K. D. (2002). The pursuit of meaningfulness in life. In C. R. Snyder & S. J. Lopez (Eds.), *Handbook of positive psychology* (pp. 608–618). New York, NY: Oxford University Press.

Bellah, R. N., Madsen, R., Sullivan, W. M., Swidler, A., & Tipton, S. M. (1985). *Habits of the heart.* Berkeley: University of California Press.

Berman, M. G., Jonides, J., & Kaplan, S. (2008). The cognitive benefits of interacting with nature. *Psychological Science, 19,* 1207–1212.

Biswas-Diener, R. M. (2008). Material wealth and subjective well-being. In M. Eid & R. J. Larson (Eds.), *The science of subjective well-being* (pp. 307–322). New York, NY: Guilford Press.

Blanchflower, D. G., & Oswald, A. J. (1999). Well-being over time in Britain and the U.S.A. In I. M. McDonald (Ed.), *Behavioural macroeconomics* (pp. 377–404). Northampton, MA: Edward Elgar.

Brickman, P., & Campbell, D. T. (1971). Hedonic relativism and planning the good society. In M. H. Appley (Ed.), *Adaptation level theory: A symposium* (pp. 287–302). New York, NY: Academic Press.

Brickman, P., Coates, D., & Janoff-Bulman, R. (1978). Lottery winners and accident victims: Is happiness relative? *Journal of Personality and Social Psychology, 36,* 917–927.

Brinkerhoff, M. B., Fredell, K. A., & Frideres, J. S. (1997). Basic minimum needs, quality of life and selected correlates: Exploration in villages in northern India. *Social Indicators Research, 42,* 245–281.

Caldwell, L. L. (2005). Leisure and health: Why is leisure therapeutic? *British Journal of Guidance and Counseling, 33,* 7–26.

Campbell, A. (1981). *The sense of well-being in America.* New York, NY: McGraw-Hill.

Caplan, R. D., Cobb, S., French, J. R. P., van Harrison, R., & Pinneau, S. R. (1975). *Job demands and worker health.* New Brunswick, NJ: Rutgers University Press.

Carsten, J. M., & Spector, P. E. (1987). Unemployment, job satisfaction, and employee turnover: A meta-analytic test of the Muchinsky model. *Journal of Applied Psychology, 72,* 374–381.

Carter, T. J., & Gilovich, T. (2010). The relative relativity of material and experiential purchases. *Journal of Personality and Social Psychology, 98*, 146–159.

Carter, T. J., & Gilovich, T. (2012). I am what I do, not what I have: The differential centrality of experiential and material purchases to the self. *Journal of Personality and Social Psychology, 102*, 1304–1317.

Caza, B. B., & Wrzesniewski, A. (2013). How work shapes well-being. In S. A. David, I. Boniwell, & A. Conley Ayers (Eds.), *The Oxford handbook of happiness* (pp. 693–710). Oxford, England: Oxford University Press.

Charles, S. T., Reynolds, C. A., & Gatz, M. (2001). Age-related differences and change in positive and negative affect over 23 years. *Journal of Personality and Social Psychology, 80*, 136–151.

Christensen, A., Herskind, A. M., & Vaupel, J. W. (2006). Why Danes are smug: Comparative study of life satisfaction in the European Union. *British Medical Journal, 333*, 1289–1291.

Crum, A. J., & Salovey, P. (2013). Emotionally intelligent happiness. In S. A. David, I. Boniwell, & A. C. Ayers (Eds.), *The Oxford handbook of happiness* (pp. 73–87). Oxford, England: Oxford University Press.

Csikszentmihalyi, M. (1975). *Beyond boredom and anxiety.* San Francisco, CA: Jossey-Bass.

Csikszentmihalyi, M. (1988). The flow experience and its significance for human psychology. In M. Csikszentmihalyi & I. S. Csikszentmihalyi (Eds.), *Optimal experience: Psychological studies of flow in consciousness* (pp. 15–35). Oxford, England: Cambridge University Press.

Csikszentmihalyi, M. (1990). *Flow: The psychology of optimal experience.* New York, NY: HarperCollins.

Csikszentmihalyi, M., Larson, R., & Prescott, S. (1977). The ecology of adolescent activity and experience. *Journal of Youth and Adolescence, 6*, 181–294.

Csikszentmihalyi, M., & LeFevre, J. (1989). Optimal experience in work and leisure. *Journal of Personality and Social Psychology, 56*, 815–822.

Diener, E., & Biswas-Diener, R. (2002). Will money increase subjective well-being? A literature review and guide to needed research. *Social Indicators Research, 57*, 119–169.

Diener, E., Horwitz, J., & Emmons, R. A. (1985). Happiness of the very wealthy. *Social Indicators Research, 16*, 263–274.

Diener, E., Nickerson, C., Lucas, R. E., & Sandvik, E. (2002). Dispositional affect and job outcomes. *Social Indicators Research, 59*, 229–259.

Diener, E., & Oishi, S. (2000). Money and happiness: Income and subjective well-being across nations. In E. Diener & E. M. Suh (Eds.), *Subjective well-being across cultures* (pp. 185–218). Cambridge: Massachusetts Institute of Technology Press.

Diener, E., Sandvik, E., Seidlitz, L., & Diener, M. (1993). The relationship between income and subjective well-being: Relative or absolute? *Social Indicators Research, 28*, 195–223.

Diener, E., & Seligman, M. E. P. (2004). Beyond money: Toward an economy of well-being. *Psychological Science in the Public Interest, 5*, 1–31.

Diener, E., Suh, E. M., Lucas, R. E., & Smith, H. L. (1999). Subjective well-being: Three decades of progress. *Psychological Bulletin, 125*, 276–302.

Diener, E., Wolsic, B., & Fujita, F. (1995). Physical attractiveness and subjective well-being. *Journal of Personality and Social Psychology, 69*, 120–129.

Dunn, E., & Norton, M. (2013). *Happy money: The science of happier spending.* New York, NY: Simon & Schuster.

Easterlin, R. A. (1974). Does economic growth improve the human lot? Some empirical evidence. In P. A. David & M. W. Reder (Eds.), *Nations and households in economic growth* (pp. 89–125). New York, NY: Academic Press.

Festinger, L. (1954). A theory of social comparison processes. *Human Relations, 7*, 117–140.

Fleming, J. H. (2000). Relating employee engagement and customer loyalty to business outcomes in the retail industry. *The Gallup Research Journal, 3*(1), 103–115.

Frijda, N. H. (1988). The laws of emotion. *American Psychologist, 43*, 349–358.

Frijda, N. H. (2007). *The laws of emotion.* Mahwah, NJ: Lawrence Erlbaum.

Fujita, F., Diener, E., & Sandvik, E. (1991). Gender differences in negative affect and well-being: The case for emotional intensity. *Journal
of Personality and Social Psychology, 61*, 427–434.

Furham, A., & Schaeffer, R. (1984). Person-environment fit, job satisfaction and mental health. *Journal of Occupational Psychology,
57*, 295–307.

Gallo, D. A., Korthauer, L. E., McDonough, I. M., Teshale, S., & Johnson,
E. L. (2011). Age-related positivity effects and autobiographical
memory detail: Evidence from a past/future source memory task.
Memory, 19, 641–652.

Gilbert, D., & Abdullah, J. (2002). A study on the impact of the expec-
tation of a holiday on an individual's sense of well-being. *Journal
of Vacation Marketing, 8*, 352–361.

Gilovich, T. (2014, June). *Two enemies of gratitude.* Invited presentation
to the Greater Good Gratitude Summit, Berkeley, CA.

Guimond, S. (Ed.). (2006). *Social comparison and social psychology:
Understanding cognition, intergroup relations, and culture.* Oxford,
England: Cambridge University Press.

Hackman, J. R., & Oldham, G. R. (1976). Motivation through the
design of work: Test of a theory. *Organizational Behavior and
Human Performance, 16*, 250–279.

Haring, M. J., Okun, M. A., & Stock, W. A. (1984). A quantitative
synthesis of literature on work status and subjective well-being.
Journal of Vocational Behavior, 25, 316–324.

Harter, J. K., Schmidt, F. L., & Hayes, T. L. (2002). Business-unit-level
relationship between employee satisfaction, employee engagement, and business outcomes: A meta-analysis. *Journal of Applied
Psychology, 87*, 268–279.

Heady, B. W., & Wearing, A. (1992). *Understanding happiness.* Mel-
bourne, Australia: Longman Cheshire.

Helliwell, J. F., & Wang, S. (2014). Weekends and subjective well-being.
Social Indicators Research, 116, 389–407.

Horley, J., & Lavery, J. J. (1995). Subjective well-being and age. *Social
Indicators Research, 34*, 275–282.

Howell, R. T., & Howell, C. J. (2008). The relation of economic status
to subjective well-being in developing countries: A meta-analysis.
Psychological Bulletin, 134, 536–560.

Hutchinson, S. L., Loy, D., Kleiber, D. A., & Dattilo, J. (2003). Leisure as a coping resource: Variations in coping with a traumatic injury and illness. *Leisure Sciences, 25*, 143–161.

Iaffaldano, M. T., & Muchinsky, P. M. (1985). Job satisfaction and job performance: A meta-analysis. *Psychological Bulletin, 97*, 251–273.

Inglehart, R. (1990). *Culture shift in advanced industrial society.* Princeton, NJ: Princeton University Press.

Jahoda, M. (1982). *Employment and unemployment.* Cambridge, England: Cambridge University Press.

Judge, T. A., & Watanabe, S. (1993). Another look at the job satisfaction–life satisfaction relationship. *Journal of Applied Psychology, 78*, 939–948.

Kasser, T. (2002). *The high price of materialism.* Cambridge: Massachusetts Institute of Technology Press.

Kasser, T., & Ryan, R. M. (1993). A dark side of the American dream: Correlates of financial success as a central life aspiration. *Journal of Personality and Social Psychology, 65*, 410–422.

Keller, M., Fredrickson, B. L., Ybarra, O., Cote, S., Johnson, K., Mikels, J., . . . Wagner, T. (2005). A warm heart and a clear head: The contingent effects of weather on mood and cognition. *Psychological Science, 16*, 724–731.

Klein, M. H., Greist, J. H., & Gurtman, A. S. (1985). A comparative outcome study of group psychotherapy vs. exercise treatments for depression. *International Journal of Mental Health, 13*, 148–177.

Kuykendall, L., Tay, L., & Ng, V. (2015). Leisure engagement and subjective well-being: A meta-analysis. *Psychological Bulletin.* doi:10.1037/a0038508

Lewis, C. S. (1982). *Screwtape letters.* New York, NY: Macmillan. (Original work published 1961)

Lloyd, K., & Auld, C. J. (2002). The role of leisure in determining quality of life: Issues of content and measurement. *Social Indicators Research, 57*, 43–71.

Lucas, R. E., Clark, A. E., Georgellis, Y., & Diener, E. (2004). Unemployment alters the set point for life satisfaction. *Psychological Science, 15*, 8–13.

Luhmann, M., Lucas, R. E., Eid, M., & Diener, D. (2013). The prospective effect of life satisfaction on life events. *Social Psychological and Personality Science, 4*, 39–45.

Luthans, F., & Youssef, C. M. (2004). Human, social, and now positive psychological capital management: Investing in people for competitive advantage. *Organizational Dynamics, 33,* 143–160.

Lyubomirsky, S., King, L., & Diener, E. (2005). The benefits of frequent positive affect: Does happiness lead to success? *Psychological Bulletin, 131,* 803–855.

Lyubomirsky, S., & Ross, L. (1997). Hedonic consequences of social comparison: A contrast of happy and unhappy people. *Journal of Personality and Social Psychology, 73,* 1141–1157.

Marks, G. N., & Fleming, N. (1999). Influences and consequences of well-being among Australian young people: 1980–1995. *Social Indicators Research, 36,* 301–323.

Massimini, F., & Carli, M. (1988). The systematic assessment of flow in daily experience. In M. Csikszentmihalyi & I. S. Csikszentmihalyi (Eds.), *Optimal experience: Psychological studies of flow in consciousness* (pp. 266–287). Cambridge, England: Cambridge University Press.

Mather, M., & Carstensen, L. L. (2005). Aging and motivated cognition: The positivity effect in attention and memory. *Trends in Cognitive Science, 9,* 496–502.

Myers, D. G. (1992). *The pursuit of happiness: Discovering the pathway to fulfillment, well-being, and enduring personal joy.* New York, NY: Avon Books.

Nawjin, J. (2011). Happiness through vacationing: Just a temporary boost or long-term benefits? *Journal of Happiness Studies, 12,* 651–665.

Newman, D. B., Tay, L., & Diener, E. (2014). Leisure and subjective well-being: A model of psychological mechanisms as mediating factors. *Journal of Happiness Studies, 15,* 555–578.

Nisbet, E. K., & Zelenski, J. M. (2011). Understanding nearby nature: Affective forecasting errors obscure the happy path to sustainability. *Psychological Science, 22,* 1101–1106.

Pavot, W., & Diener, E. (2013). Happiness experienced: The science of subjective well-being. In S. A. David, I. Boniwell, & A. C. Ayers (Eds.), *The Oxford handbook of happiness* (pp. 134–151). Oxford, England: Oxford University Press.

Peterson, C. (2006). *A primer in positive psychology.* New York, NY: Oxford University Press.

Pinquart, M., & Silbereisen, R. K. (2010). Patterns of fulfillment in the domains of work, intimate relationship, and leisure. *Applied Research in the Quality of Life, 5*, 147–164.

Rosenzweig, E., & Gilovich, T. (2012). Buyer's remorse or missed opportunity? Differential regrets for material and experiential purchases. *Journal of Personality and Social Psychology, 102*, 215–223.

Russell, B. (1930). *The conquest of happiness.* London, England: George Allen and Unwin Ltd.

Ryan, R. M., & Deci, E. L. (2000). Self-determination theory and the facilitations of intrinsic motivation, social development, and well-being. *American Psychologist, 55*, 68–78.

Schkade, D. A., & Kahneman, D. (1998). Does living in California make people happy? A focusing illusion in judgments of life satisfaction. *Psychological Science, 9*, 340–346.

Scott, K. D., & Taylor, G. S. (1985). An examination of conflicting findings on the relationship between job satisfaction and absenteeism: A meta-analysis. *Academy of Management Journal, 28*, 599–612.

Shin, Y., Kim, D. J., Jung-Choi, K., Son, Y., Koo, J., Min, J., & Chae, J. (2013). Differences of psychological effects between meditative and athletic walking in a forest and gymnasium. *Scandinavian Journal of Forest Research, 28*, 64–72.

Spector, P. E. (1997). *Job satisfaction.* Thousand Oaks, CA: Sage.

Suh, E., & Koo, J. (2008). Comparing subjective well-being across cultures and nations. In M. Eid & R. J. Larson (Eds.), *The science of subjective well-being* (pp. 414–427). New York, NY: Guilford Press.

Suls, J., Martin, R., & Wheeler, L. (2002). Social comparison: Why, with whom, and with what effect? *Current Directions in Psychological Science, 11*, 159–163.

Tait, M., Padgett, M. Y., & Baldwin, T. T. (1989). Job satisfaction and life satisfaction: A reexamination of the strength of the relationship and gender effects as a function of the date of the study. *Journal of Applied Psychology, 74*, 502–507.

Thayer, R. E. (1989). *The biopsychology of mood and arousal.* New York, NY: Oxford University Press.

Tsang, J., Carpenter, T. P., Roberts, J. A., Frisch, M. B., & Carlisle, R. D. (2014). Why are materialists less happy? The role of gratitude and need satisfaction in the relationship between materialism and life satisfaction. *Personality and Individual Differences, 64,* 62–66.

Van Boven, L. (2005). Experientialism, materialism, and the pursuit of happiness. *Review of General Psychology, 9,* 132–142.

Van Boven, L., & Gilovich, T. (2003). To do or to have? That is the question. *Journal of Personality and Social Psychology, 85,* 1193–1202.

van der Doef, M., & Maes, S. (1999). The job demands-control (-support) model and psychological well-being: A review of 20 years of empirical research. *Work and Stress, 13,* 87–115.

Veenhoven, R., & Choi, Y. (2012). Does intelligence boost happiness? Smartness of all pays more than being smarter than others. *International Journal of Happiness and Development, 1*(1), 5–27.

Warr, P. (2013). Jobs and job-holders: Two sources of happiness and unhappiness. In S. A. David, I. Boniwell, & A. C. Ayers (Eds.), *The Oxford handbook of happiness* (pp. 733–750). Oxford, England: Oxford University Press.

Warr, P. B. (1978). A study of psychological well-being. *British Journal of Psychology, 69,* 111–121.

Warr, P. B. (1982). A national study of non-financial employment commitment. *Journal of Occupational Psychology, 55,* 297–312.

Warr, P. B. (1984). Work and unemployment. In P. J. D. Drenth et al. (Eds.), *Handbook of work and organizational psychology* (Vol. 1, pp. 413–443). Chichester, England: Wiley.

Watkins, P. C. (2014). *Gratitude and the good life: Toward a psychology of appreciation.* Dordrecht, The Netherlands: Springer.

West, M. A., Borrill, C. S., & Unsworth, K. L. (1998). Team effectiveness in organizations. In C. Cooper & I. T. Robertson (Eds.), *International review of industrial and organizational psychology* (Vol. 13, pp. 1–48). Chichester, England: Wiley.

Wilson, W. R. (1967). Correlates of avowed happiness. *Psychological Bulletin, 67*(4), 294–306.

Winefield, A. H., Tiggermann, M., & Winefield, H. R. (1992). Spare time use and psychological well-being in employed and unemployed young people. *Journal of Occupational and Organizational Psychology,* *65,* 307–313.

Wood, W., Rhodes, N., & Whelan, M. (1989). Sex differences in positive well-being: A consideration of emotional style and marital status. *Psychological Bulletin, 106,* 249–264.

Wright, T. A. (2013). Encouraging employee happiness. In S. A. David, I. Boniwell, & A. Conley Ayers (Eds.), *The Oxford handbook of happiness* (pp. 783–797). Oxford, England: Oxford University Press.

Wrzesniewski, A., McCauley, C., Rozin, P., & Schwartz, B. (1997). Jobs, careers, and callings: People's relations to their work. *Journal of Research in Personality, 31,* 21–33.

What Are Happy
People Like?
The Characteristics
of Happiness

Right now, identify two or three people you know
well whom you consider to be happy people.
Think about what they are like. What are their
personalities like? How do they typically act?
What are their lifestyles like? What motivates them in life? What
are their worldviews? Reflecting on the happy people you know
should help you comprehend the information contained in this
chapter—an exploration of the characteristics of happy people.
First, we investigate the genetic makeup of happy people,
and draw some conclusions about biological contributions to
happiness. Next, we discuss the behavioral characteristics of

those who are happy. Then we delve into an important area of research in positive psychology: looking at the personality traits that predict happiness. Your life goals are a crucial component of your personality and, as it turns out, your goals are important to your happiness. I spend some time here considering the goals of happiness. Finally, we examine the spirituality of happiness: What are the spiritual and religious characteristics of happy people?

So why is it vital to comprehend the characteristics of happiness? Understanding the personality, the characteristic behaviors, the goals, and the spiritualty of happy people provides us with crucial clues as to how we might proceed to change people's happiness. For instance, if we find that happy people like to get along and cooperate with other people, this might give us an important suggestion for how you approach others. If we see that happy people tend to be active people, this supplies a useful principle for evaluating the use of your own leisure time. So as we explore the characteristics of happy people, you might find it helpful to think about what these traits imply for how you can change your life to improve your happiness.

BIOLOGICAL CHARACTERISTICS OF HAPPY PEOPLE: GENETIC CONTRIBUTIONS TO HAPPINESS

Is happiness simply a product of the genes you've inherited from your parents? Are we genetically programmed to a certain set point of happiness, so that trying to change my happiness is about as useful as trying to change the color of my eyes? Are we doomed to inevitably return to this genetic set point of happiness, regardless of what we do to improve our well-being? As you can see, understanding the genetic contributions to happiness has critical practical implications.

So is there a genetic contribution to happiness? The simple answer to this question is that research shows that genetics play a large part in explaining our happiness. Figure 4.1 demonstrates the findings from one study (Lykken & Tellegen, 1996), clearly showing the genetic contribution to happiness. As you may know, monozygotic twins (identical twins) share an identical genetic structure, whereas dizygotic twins (fraternal twins) do not. As you can see from this figure, the correlations between the identical twins' happiness scores are much higher than the correlations between fraternal twins, regardless of whether they were raised apart or together. This provides strong evidence for a genetic contribution to happiness. How much of our happiness is controlled by our genetics? Estimates vary widely—from

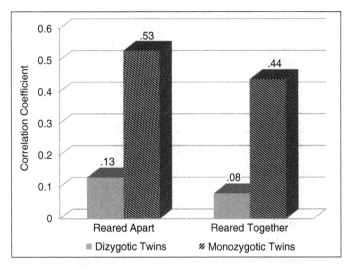

FIGURE 4.1 Correlations between twins' happiness scores.
Source: Lykken and Tellegen (1996).

38% (Diener, Emmons, Larsen, & Griffin, 1985) to 80% (Lykken & Tellegen, 1996)—but the most reasonable estimates seem to be that genetics contribute about 40% to 50% of our happiness (Lucas, 2008). So although genetics account for a significant proportion of our happiness, there is much of our subjective well-being (SWB) that is left to be explained.

Of course, simply saying that a certain amount of our happiness is due to genetics doesn't really explain much. Genetics must be expressed in some biological tendencies that influence our happiness. So how is the genetic contribution to happiness expressed? We get some clues by looking at the genetic contribution to positive and negative affectivity. Remember that high SWB can be seen as having three primary components: frequent positive emotions, infrequent negative emotions, and high judgments of life satisfaction. Although estimates vary, about 40% of people's dispositions for positive emotions is inherited (i.e., *positive affectivity*), whereas about 50% to 55% of their tendency to experience negative emotions is due to their genetics (i.e., *negative affectivity*; Bouchard, 2004; Peterson, 2006; Tellegen et al., 1988). There are some important implications to be drawn from these findings. First, negative affectivity is more heritable than positive affectivity (Baker, Cesa, Gatz, & Mellins, 1992). This implies that one's tendency to experience positive emotions might be more trainable than one's disposition for negative affect. In general, this is good news for positive psychology because your tendency to experience positive emotions is more important to your happiness than the frequency of unpleasant emotions. There are also meaningful implications for negative psychology. Because positive affectivity may be more trainable than negative affectivity, clinical psychologists may want to focus more on enhancing positive emotion as a target in treatment. Indeed, recent theories of clinical depression have argued that depression may be more the consequence of an absence of positive affect rather than excess negative affect (see Chapter 8 in Watkins, 2014). Thus a *positive clinical psychology* may have much to offer in the treatment of psychological disorders (Wood & Johnson, in press; Wood & Tarrier, 2010), and this is a theme that I return to throughout this book.

The findings about the heritability of positive and negative affectivity may also have important implications for how the genetics of happiness are expressed biologically. Here I have found the biological theory of emotion by Gray to be very helpful (Gray, 1990, 1991). He argues that two different independent systems in the brain mediate most of our positive and negative emotional responses. The *behavioral activation system* (BAS) is essential to our experience of positive emotions, and the *behavioral inhibition system* (BIS) mediates our negative emotional responses. The idea is that our brains need to have two distinct motivational systems: one to encourage us to approach and secure things that benefit our survival—namely, the BAS—and one to inhibit responses that might end up harming us—that is, the BIS. It is important to state that Gray also theorized a third emotional system—one that motivates us to flee or fight—but most happiness researchers have emphasized the importance of the BAS and the BIS. The BAS is sensitive to reward and nonpunishment, whereas the BIS is sensitive to signals in the environment that indicate the possibility of punishment. Because the BAS is vital for motivating us to approach benefits that are necessary to survival, some have referred to this as the *behavioral approach system*, and the BAS is probably mediated by the dopamine system in the midbrain (Depue & Collins, 1999). According to Gray, although the BAS and BIS tend to inhibit each other in the moment (i.e., when our positive emotion system is activated it tends to deactivate our negative emotion system and vice versa), because these systems are largely independent, over the long run you won't find that the frequency of negative emotional experiences predicts the frequency of positive emotions. Research largely supports this pattern. If you're feeling grateful and happy right now, you're probably not feeling sad and anxious. Studies also suggest, however, that if I know how much you are inclined to experience positive emotions, this tells me very little about your disposition to experience negative emotions. Some people are high on positive affectivity and low on negative affectivity; however, others are high on both positive and negative affectivity, and still others might be low on both. Thus Gray's theory states that we're all different in how easily our BAS and BIS become activated and we're all somewhat different in how long these systems might remain activated. Genetics probably play a significant part in terms of how easily these systems are activated, but research suggests that heritability has more to do with the sensitivity of the BIS than the BAS.

So what does all this have to do with happiness? Gray's theory proposes that individuals who have a sensitive BAS but, at the same time, a somewhat insensitive BIS should end up being the happiest people, and indirect evidence largely supports this idea. Conversely, those who have an easily activated BIS and an insensitive BAS should be somewhat anxious and relatively unhappy. In sum, genetics play an important part in our happiness and, very likely, the way genetics are expressed is through how easily our BAS and BIS brain emotional systems are activated.

Thus far we have seen that genetics are a significant aid to our happiness. So is our happiness doomed by our heredity? Lykken and Tellegen (1996) estimated that about 80% of one's stable SWB was genetically determined, and hence they concluded: "It may be that trying to be happier is as futile as trying to be taller and therefore is counterproductive" (p. 189). Are they right? Is our happiness so determined by heredity that any attempt at improving it is bound to fail? I suspect that if they're right, you'd be tempted to put this book down right now and ask for a refund from the bookstore. Fortunately, there are several notable problems with this determination. First, note how Lykken and Tellegen's conclusion essentially cuts its own throat. Because our happiness is so genetically determined, they argue, trying to be happier is "counterproductive" and thus will actually make us less happy. So in this interpretation itself, they admit that you can do things to change your happiness (in this case decrease your happiness), which of course goes against their supposition that it's "futile" to attempt to change your happiness. There are several additional problems to their rather gloomy prognosis. First, we should note that even if we do accept the notion of a genetic set point for our happiness, that point is actually set pretty high. As a number of studies have clearly shown, "Most people are happy" (Diener & Diener, 1996), and so this set point is pretty high for most people. Second, although the heritability estimates achieved by Lykken and Tellegen were higher than most studies have found, there were questions about how they chose to look at their data. If you think about it, a stable factor such as your genetics is bound to correlate higher with stable happiness than it would with changing circumstances, and so we might complain that the analysis itself was a bit biased. Indeed, as Lykken later admitted (Lykken & Csikszentmihalyi, 2001), only about 50% of the variance of happiness was stable over a 10-year period. Thus the better conclusion might be: "It is more accurate to say that trying to change the part of our happiness that does not change is like trying to be taller" (Lucas, 2008, p. 176).

There are other issues with Lykken and Tellegen's (1996) conclusions that I won't delineate here (see Lucas, 2008); nevertheless, to be fair to the memory of an excellent psychological scientist like David Lykken, he later admitted that his earlier determination was too strong (Lykken & Csikszentmihalyi, 2001). So Lyubomirsky's proposition that was covered earlier still holds: Although 50% of our happiness may be inherited, about 40% is still up to us (Lyubomirsky, 2007; Lyubomirsky, Sheldon, & Schkade, 2005). Before we just dismiss Lykken's conclusion, I think there's still something important to take away from his work. Although there are things we could do to improve our happiness, I worry that our current obsession with

147

happiness leads us to believe that we can achieve whatever level of happiness we desire. And this emphasis leads us to pursue an unrealistic level of happiness—a happiness too lofty for the SWB that our genetics might allow. If we strive too hard for an unrealistic level of happiness, we are bound to be disappointed, and that will probably make us less happy. As Fontenelle, the 17th- through 18th-century French author, philosopher, and scientist, said: "A great obstacle to happiness is to anticipate too great a happiness."

BEHAVIORAL CHARACTERISTICS OF HAPPY PEOPLE: HAPPY PEOPLE ARE ACTIVE PEOPLE

In Chapter 3, we saw that life circumstances such as one's gender, age, income, and location explain very little of one's happiness. Activities such as work and leisure, however, predict much more of the variance in happiness. In this, we see that happy people are active in their work and leisure life. Indeed, we may extend this to a more general conclusion: Happy people tend to be active people. Contrary to the stereotype of happiness producing "contented cows," happy people appear to be actively engaged in life (Veenhoven, 1988). This is not to suggest, however, that the lives of happy people may be characterized by mindless business. Although more studies could investigate this area, I suggest two reasons why happy people are not merely busy people. First, indirect evidence implies that the activities of happy people tend to be driven by purpose and meaning. I review these findings in more detail later, but this goes against the picture of happy people simply being active for the sake of being active. Second, I propose that happy people are able to find the time for experiences of solitude and serenity. Although happy people have a tendency to be social people, this should not imply that they can't tolerate being alone; I believe more research could be devoted to exploring how occasions of reflection and contemplation might be beneficial to happiness. But the bottom line is that happy people tend to be active people; they are actively *engaged* in the endeavors of life, and much of the remainder of this book is devoted to describing these activities.

PERSONALITY CHARACTERISTICS OF HAPPY PEOPLE

Broad Personality Characteristics of Happy People: The Big Five Approach

How can we understand a person? How do we know a person as a unique individual? These questions are the domain of the psychology of personality, and personality psychologists argue that we may know a person at several different levels of explanation. One way of knowing people is by knowing their broad personality traits. Perhaps one of the most significant advancements in personality science in the last 30 years has been the discovery that most of our personality traits can be described in terms of five relatively independent features of personality: the so-called "Big Five" personality traits (Goldberg, 1981, 1993; McCrae & Costa, 1999). Following is a brief description of these characteristics (adapted from John & Srivastava, 1999):

- *Extraversion* (vs. *Introversion*)—These are people who are active, outgoing, sociable, and seem to have an energetic approach to life.
- *Neuroticism* (vs. *Emotional stability*)—Often called trait anxiety, these individuals tend to be anxious, tense, and sad.

- *Agreeableness*—Persons who are prosocial in nature; they enjoy getting along with and giving to others.
- *Conscientiousness*—Individuals with good self-control, they're good at managing their impulses so that they can achieve their goals.
- *Openness*—These people are inclined to be original, creative, somewhat nonconventional, and are open to new experiences.

These factors have been found to be largely independent, meaning that they don't correlate strongly with each other. This means, for example, that one can be high in extraversion but low in agreeableness. One can be high in extraversion but high in neuroticism as well. So how do these Big Five traits help us understand the happy person? In a nutshell, happy people have a tendency to be higher in extroversion, lower in neuroticism, higher in agreeableness, and higher in conscientiousness. Figure 4.2 presents these relationships by illustrating average correlations from a number of studies cited by a recent review (Steel, Schmidt, & Shultz, 2008). As demonstrated by this figure, the strongest relationships with happiness are found with extraversion and neuroticism, followed by associations with agreeableness and conscientiousness. Openness tends to show small and inconsistent associations with happiness. Let's explore each of these traits in turn.

As seen in Figure 4.2, one of the traits that most strongly correlates with happiness is extraversion, but what does this mean? Just knowing that extraverted people tend to be happy doesn't tell us a great deal about happiness. In order to really understand this relationship, we must comprehend what extraversion actually is. One of the central characteristics of extraverted people is that they're high in positive affectivity—they experience positive emotions much more frequently than introverts—so much that some have suggested that positive affectivity is at the core of

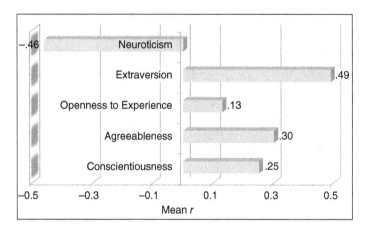

FIGURE 4.2 Mean correlations of the Big Five traits with happiness, a meta-analysis.

Source: Steel et al. (2008).

Note: The results in the graph are from the Neuroticism-Extroversion-Openness Inventory. Relationships of the Big Five traits with life satisfaction showed a pattern similar to the one seen here, with the caveat that the associations were weaker.

extraversion (e.g., Lucas, Le, & Dyrenforth, 2008). Why is it that extraverts seem so often to be in a good mood? There are several theories that have tried to explain the contribution of extraversion to positive affectivity. The *Person-by-Situation Fit* perspective argues that extraverts are happier than introverts because society requires frequent social interactions. Due to the fact that extraverts enjoy being with people but introverts prefer being alone, this results in extraverts experiencing more positive emotions, and thus they end up being happier people (Pavot, Diener, & Fujita, 1990). The evidence for this idea is rather mixed, and Figure 4.3 illustrates the results of one relevant study (Pavot et al., 1990). First, note that across situations, extraverts reported more positive emotion than introverts. Even when alone, extraverts are happier than introverts. Second, note that both extroverts and

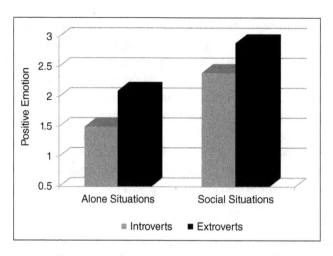

FIGURE 4.3 Introversion/extraversion, social contact, and happiness. *Source*: Pavot et al. (1990).

introverts are happier when they're with others. These results don't quite adhere to the Person-by-Situation Fit model. It's not that introverts are happier when they're alone and extroverts are happier when they're with others, all of us get a positive mood boost when we're with other people. I have several friends who claim to be introverts, and they maintain that they're always happier when they can be alone. The data just don't support that idea, and the importance of social contact to your happiness is examined further in Chapter 5. The fact that extroverts are in a better mood than introverts even when they're alone implies that there's something else besides their social nature that explains the happiness of extraverts (Lucas et al., 2008).

Others have proposed that extroverts are happier because they experience more positive affect in pleasant situations than do introverts. This is called the *affective-reactivity hypothesis* and this theory appears to have some traction (e.g., Larsen & Ketelaar, 1991). Earlier, when discussing the biological contribution to happiness, I introduced Gray's neuropsychological theory of emotion, which proposes that happy people have a sensitive BAS. If positive affectivity is a core feature of extraversion and positive affectivity is essentially the reflection of a sensitive BAS, then extraversion might simply be the measurement of an active BAS. In other words, extroverts essentially have a sensitive reward system in their brains, and this is why they experience frequent positive emotions and hence prove to be happier people than introverts. Taken together, these findings appear to converge on the conclusion that a sensitive BAS is at the heart of extraversion.

One problem with this conclusion is that recent research has shown that extroverts do not respond more strongly than introverts to all pleasant events. Indeed, there are some positive events that introverts are as happy about as extraverts. This has led some to reconsider what the BAS actually entails (Smillie, 2013). It is now clear that the BAS is not simply a "pleasure center" that mediates all pleasurable responses. Rather, if one looks at Gray's theory more carefully (see also Depue & Collins, 1999), the BAS is a motivational system—the structure activated in the brain when we are motivated to approach things that help us live well. Thus the BAS should be important for goal-directed pleasurable pursuits, but it is clear that not all pleasures are goal directed. This has led researchers to differentiate between activities that can be characterized as *reward approach activities* and those that are *consumptive activities*. More simply, the distinction between *reward approach activities* and *consumptive activities* can also be characterized as activities of *wanting* and *liking*, respectively. Reward approach activities are pleasurable activities that also involve high effort (physically or cognitively). Conversely, consumptive activities are those that are pleasurable but involve low effort. Exercise, dancing, and enjoyable work-related activities are considered to be reward approach, whereas watching television, listening to music, and shopping are consumptive activities

(Waterman, 2005). Because the BAS is supposed to be specifically involved in the motivation to pursue reward, this formulation implies that extraversion should distinguish the pleasure experienced when involved in reward approach activities, but not in consumptive activities. In other words, extroverts should enjoy exercising, dancing, and work-related activities more than introverts, but introverts should enjoy shopping and watching television as much as extraverts.

Some research now supports this idea. For instance, Figure 4.4 illustrates the results from one study that investigated whether or not extraversion differentiated the enjoyment experienced during reward approach activities but not the pleasure experienced during consumptive activities (Smillie, Cooper, Wilt, & Revelle, 2012; see also Smillie, Geaney, Wilt, Cooper, & Revelle, 2013). In this experiment participants were randomly assigned

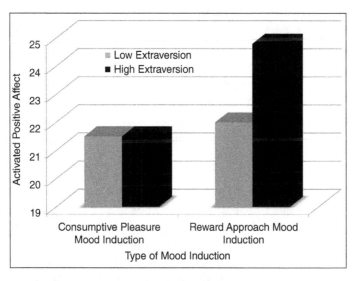

FIGURE 4.4 Amount of activated positive affect by extraversion and type of mood induction.

Source: Smillie et al. (2012).

to one of two pleasant mood inductions, in addition to a neutral mood induction. As the graph clearly shows, in the consumptive mood induction introverts showed just as much enjoyment as extraverts, whereas extraverts experienced significantly more positive affect in the reward approach positive mood induction.

That's a nice effect in the laboratory, but what about real life? More recently, Oerlemans and Bakker (2014) replicated this effect in a daily diary study. They asked their participants to chronologically map out the events of the previous day and report how much "happiness" they experienced with each event. The researchers divided up the activities in terms of whether they were consumptive (low-effort pleasurable activities, e.g., watching television, listening to music, relaxing), or reward approach (high-effort pleasurable activities, e.g., athletic activities, financial-reward–associated activities). They also determined whether or not they were alone or with others with each activity. As with other studies, both extraverts and introverts reported more happiness when they were with others than when alone, and extraverts reported more happiness than introverts in both situations. More significant for our discussion here, although both introverts and extraverts enjoyed reward-pursuit activities more than consumptive activities, there was only a small bump of happiness for introverts but extraverts experienced a much larger increase in happiness. Thus these results are largely consistent with those of Smillie and colleagues (2012, 2013), and we can see that both in and out of the laboratory, extraverts enjoy reward-pursuit activities more than introverts, but extraversion does not differentiate the enjoyment of consumptive activities. Taken together, this suggests that extraversion is indeed due to a sensitive BAS; however, the BAS must be a brain system that specifically is involved with the motivation to pursue rewards.

The other Big Five trait that shows a strong association with happiness is neuroticism. Refer back to Figure 4.2, and note that neuroticism is the only Big Five factor that shows negative associations with happiness. Thus, the more neurotic a person is, the less happy this individual tends to be. People high in neuroticism are inclined to experience unpleasant emotions such as anxiety, guilt, frustration, and sadness more often than emotionally stable individuals. Because of this, many have proposed that just as extraversion is reflective of positive affectivity, so neuroticism is reflective of negative affectivity. Hence the neuroticism characteristic of the Big Five is likely a reflection of the sensitivity of the BIS.

As seen in Figure 4.2, agreeableness also shows moderate positive relationships with happiness. This suggests that those who enjoy getting along with others, and are willing to give up some of their own rights for the sake of others, also tend to be happier. Agreeableness is really the prosocial trait of the Big Five and, as is shown in Chapter 5, giving people are inclined to be happy people. Just like extraversion and neuroticism, research has found that the agreeableness trait is cross-cultural; this implies that there may be a brain system that underlies agreeableness just as the BAS and BIS underlie extraversion and neuroticism.

For me, perhaps the most surprising finding of the happiness Big Five research is that conscientiousness is positively related to happiness (see Figure 4.2). This means that those who are good at controlling their impulses and resisting temptation have the tendency to be happier people. You might think that the picture of the conscientious person who is careful to plan out life and controls impulses is the opposite of the person who is "happy-go-lucky." But studies demonstrate that conscientiousness is consistently predictive of greater happiness. At the heart of conscientiousness is the ability to delay gratification. For example, the conscientious student is able to put off consumptive enjoyments such as watching television, partying, or playing video games for the sake of studying course material. I believe that, more than anything else, it is the ability of conscientious persons to delay gratification that enhances their happiness. Conscientious people are able to endure a little short-term pain in order to achieve long-term gain. It is popular today to assert that in order to be happy you must "be in the moment"; you must "live for the now." As will be discussed, there's a great deal of truth in this statement, but often this dictum is interpreted as "if it feels good now, just do it, and don't worry about the consequences it has for you in the future." This approach to life, however, is bound to lead to unhappiness. Having three more drinks now, because it feels good, is likely to lead to a head that doesn't feel so good in the morning. Buying an expensive dress now because "I want to spontaneously live in the moment" might feel good right now, but when the interest and finance charges start to mount up on one's credit card, one isn't likely to be so happy. Watching television now rather than studying might provide some needed relaxation, but you might not feel so good when you receive that not-so-appealing grade on your next test. It's not that conscientious people never allow themselves to enjoy the moment; however, they're probably good at knowing when to control their impulses in the moment for the sake of gaining some goal in the future, and that's likely to enhance their happiness.

Perhaps the most surprising result for my students in this area is that openness does not reliably predict greater happiness. Being open to new experiences may not produce more happiness because not all novel experiences turn out to be good experiences. Being somewhat unconventional in your thinking may not enhance happiness because although some unconventional thoughts result in creative solutions to problems, other unusual thoughts are simply unusual, and may even be counterproductive. Whereas openness is not reliably related to happiness, I believe that there is a type of openness that is important to happiness. Those who are open to seeing goodness in their lives that they did not expect or did not initially see as good are likely to be happier people. Often in my life, I fail to appreciate something that is really good simply because I expected some other good result.

157

Many years ago I ran for a second term for chair of my psychology department. At the time, I thought that being chair for 4 more years would be a good thing, and losing the election would be a bad thing. In brief, I lost the election and, in retrospect, this was one of the best things that ever happened to me in my career. By losing the election this turned my attention back to what I loved most about my job—teaching students and conducting research. If I had been able to be open to that goodness in my life at the time, I think I might have been a happier camper. Moreover, losing that election allowed me to pursue research in gratitude and to become involved in the positive psychology movement—two "goods" that I did not foresee, but have been benefits that have made my career so fulfilling. Perhaps future research can investigate this form of openness that is not currently tapped in Big Five measures: being open to good things in my life that I might not have expected or foreseen. So many times we miss important good things in our lives because we expected and wanted a good that was very different from what actually ensued.

To summarize, how can we characterize the broad personality characteristics of happy people? These individuals tend to be characterized by high extraversion and low neuroticism, they are moderately agreeable, and they are somewhat conscientious. However, describing people merely in terms of broad personality traits misses subtle but meaningful characteristics that can help us understand what happy people are like.

Specific Personality Characteristics of Happiness

Satisfied With Self, Satisfied With Life

In Angus Campbell's landmark study of American happiness, he found that one's satisfaction with self was more predictive of life satisfaction than any other fulfillment domain (1981). Indeed, some studies have found that self-esteem correlates as high as .78

with happiness (Hills & Argyle, 1998), leading some to wonder whether self-esteem and happiness might be the same thing. The evidence, however, indicates that happiness and self-esteem are distinct, but obviously they are strongly related (Lyubomirsky, Tkach, & Dimatteo, 2006). Some interesting cultural differences have been found in the relationship between self-esteem and SWB. Several studies have found that the correlation between self-esteem and happiness is stronger in individualistic cultures like the United States, as opposed to more collectivist countries like Japan (Diener & Diener, 1995; Yuki, Sato, Takemura, & Oishi, 2013). Some have taken these findings to mean that self-esteem is important to happiness in individualistic but not in collectivist cultures, but this would be a misreading of the data. Self-esteem appears to be crucial to happiness in the East and the West; nevertheless, it appears to be more essential to those of us who live in more individualistic countries.

The strength of these results has led some with a more pop psychology bent to urge that improving self-esteem is the elixir to all ailments. To illustrate, some states have literally spent billions of dollars with the idea that improving the self-esteem of our children will improve their academic performance (Baumeister, Campbell, Krueger, & Vohs, 2003). This was based on the finding that self-esteem is positively correlated with academic performance, but here we can see the classic correlation equals causation fallacy. Baumeister and colleagues (2003) found that programs designed to improve self-esteem had no impact on objective measurements of academic performance. Of course, when we feel good about ourselves, we also feel that we're doing well, we're healthier than others, and others like us more. But when objective measures of these domains are used, high self-esteem is not clearly related to better job performance, healthier behaviors, or better relationships. About the only clear benefit of self-esteem appears to be that it improves our mental health and, in particular, our happiness (Baumeister et al., 2003), but even here there are some important caveats. Those with high but unstable self-esteem are not happier. Similarly, narcissistic individuals have higher self-esteem than most of us, but they aren't inclined to be happier people.

One of the problems with global self-esteem is that it is simply a measurement of how you feel about yourself, and there may be many different reasons why people feel good about themselves. For instance, one individual may be satisfied with self because of the belief in his or her inherent value, whereas others may feel good about themselves because they believe that they're better than others. Those who feel good about themselves because they believe they are superior to others are often high in narcissism and, as we've seen, narcissists aren't reliably happier than most folks. Why aren't narcissists generally happy people? Baumeister argues that it is because narcissists have an unrealistically high view of themselves, and the reality of the world—and the feedback of others—just can't keep up with their high expectations of themselves (Baumeister, Bushman, & Campbell, 2000). If your professor tells you that you have written a fine paper, you'll probably feel quite good about this feedback. If, however, you happen to believe that you're a Pulitzer Prize winning author-in-waiting, you might actually be offended by this comment on your work because you hadn't been told that it was the best paper your professor had ever seen. I may feel good if colleagues from another university tell me that they really appreciate my research unless, of course, I believe that I'm one of the world's top psychologists. In that case, I'm likely to be insulted that they didn't tell me that my research was the best in the field. This might be why some self-esteem treatment programs have even backfired (Baumeister et al., 2003). For example, many self-esteem improvement programs involve the instructor encouraging children to believe extraordinary things about themselves: "You're a wonderful person"; "You're an extremely smart boy"; "You can do anything you put your mind to"; "There are no limits to what you can accomplish." The problem is that, for most of us, reality has a hard time keeping up with these exceptional affirmations. Although it might feel good to say these things to ourselves, when we don't get the highest test grade in the class, when we do something wrong, when we don't win the prize, when the teacher doesn't tell us that we're the best writer in the class, our satisfaction with ourselves is likely to plummet—along with our happiness.

So although, generally speaking, self-esteem is strongly predictive of SWB, because there are varying sources of high self-esteem this creates some ambiguities with this finding. The critical question is: What type of self-esteem is best for your happiness? I submit that self-esteem borne out of self-acceptance is the type that produces enduring happiness. *Self-acceptance* involves having a fairly accurate view of yourself—with all your strengths and weaknesses—and still accepting yourself as a valuable person. Some studies have found that self-compassion is more strongly related to happiness than global self-esteem (Neff & Vonk, 2009). If I can accept myself—warts and vices included—I should be able to be compassionate toward myself.

Moreover, other investigations have found that if you want the strengths that you have (called *actual self-regard*), this is more important to your happiness than having the strengths that you want (called *ideal self-actualization;* Hardin & Larsen, 2014). This might sound like the same thing to you, but research shows that these are really quite distinct. First, imagine listing the traits that ideally you would like to have, and then rating each of these characteristics as to how much each of these factors actually describes you now. This is the measurement that Hardin and Larsen (2014) used for ideal self-actualization, or how much you have the traits that you want. On the other hand, imagine yourself listing the traits that you have right now, and then rating each factor for how much you want each characteristic. This is how they measured actual self-regard, or how much you want the traits that you have. Across several studies, Hardin and Larsen found that wanting the traits you have was more important to happiness than having the traits you want. Moreover, wanting the traits you have (actual self-regard) was predictive of one's future happiness, whereas having the traits you want (ideal self-actualization) was not. Why is actual self-regard more important to SWB than ideal self-actualization? I believe it is because actual self-regard is closely related to self-acceptance. Wanting the traits that you have is probably a good measurement of how much you accept who you really are.

But our discussion thus far begs an important question: How does one accept oneself—with all of one's strengths and weaknesses? And here is where I believe it is important to return to a consideration of humility and how it might impact your happiness. Recall in Chapter 2 I defined humility as "the ability to acknowledge and accept your weaknesses and limitations, as well as your strengths." As you can see, my views of humility and self-acceptance are very close and, indeed, I propose that humility should be related to healthy self-acceptance. Although the study of humility has proven to be somewhat humiliating, recently researchers have made significant progress in measuring this construct and it has been found that humility is positively correlated with happiness (e.g., Uhder, Watkins, & Hammamoto, 2010). So humble people tend to be happy people, but the jury is still out as to whether humility *causes* increased happiness. Recent advances in the understanding and measurement of humility should push research forward in this area (Chancellor & Lyubomirsky, 2013; Davis et al., 2011; Wayment, Bauer, & Sylaska, 2014).

Why should humility enhance happiness? First and perhaps foremost, humility should promote a *balanced view of self*. Acknowledging your strengths and weaknesses implies that you have a fairly accurate understanding of who you are. Accurate comprehension is bound to protect you from having an unreasonably high view of yourself, which should not set up expectations for unreasonably high praise from others. Humility involves not just acknowledging one's strengths and weaknesses, but accepting them as well. Knowing that I am more emotional than most men is one thing; being able to accept this fact about myself is something more. When I can accept my weaknesses as well as my strengths, this should result in more stable self-esteem, which some have called a *quiet ego* (Wayment et al., 2014), or a *secure accepting identity* (Chancellor & Lyubomirsky, 2013). When people can accept themselves, with all their strengths and weaknesses, this helps them get past their self, so to speak. Humble people accept who they really are, and this provides the luxury of not having to be self-preoccupied, which leads us to consider another quality of humility: self-forgetfulness. In Chancellor and Lyubomirsky's (2013) words, humble people are *other-focused*. When I have accepted who I really am, then I don't have to be preoccupied with what others are thinking about me, and I won't be constantly comparing myself with others. As we will see in Chapter 5, happy people are focused on others. Humility should free us from being preoccupied with our own reputation or with respect from others, which frees us to be focused on the needs of others rather than our own needs. I look forward to more research investigating the contribution of humility to the good life. In short, humility should produce a balanced sense of self, a quiet and stable ego, and a self-forgetfulness that supports greater happiness. In the words of C. S. Lewis (1952/2002, p. 72), the humble person "will not be thinking about humility: he will not be thinking about himself at all."

So in a curious paradox, humility might produce the kind of self-acceptance that is most conducive to happiness. Because humble persons have accepted their limitations, this should counteract the somewhat unreasonable self-statements that the self-esteem movement seems to be encouraging. If I really believe that "There are no limits to what I can accomplish," I'm set up for the fall. When I don't achieve the heights of accomplishment that my boundless ego has set for myself, I'm likely to be gravely disappointed. Thus, many of the wonderful self-esteem–bolstering statements we say to ourselves ironically end up in discouragement. Humility should counteract the pitfalls of the boundless self, and should promote the kind of self-acceptance that enhances SWB. In sum, people who are satisfied with their self tend to be satisfied with life, and those who can accept themselves as they really are should be most comfortable—and most satisfied—with themselves.

Optimism And Hope In Happy People

Among the most robust personality correlates of happiness are optimism and hope. Although there are varying forms of this construct, all of these have a future-mindedness in common: Optimistic people see the future in a positive way; they see desirable things in their future. Dispositional optimism is a global belief that the future will bring many good things, and undesirable events will be infrequent (Carver & Scheier, 1981). Another approach to optimism has emphasized *explanatory style*, or the habitual way that you choose to explain events in your life (Peterson & Seligman, 1984). If you have a *pessimistic explanatory style*, then you tend to explain bad events as happening to you because of internal (i.e., you caused it), stable (i.e., the cause is long lasting), and global causes. For example, if you were to get a bad test grade in one of my classes, a more pessimistic explanation for your results would be: "I got a bad grade because I'm just stupid." Note that this explanation is internal because you're blaming yourself, stable because most people believe that stupidity is rather long-lasting, and global because you're not just saying that you have difficulty with psychology tests but your stupidity transcends to all college courses. Presumably this type of thinking leads to a more hopeless view of the future because there's not much that you can do about it. A more optimistic explanation might say: "That was a really bad test Dr. Watkins administered this time, but I don't think he'll give another one like that." Optimistic explanatory styles are generally predictive of SWB (Peterson & Chang, 2003), although some research has questioned the importance of internal attributions, and other studies have suggested that pessimistic and optimistic explanatory styles may be somewhat independent.

From a somewhat different perspective, Rick Snyder and associates have emphasized the future-minded perspective of *hope*. According to this approach, hope is defined as a form of goal-directed thinking that involves two distinct aspects (Lopez, Pedrotti, & Snyder, 2015, p. 204). First, hope involves *pathways thinking*, which relates to how effective you think you are at finding routes to achieve your goals. Snyder and colleagues call the second aspect of hope *agency thinking*, which refers to whether you have the required motivation to use those routes to realize your goals. So if you have a goal to get into graduate school, one aspect of hope is that you believe that you will be effective in finding the best way to get into graduate school (i.e., pathways thinking). Furthermore, if you have hope, then you will be motivated to actually pursue those routes to get into graduate school. It is one thing to say that you have hope that you can find the best ways to get accepted into graduate school; it is quite another thing to actually have the motivation to pursue those roads to acceptance. Snyder is quick to point out that hope only applies to those goals that you really value. If graduate school is not all that important to you, then hope is not likely to come into play; however, if a PhD has always been your lifetime goal, hope should be very important as to whether you succeed in reaching your goal. Hope has been shown to predict a number of positive variables, including SWB (Snyder, 2002). Moreover, many of these effects are retained even after controlling for self-esteem and optimism. There is some evidence that the agency aspect of hopeful thinking is more important to achieving goals (Feldman,

Rand, & Kahle-Wrobleski, 2009), although there are also findings that ethnic and cultural factors show significant interactions (e.g., Chang & Banks, 2007). Investigations on hope have been active and encouraging in positive psychology, and taken together we may conclude that, indeed, hopeful people tend to be happy people.

The Importance of a Belief in Personal Control for Happiness
If individuals believe that the future holds good things for them, then they are likely to believe that they are in control of their future. Rather than believing that one's future is determined by others or by chance, happy people believe that they are basically in charge of their future. This is often referred to as an *internal locus of control* (Rotter, 1966), and it has been one of the most robust predictors of SWB (e.g., Lu, Shih, Lin, & Ju, 1997). Interestingly, it is more of a generalized expectancy of personal control that is most predictive of happiness, rather than an unrealistic belief that one is in control of every aspect of one's life (Watkins, Woodward, Stone, & Kolts, 2003). So, happy people don't believe that life is good because they're just lucky. They don't believe that they're mere reeds in the winds of fate. Rather, happy people believe that they can influence what happens to them in the future, and they tend to take responsibility for the important events in their lives.

Gratitude and Happiness
In terms of emotional dispositions, the trait of gratitude has shown some of the most robust correlations with SWB. Two trait gratitude measures have been developed (McCullough, Emmons, & Tsang, 2002; Watkins et al., 2003), and these instruments show moderate to strong correlations with various indices of SWB. Furthermore, gratitude predicts SWB above and beyond the Big Five personality traits, meaning that gratitude is more strongly correlated with happiness than any of the traits of the Big Five, and still predicts happiness after controlling for the Big

Five (McComb, Watkins, & Kolts, 2004; McCullough et al., 2002; Wood, Joseph, & Maltby, 2008). In short, grateful people are inclined to be happy people.

Of course, it is quite possible that gratitude is simply a happy consequence of SWB, but prospective studies have shown that gratitude predicts subsequent increases in happiness (Wood, Maltby, Gillett, Linley, & Joseph, 2008). Indeed, Wood and colleagues (2008) showed that gratitude predicted increases in happiness but happiness did not predict greater gratitude, supporting the idea that being grateful actually does make you a happier person. Why are grateful people happy people? There may be several reasons that gratitude is important to the good life (Watkins, 2014), but we have argued that gratitude supports happiness because it amplifies the good in one's life (Watkins, 2008, 2014). In short, gratitude increases the signal strength of what is good in your life.

A Happy Life Is a Meaningful Life

As Nietzche famously wrote: "Those who have a 'why' to live, can bear with almost any 'how'" (cited in Frankl, 1959). Indeed, those who find meaning and purpose in their lives also find their lives to be satisfying. A number of studies show strong correlations with self-reports of meaning in life and happiness (e.g., Freedman, 1978; Schulenberg, Schnetzer, & Buchanan, 2011; Steger, Frazier, Oishi, & Kaler, 2006; for a review, see Emmons, 2003). These studies support the idea that when one lives with a sense of purpose and meaning, this enhances happiness. There are several problems with this conclusion, however. First, the primary way that purpose is measured is through the Purpose in Life test. The difficulty here is that many of the items on this measure seem to relate more directly to SWB than to purpose. For example, one might argue that items such as "I am usually: bored/enthusiastic," "Life to me seems: completely routine/always exciting," and "Facing my daily tasks is: a painful and boring experience/a source of pleasure and excitement" are more directly related to happiness than to purpose in life. Thus method invariance may partially explain the purpose in life/happiness relationship. Second, most studies investigating purpose and SWB have used cross-sectional designs. Hence it is difficult to say whether it is meaning and purpose that are producing happiness, or that happiness affords one more meaning in life. Although it would seem more intuitive to conclude that purpose promotes happiness rather than the converse, there is now evidence that inducing positive emotions enhances one's ability to see meaning in life (e.g., Hicks, Cicero, Trent, Burton, & King, 2010). Consequently, it might be that one of the major benefits of happiness is that it enhances your ability to see purpose and meaning in your life. More than likely, however, purpose and happiness is a two-way street: Purpose in your life enhances your happiness, and happiness enables a meaningful life. Indeed, a recent study found that purpose in life predicted satisfaction with life above and beyond daily positive emotional balance and physical pleasure. In short, a meaningful life tends to be a happy life (Diener, Fujita, Tay, & Biswas-Diener, 2012).

THE GOALS OF HAPPY PEOPLE

It would seem that if one's life is purpose-driven, then one would also have meaningful goals. Accordingly, it seems reasonable to propose that happy people should be goal-oriented and, certainly, research supports this conclusion (Emmons, 2003). What are personal goals? Very simply, your goals are what you are trying to do in life (Austin & Vancouver, 1996). In fact, if you took a few minutes right now to simply list what you're trying to do in your life, this would help you make some sense of the research that is about to be explained.

Although happy people tend to be more goal-oriented (they report more goals than unhappy folks), research has found that the content of your goals matters. When it comes to your happiness: "Not all goals are created equal" (Emmons, 2003, p. 114). Some goals are positively associated with SWB, others seem to have no relationship with happiness, and still others actually appear to cause decrements in SWB. First, *relationship goals* predict greater happiness. To illustrate, "spending more time with my kids" is the type of goal that seems to be conducive to SWB. Second, a number of studies have found that *generativity strivings*—goals related to helping others and influencing future generations—are associated with higher SWB (e.g., Ackerman, Zuroff, & Moskowitz, 2000). Third, *spiritual strivings* are also associated with happiness. Happy people are more likely to have self-transcendent and sacred goals than unhappy folks. Examples of spiritual goals might be: "I want to be more aware of God in my life," and "I want to be more aware of Divine good in the world." Finally, observations have shown that power-oriented goals—for instance, "I want to get others to agree with my point of view"—are actually associated with lower SWB (Emmons, 2003).

So the content of your goals matters, but how can we make some sense of these findings? Here, I believe that Ryan and Deci's (2000) *self-determination theory* (SDT) of SWB is most helpful for understanding this pattern of results. Recall from Chapter 1 that SDT argues that three fundamental psychological needs must be met in order for SWB to be achieved: *competence, autonomy,* and *relatedness*. So SDT should hypothesize that goals that are more directly related to these fundamental needs should be more likely to produce happiness. Clearly, relationship goals and generativity goals relate fairly directly to the needs of relatedness and competence. Power goals on the other hand—which appear to reduce happiness—are not directly related to these fundamental goals. It is a bit more difficult to see how spiritual goals relate to Ryan and Deci's framework. If, however, spiritual goals are seen as the fulfillment of a need to relate to the ultimate Other (Buber, 1996), then we can see how spiritual goals might directly fulfill the need for relatedness. Studies have more directly tested SDT as it relates to goals. Kasser and Ryan (1993, 1996) initially described the difference between intrinsic goals—aims that are directly relevant to our fundamental psychological needs—and extrinsic goals—our strivings that are not fulfilling our inherent needs. Examples of intrinsic goals would be things such as "I want to be a better husband" and "I want to listen to my students better." On the other hand, extrinsic goals are related to wealth, beauty, and social status. Indeed, Kasser and Ryan found that SWB was positively correlated with intrinsic goals, but extrinsic goals predicted lower well-being. You might rightly complain that intrinsic goals are more realistic and achievable than extrinsic goals. After all, it's more likely that I can become a better husband as opposed to becoming a billionaire (although some might disagree . . .). But subsequent studies have found that even when the factor of perceived goal attainability is controlled for, intrinsic goals still predict SWB, whereas extrinsic goals do not (e.g., Sheldon & Kasser, 1998).

So the content of your goals matters when it comes to your happiness; nevertheless, additional research suggests that your goal orientation is important as well. People can claim what is essentially the same goal, but the way they frame the goal—how they orient the goal—has important implications for how it impacts their happiness. Some people tend to report their goals in an approach orientation, while others state their goals with an avoidance orientation. With an *approach goal orientation*, individuals strive for approaching something desirable, whereas with an *avoidance goal orientation* people are pursuing something in order to avoid something they deem unpleasant. Let's say your desire is to get a good job after graduating. With an approach orientation you would frame your goal with a statement such as: "I really want to pursue a fulfilling job for my career." On the other hand, if you had an avoidance orientation you might say: "I want to make sure that I'm not unemployed after college." Both of these goals have the same objective—being employed—but the way they are framed appears to have important consequences for your happiness. As you might have guessed, happy people tend to frame their goals with an approach orientation, whereas unhappy people are more likely to use an avoidance orientation with their goals (Elliot & Sheldon, 1998; Emmons & Kaiser, 1996).

Another important issue as it relates to happiness is how well your goals fit together. If your goals have a tendency to conflict with each other, then you'll tend to be less happy; however, if your goals are supportive of each other, then you'll be more inclined to report greater SWB. For example, if I have a goal to be a top business executive, but I also have a goal to spend meaningful time with my children, these two goals may well conflict with each other and thus degrade my happiness. Alternatively, the goal of spending more time outside may fit well and support my goal of spending more time with my kids, particularly if they want to spend more time out of doors as well. In short, conflicting goals tend to degrade happiness, whereas goals that are supportive and congruent have a tendency to encourage emotional well-being.

Although goals have been and will continue to be a critical issue for happiness research, there are crucial unresolved problems in this area. First, most of the studies cited earlier are cross-sectional in nature and, as is frequently emphasized in this book, this poses a number of problems for understanding the causal relationship among these variables. Most authors assume that the causal direction is from goals to happiness; still, it is equally reasonable to propose that happiness gives people the motivation and energy to be more goal-oriented. Moreover, intervention programs designed to enhance people's goal orientation have shown mixed results with regard to happiness. Thus additional research needs to more directly establish the causal status of goals to happiness.

Goals provide an important window into understanding a person, and goals have been shown to have significant relationships with happiness. What characterizes the goals of happy people? First, happy people tend to be goal-oriented; however, their goals are usually intrinsic in nature—they relate more directly to their psychological needs. The goals of happy people may be characterized as relational and more related to personal growth, rather than extrinsic goals that are concerned with riches, fame, and beauty. Finally, happy people tend to be approach-oriented in their goals; they frame their goals in terms of approach to desirable circumstances, rather than an avoidance of unpleasant situations. We have seen that happy people tend to lead more meaningful lives that are characterized by striving for significant goals. If the happy life is a meaningful life, might people's religious beliefs and spiritual worldviews be crucial to their happiness? Now we turn to this critical characteristic of happy people.

SPIRITUAL CHARACTERISTICS OF HAPPY PEOPLE

In general, research has confirmed that a prominent characteristic of happy people is that they tend to be religious and spiritual. Although there are plenty of examples of happy atheists and miserable Christians, studies have consistently shown that religiosity is positively correlated with happiness (see Myers, 2013, for a review). Although often the opposite relationship is found when the unit of analysis is at the societal level (Diener, Tay, & Myers, 2011; Myers, 2013), even within these societies, when analyzed at the individual level, religiosity predicts greater SWB. Furthermore, it appears that intrinsic, committed religiosity is more important to well-being than uncommitted individualistic religion (Myers, 2013).

Whereas this relationship has been well established, it is not altogether clear how religiosity promotes well-being. First, it is essential to point out that, once again, most of the examinations that have investigated the relationship between spirituality and happiness have done so with cross-sectional correlational designs. Thus the same issue may exist here that was explained with purpose and meaning: It is possible that being happy encourages one to see more meaning in life, and hence encourages religiosity. But most researchers assume that at least a good part of the causal direction of this relationship is from religion to SWB, so let's explore how spirituality might promote happiness.

Some have argued that religious people tend to be happier because faith communities provide committed social networks. A person who regularly attends synagogue, temple, or church has a built-in community of like-minded advocates. Indeed, research has found that this provides some explanation of the religiosity/ SWB connection, but enhanced social networks cannot explain all of the religiosity and happiness relationship (Ellison, Gay, & Glass, 1989). Other factors must also be at work.

A second possibility is that religion offers people an adaptive way of coping with difficult life events, and this promotes happiness. First, if one is part of a provide community of faith, then there should be individuals who are committed to helping the person who is navigating through a stressful situation. Second, religion may help individuals cognitively deal with unpleasant events in their lives by helping them see meaning in the events. If religious people believe that "all things work together for good" for those who love God (*The Bible*, New Revised Standard Version, Romans 8:28), this might help them endure difficult situations because they see these as something that the Divine is using to produce good in their lives.

If religiosity helps people cope by encouraging individuals of faith to see meaning in difficult life events, religiosity could enhance happiness by aiding people in seeing meaning and purpose in their lives more generally. We have seen that happy people view their lives as meaningful and full of purpose and, indeed, research has demonstrated that religiosity assists people in identifying more meaning in their life tasks (e.g., Mooney, 2008; Myers, 2013). Thus religious people might tend to be happier than those less religious because religion helps them see meaning in their lives.

A third possibility is that spirituality enhances happiness because it helps people manage the terror of death. According to *terror management theory* (Greenberg & Arndt, 2012), we do all sorts of things to avoid the fact that we're going to die. Many of these things can be described as striving for *symbolic immortality* and, for the most part, what we do to avoid our mortality is not very attractive. Striving to show that I'm better than you in any number of areas (my gender is better than yours; my race is better than yours; my school is better than yours; I've got more stuff than you have) has been shown to result from exposing people to cues suggesting their own mortality (Pyszczynski, Greenberg, Solomon, Arndt, & Schimel, 2004). Because almost all religions emphasize life after death—a literal, not symbolic immortality—religious belief may help protect people from the terror of their own demise, or what is sometimes referred to as *death anxiety*. Indeed, research has consistently found that belief in the afterlife is associated with emotional well-being (e.g., Flannelly, Koenig, Ellison, Galek, & Krause, 2006). In short, one reason religious people might tend to be happier than those less religious is because their faith helps them deal with the reality of their own death.

Another mechanism that might help explain the association between religiosity and happiness is self-control. It might be that religious people are inclined to be happier because religion encourages self-discipline (DeWall et al., 2014; McCullough & Willoughby, 2009). Earlier, I argued that the reason conscientious people have a tendency to be happier is because they have greater self-control—they are able to resist temptation and delay gratification. If religion aids people in putting off the pleasure of the moment for the sake of their long-term well-being, this might be an important way that religiosity promotes SWB.

One of the most robust personality characteristics of happy people is gratitude. Is it possible that religious people tend to be happier because they are more grateful? Virtually all major religions promote gratitude as a virtue (Emmons & Crumpler, 2000). Some have pointed out that religious folks might have a built-in advantage when it comes to gratitude because if they believe in God, they always have a benevolent source to be grateful to for any good thing (McCullough et al., 2002; Watkins, 2014). In fact, research has frequently found that religious people tend to be more grateful than those less religious (Emmons & Kneezel, 2005; McCullough et al., 2002; Watkins et al., 2003). So religion might promote happiness by encouraging gratitude that in turn enhances SWB.

Finally, religiosity might encourage happiness by promoting a more balanced view of self (Myers, 1992). We have seen that self-esteem is strongly correlated with happiness; however, unbalanced self-concepts that promote unrealistic self-esteem, such as that characterized by narcissism, appear to backfire when it comes to happiness. Happy people seem to be those who have a realistic understanding of who they really are, and yet they are able to accept themselves, with all of their strengths and weaknesses. David Myers argues that the prominent monotheistic religions (Judaism, Christianity, and Islam) appear to promote this balanced view of self. In his words, Abrahamic religions emphasize that we are "Creatures formed of the earth, *creatures having dignity but not deity*" (Myers, 1992, p. 89, italics in original). Thus, if religiosity promotes a balanced view of self, then it is likely to promote happiness as well. As Myers points out, when religions also promote a loving God who accepts a person unconditionally, that person is even more likely to be happy.

In sum, religious and spiritual people tend to be happier than those who are not. Although this seems to be a reliable relationship, we don't yet fully understand *why* religious people tend to be happier. So should you "get religion" so as to get happiness? Like many things, that pursuit is likely to backfire. Remember that intrinsic religion is more associated with happiness than extrinsic religion, and a religious practice that is simply focused on your own happiness is really the definition of extrinsic religiosity. Although religion seems to promote SWB, paradoxically, becoming religious just to become happy is likely to be counterproductive.

SUMMARY AND CONCLUSIONS: WHAT ARE HAPPY PEOPLE LIKE?

This chapter attempts to describe the characteristics of happy people. First, recall from Chapter 3 that your external characteristics tell us very little about your happiness. Knowing your age, gender, ethnicity, education, and income doesn't tell me much about your happiness. Although there is a small positive correlation between income and happiness, after the essentials in life have been purchased, there's not much happiness left to be bought. We see here that although there is a genetic contribution to your happiness, about half of your happiness comes from other sources. We learn also that happy people tend to be active people. Moreover, personality characteristics show moderate to strong correlations with happiness. In terms of broad personality characteristics, happy people are inclined to be more extraverted, less neurotic, more agreeable, and somewhat more conscientious. We have also seen that more specific personality characteristics are predictive of happiness. Perhaps most prominently, people who are satisfied with life have the tendency to be satisfied with their self. Happy people can also be described as being more optimistic and hopeful; they believe they have some control over their lives; they are more grateful; and they feel that there is more meaning and purpose in their lives. Happy people are goal-oriented people. They tend to have intrinsic goals, and their goals tend to support rather than conflict with each other. Finally, happy people are inclined to be more religious and spiritual. Happy people seem to be focused on things beyond themselves.

So what conclusions can be drawn about the happy person? How can the happy person best be described? For me, the theme that keeps running through these characteristics of happiness is that happy people seem to be remarkably devoid of self-preoccupation. Happy people are not focused on themselves; they're focused on others, on the beauty of life, the activities of life, and on things beyond themselves. Happy people seem to be peculiarly self-forgetful. In short, happy people tend to be humble people.

At the facility where I work out there are elliptical machines with video screens where you can watch various virtual programs. I like to watch the videos where you can bike through the Italian Alps, run through the streets of Venice, or hike up to Angel's Landing in Zion National Park (to name a few locations). When I'm watching these videos they seem to make the workout flow, the session feels shorter, and I look forward to the next jaunt through the virtual wilderness. One day when I was exercising on the elliptical and watching a trail run around Lake Tahoe, I noticed that I could see a reflection of myself on the screen. For the next 5 minutes or so I focused on how I looked, tried to look like I was enjoying my workout, and wondered how my hair had gotten so messy that morning. Then I realized I was focusing on myself and was completely missing the beauty of Lake Tahoe. My workout seemed to be more of a task and it appeared to go much more slowly. I think this is a good metaphor for under-standing the characteristics of happiness. What is the main thing that inhibits my happiness? Unfortunately, it's usually *me* that gets in the way. By incessantly focusing on myself, by being pre-occupied with whether others respect me or whether I'm getting my just rewards, by being preoccupied with how I look to others, I'm distracted from the good and the beautiful that is all around me. It's not that we should ignore the bad in our lives; however, there is so much good in life that I miss because I'm caught up in gazing at my own reflection. And here's where I think that healthy humility may have such an important role to play in our happiness: Humility helps us accept who we really are, so we can get past ourselves to focus on others and the beauty all around us. C. S. Lewis said it so well: "Be humble—delightedly humble, feeling the infinite relief of having for once got rid of all the silly nonsense about your own dignity which has made you so restless and unhappy all your life" (1952/2002, p. 71).

REFERENCES

Ackerman, S., Zuroff, D. C., & Moskowitz, D. S. (2000). Generativity in midlife and young adults: Links to agency, communion, and subjective well-being. *International Journal of Aging & Human Development, 50,* 17–41.

Austin, J. T., & Vancouver, J. B. (1996). Goal constructs in psychology: Structure, process, and content. *Psychological Bulletin, 120,* 338–375.

Baker, L. A., Cesa, I. L., Gatz, M., & Mellins, C. (1992). Genetic and environmental influences on positive and negative affect: Support for a two-factor theory. *Psychology and Aging, 7,* 158–163.

Baumeister, R. F., Bushman, B. J., & Campbell, W. K. (2000). Self-esteem, narcissism, and aggression: Does violence result from low self-esteem or from threatened egotism? *Current Directions in Psychological Science, 9,* 26–29.

Baumeister, R. F., Campbell, J. D., Krueger, J. I., & Vohs, K. D. (2003). Does self-esteem cause better performance, interpersonal success, happiness, or healthier lifestyles? *Psychological Science in the Public Interest, 4*, 1–44.

Bouchard, T. J., Jr. (2004). Genetic influence on human psychological traits: A survey. *Current Directions in Psychological Science, 13*, 148–151.

Buber, M. (1996). *I and thou.* New York, NY: Touchstone.

Campbell, A. (1981). *The sense of well-being in America.* New York, NY: McGraw-Hill.

Carver, C. S., & Scheier, M. F. (1981). *Attention and self-regulation: A control theory approach to human behavior.* New York, NY: Springer Publishing Company.

Chancellor, J., & Lyubomirsky, S. (2013). Humble beginnings: Current trends, state perspectives, and hallmarks of humility. *Social and Personality Psychology Compass, 7*, 819–833.

Chang, E. C., & Banks, K. H. (2007). The color and texture of hope: Some preliminary findings and implications for hope theory and counseling among diverse racial/ethnic groups. *Cultural Diversity and Ethnic Minority Psychology, 13*, 94–103.

Davis, D. E., Hook, J. N., Worthington, E. L., Van Tongeren, D. R., Gartner, A. L., Jennings, D. J., & Emmons, R. A. (2011). Relational humility: Conceptualizing and measuring humility as a personality judgment. *Journal of Personality Assessment, 93*, 225–234.

Depue, R. A., & Collins, P. F. (1999). Neurobiology of the structure of personality: Dopamine, facilitation of incentive motivation, and extraversion. *Behavioral and Brain Sciences, 22*, 491–569.

DeWall, C., Pond, R. R., Carter, E. C., McCullough, M. E., Lambert, N. M., Fincham, F. D., & Nezlek, J. B. (2014). Explaining the relationship between religiousness and substance use: Self-control matters. *Journal of Personality and Social Psychology, 107*, 339–351.

Diener, E., & Diener, C. (1996). Most people are happy. *Psychological Science, 7*, 181–185.

Diener, E., & Diener, M. (1995). Cross-cultural correlates of life satisfaction and self-esteem. *Journal of Personality and Social Psychology, 68*, 653–663.

Diener, E., Emmons, R. A., Larsen, R. J., & Griffin, S. (1985). The Satisfaction with Life Scale. *Journal of Personality and Social Psychology, 49*, 71–75.

Diener, E., Fujita, F., Tay, L. & Biswas-Diener, R. (2012). Purpose, mood, and pleasure in predicting satisfaction judgments. *Social Indicators Research, 105*, 333–341.

Diener, E., Tay, L., & Myers, D. G. (2011). The religion paradox: If religion makes people happy, why are so many dropping out? *Journal of Personality and Social Psychology, 101*, 1278–1290.

Elliot, A. J., & Sheldon, K. M. (1998). Avoidance personal goals and the personality-illness relationship. *Journal of Personality and Social Psychology, 75*, 1281–1299.

Ellison, C. G., Gay, D. A., & Glass, T. A. (1989). Does religious commitment contribute to individual life satisfaction? *Social Forces, 68*, 100–123.

Emmons, R. A. (2003). Personal goals, life meaning, and virtue: Wellsprings of a positive life. In C. L. Keyes & J. Haidt (Eds.), *Flourishing: Positive psychology and the life well-lived* (pp. 105–128). Washington, DC: American Psychological Association.

Emmons, R. A., & Crumpler, C. A. (2000). Gratitude as a human strength: Appraising the evidence. *Journal of Social and Clinical Psychology, 19*, 56–69.

Emmons, R. A., & Kaiser, H. (1996). Goal orientation and emotional well-being: Linking goals and affect through the self. In A. Tesser & L. L. Martin (Eds.), *Striving and feeling: Interactions among goals, affect, and self-regulation* (pp. 79–98). New York, NY: Plenum Press.

Emmons, R. A., & Kneezel, T. T. (2005). Giving thanks: Spiritual and religious correlates of gratitude. *Journal of Psychology and Christianity, 24*, 140–148.

Feldman, D. B., Rand, K. L., & Kahle-Wrobleski, K. (2009). Hope and goal attainment: Testing a basic prediction of hope theory. *Journal of Social and Clinical Psychology, 28*, 479–497.

Flannelly, K. J., Koenig, H. G., Ellison, C. G., Galek, K., & Krause, N. (2006). Belief in life after death and mental health—Findings from a national survey. *Journal of Nervous and Mental Disease, 194*, 524–529.

Frankl, V. (1959). *Man's search for meaning.* New York, NY: Pocket Books.

Freedman, J. L. (1978). *Happy people.* New York, NY: Harcourt, Brace, Jovanovich.

Goldberg, L. R. (1981). Language and individual differences: The search for universals in personality lexicons. In L. Wheeler (Ed.), *Review of personality and social psychology* (Vol. 2, pp. 141–166). Beverly Hills, CA: Sage.

Goldberg, L. R. (1993). The structure of phenotypic personality traits. *American Psychologist, 48,* 26–34.

Gray, J. A. (1990). Brain systems that mediate both emotion and cognition. *Cognition and Emotion, 4,* 269–288.

Gray, J. A. (1991). The neuropsychology of temperament. In J. Strelau & A. Angleitner (Eds.), *Explorations in temperament: International perspectives on theory and measurement.* New York, NY: Plenum Press.

Greenberg, J., & Arndt, J. (2012). Terror management theory. In P. M. Van Lange, A. W. Kruglanski, & E. Higgins (Eds.), *Handbook of theories of social psychology* (Vol. 1, pp. 398–415). Thousand Oaks, CA: Sage.

Hardin, E. E., & Larsen, J. T. (2014). Distinct sources of self-discrepancies: Effects of being who you want to be and wanting to be who you are on well-being. *Emotion, 14,* 214–226.

Hicks, J. A., Cicero, D. C., Trent, J., Burton, C. M., & King, L. A. (2010). Positive affect, intuition, and feelings of meaning. *Journal of Personality and Social Psychology, 98,* 967–979.

Hills, P., & Argyle, M. (1998). Positive moods derived from leisure and their relationship to happiness and personality. *Personality and Individual Differences, 30,* 595–608.

John, O. P., & Srivastava, S. (1999). The big-five taxonomy: History, measurement, and theoretical perspectives. In L. Pervin & O. John (Eds.), *Handbook of personality: Theory and research* (pp. 102–138). New York, NY: Guilford Press.

Kasser, T., & Ryan, R. M. (1993). A dark side of the American dream: Correlates of financial success as a central life aspiration. *Journal of Personality and Social Psychology, 65,* 410–422.

Kasser, T., & Ryan, R. M. (1996). Further examining the American dream: Differential correlates of intrinsic and extrinsic goals. *Personality and Social Psychology Bulletin, 22,* 280–287.

Larsen, R. J., & Ketelaar, T. (1991). Personality and susceptibility to positive and negative emotional states. *Journal of Personality and Social Psychology, 61,* 132–140.

Lewis, C. S. (2002). Mere Christianity. In C. S. Lewis, *The complete C. S. Lewis signature classics* (pp. 1–118). San Francisco, CA: HarperSanFrancisco. (Original work published 1952)

Lopez, S. J., Pedrotti, J. T., & Snyder, C. R. (2015). *Positive psychology: The scientific and practical explorations of human strengths.* Los Angeles, CA: Sage.

Lu, L., Shih, J. B., Lin, Y., & Ju, L. S. (1997). Personal and environmental correlates of happiness. *Personality and Individual Differences, 23,* 453–462.

Lucas, R. E. (2008). Personality and subjective well-being. In M. Eid & R. J. Larson (Eds.), *The science of subjective well-being* (pp. 171–194). New York, NY: Guilford Press.

Lucas, R. E., Le, K., & Dyrenforth, P. S. (2008). Explaining the extraversion/positive affect relation: Sociability cannot account for extraverts' greater happiness. *Journal of Personality, 76,* 385–414.

Lykken, D., & Csikszentmihalyi, M. (2001). Happiness—Stuck with what you've got? *The Psychologist, 14,* 470–472.

Lykken, D., & Tellegen, A. (1996). Happiness is a stochastic phenomenon. *Psychological Science, 7,* 186–189.

Lyubomirsky, S. (2007). *The how of happiness: A scientific approach to getting the life you want.* New York, NY: Penguin Press.

Lyubomirsky, S., Sheldon, K. M., & Schkade, D. (2005). Pursuing happiness: The architecture of sustainable change. *Review of General Psychology, 9,* 111–131.

Lyubomirsky, S., Tkach, C., & Dimatteo, M. R. (2006). What are the differences between happiness and self-esteem? *Social Indicators Research, 78,* 363–404.

McComb, D., Watkins, P., & Kolts, R. (2004, April). *Personality and happiness: The importance of gratitude.* Paper presented at the 84th Annual Convention of the Western Psychological Association, Phoenix, AZ.

McCrae, R. R., & Costa, P. T., Jr. (1999). A five-factor theory of personality. In L. Pervin & O. John (Eds.), *Handbook of personality: Theory and research* (pp. 139–153). New York, NY: Guilford Press.

McCullough, M. E., Emmons, R. A., & Tsang, J. (2002). The grateful disposition: A conceptual and empirical topography. *Journal of Personality and Social Psychology, 82,* 112–127.

McCullough, M. E., & Willoughby, B. B. (2009). Religion, self-regulation, and self-control: Associations, explanations, and implications. *Psychological Bulletin, 135,* 69–93.

Mooney, M. (2008). *Religion, college grades, and satisfaction among students at elite colleges and universities* (Unpublished doctoral dissertation). Department of Sociology, University of North Carolina, Chapel Hill, North Carolina.

Myers, D. G. (1992). *The pursuit of happiness: Discovering the pathway to fulfillment, well-being, and enduring personal joy.* New York, NY: Avon Books.

Myers, D. G. (2013). Religious engagement and well-being. In S. A. David, I. Boniwell, & A. C. Ayers (Eds.), *The Oxford handbook of happiness* (pp. 88–100). Oxford, England: Oxford University Press.

Neff, K. D., & Vonk, R. (2009). Self-compassion versus global self-esteem: Two different ways of relating to oneself. *Journal of Personality, 77,* 23–50.

Oerlemans, W. G. M., & Bakker, A. B. (2014). Why extraverts are happier: A day reconstruction study. *Journal of Research in Personality, 50,* 11–22.

Pavot, W., Diener, E., & Fujita, F. (1990). Extraversion and happiness. *Personality and Individual Differences, 11,* 1299–1306.

Peterson, C. (2006). *A primer in positive psychology.* New York, NY: Oxford University Press.

Peterson, C., & Chang, E. C. (2003). Optimism and flourishing. In C. L. M. Keyes & J. Haidt (Eds.), *Flourishing: Positive psychology and the life well-lived* (pp. 55–79). Washington, DC: American Psychological Association.

Peterson, C., & Seligman, M. E. P. (1984). Causal explanations as a risk factor for depression: Theory and evidence. *Psychological Review, 91,* 347–474.

Peterson, C., & Seligman, M. E. P. (2004). *Character strengths and virtues: A handbook and classification.* Washington, DC: American Psychological Association; and New York, NY: Oxford University Press.

Pyszczynski, T., Greenberg, J., Solomon, S., Arndt, J., & Schimel, J. (2004). Why do people need self-esteem? A theoretical and empirical review. *Psychological Bulletin, 130*, 435–468.

Rotter, J. B. (1966). Generalized expectancies for internal versus external control of reinforcement. *Psychological Monographs: General and Applied, 80*(1), 1–28.

Ryan, R. M., & Deci, E. L. (2000). Self-determination theory and the facilitations of intrinsic motivation, social development, and well-being. *American Psychologist, 55*, 68–78.

Schulenberg, S. E., Schnetzer, L. W., & Buchanan, E. M. (2011). The Purpose in Life test-short form: Development and psychometric support. *Journal of Happiness Studies, 12*, 861–876.

Smillie, L. D. (2013). Extraversion and reward processing. *Current Directions in Psychological Science, 22*, 167–172.

Smillie, L. D., Cooper, A. J., Wilt, J., & Revelle, W. (2012). Do extraverts get more bang for the buck? Refining the affective-reactivity hypothesis of extraversion. *Journal of Personality and Social Psychology, 103*, 306–326.

Smillie, L. D., Geaney, J. T., Wilt, J., Cooper, A. J., & Revelle, W. (2013). Aspects of extraversion are unrelated to pleasant affective-reactivity: Further examination of the affective-reactivity hypothesis. *Journal of Research in Personality, 47*, 580–587.

Snyder, C. R. (2002). Hope theory: Rainbows of the mind. *Psychological Inquiry, 13*, 249–275.

Steel, P., Schmidt, J., & Shultz, J. (2008). Refining the relationship between personality and subjective well-being. *Psychological Bulletin, 134*, 138–161.

Steger, M. F., Frazier, P., Oishi, S., & Kaler, M. (2006). The Meaning in Life Questionnaire: Assessing the presence of and search for meaning in life. *Journal of Counseling Psychology, 53*, 80–93.

Tellegen, A., Lykken, D., Couchard, T. J., Wilcox, K. J., Segal, N. J., & Rich, S. (1988). Personality similarity in twins reared apart and together. *Journal of Personality and Social Psychology, 54*, 1031–1039.

Uhder, J., Watkins, P. C., & Hammamoto, D. (2010, August). *Would the humble please stand: Can self-reported humility be valid?* Paper presented at the Annual Convention of the American Psychological Association, San Diego, CA.

Veenhoven, R. (1988). The utility of happiness. *Social Indicators Research, 20,* 333–354.

Waterman, A. S. (2005). When effort is enjoyed: Two studies of intrinsic for personality salient activities. *Motivation and Emotion, 29,* 165–188.

Watkins, P. C. (2008). Gratitude: The amplifier of blessing. In A. Przepiorka (Ed.), *Closer to emotions II* (pp. 49–62). Lublin, Poland: Publishing House of Catholic University of Lublin.

Watkins, P. C. (2014). *Gratitude and the good life: Toward a psychology of appreciation.* Dordrecht, The Netherlands: Springer.

Watkins, P. C., Woodward, K., Stone, T., & Kolts, R. (2003). Gratitude and happiness: Development of a measure of gratitude, and relationships with subjective well-being. *Social Behavior and Personality, 31,* 431–452.

Wayment, H. A., Bauer, J. J., & Sylaska, K. (2014). The Quiet Ego Scale: Measuring the compassionate self-identity. *Journal of Happiness Studies.* doi:10.1007/s10902-014-9546-z

Wood, A. M., & Johnson, J. (Eds.). (in press). *The Wiley handbook of positive clinical psychology.* Chichester, England: Wiley.

Wood, A. M., Joseph, S., & Maltby, J. (2008). Gratitude uniquely predicts satisfaction with life: Incremental validity above the domains and facets of the five factor model. *Personality and Individual Differences, 45,* 49–54.

Wood, A. M., Maltby, J., Gillett, R., Linley, P. A., & Joseph, S. (2008). The role of gratitude in the development of social support, stress, and depression: Two longitudinal studies. *Journal of Research in Personality, 42,* 854–871.

Wood, A. M., & Tarrier, N. (2010). Positive clinical psychology: A new vision and strategy for integrated research and practice. *Clinical Psychology Review, 30,* 819–829.

Yuki, M., Sato, K., Takemura, K., & Oishi, S. (2013). Social ecology moderates the association between self-esteem and happiness. *Journal of Experimental Social Psychology, 49,* 741–746.

Are Relationships Important to Happiness?

The conclusions from the authors of an important recent article stand as an apt illustration of the importance of relationships to our happiness: "Humans may indeed be social animals but may not always be social enough for their own well-being" (Epley & Schroeder, 2014, p. 1993). In a series of studies, these researchers showed that people experienced more happiness when they were told to "connect" with strangers near them, rather than when they were told to be in solitude. They demonstrated this in several different contexts; however, they focused on situations where you are close to others you don't know and you don't usually speak to (on commuter trains, on buses, and in taxis). Not only did their participants experience more positive emotions when they tried to talk to strangers rather than when they were told to "keep to yourself," they also were happier when connecting with others rather than doing what they would normally do on their commute. Perhaps these findings aren't surprising to you, but they were surprising to other commuters: They thought they would be happier if they kept to themselves rather than being forced to talk to strangers. Even when it comes to strangers, it appears we're better off relating to them rather than isolating ourselves.

This chapter examines the question: Are relationships important to your happiness? The short response to this query appears to be "yes," but this simple answer hides a great deal of important information that is relevant to your happiness. Is quality more crucial than quantity when it comes to your relationships? Is actual social support vital to your happiness, or is it simply your *perception* of social support? Are some types of relationships more essential to subjective well-being (SWB) than others? Is marriage an important relationship to one's happiness? Are parents with children really less happy than couples without kids? What are the dynamics of happy relationships? When it comes to your happiness, is it more important to give to yourself or to give to others? These are some of the questions this chapter explores.

RESEARCH ON THE IMPORTANCE OF RELATIONSHIPS TO HAPPINESS

As we'll see, relationships are important to your happiness but, as it turns out, things aren't quite as straightforward as this proposition would seem to imply. The first important observation that we can make of this association is that the *perception of social support* appears to be more significant to happiness than objective indicators of social support. Objective indicators of social support such as number of friends and frequency of social activity show small and sometimes nonsignificant relationships with happiness (e.g., Lucas & Dyrenforth, 2006; Okun, Stock, Haring, & Witter, 1984), whereas subjective indicators of social support often show moderate to strong relationships with happiness (for a review, see Saphire-Bernstein & Taylor, 2013). In an illustrative study that directly compared these variables, Cooper, Okamura, and Gurka (1992) found that people's satisfaction with their social activities was moderately related to life satisfaction ($r = .38$), whereas frequency of social activities showed only a small relationship ($r = .19$). Moreover, whereas satisfaction with social activities showed significant relationships with positive and negative affect in the expected directions, frequency of social activity failed to show any meaningful relationships with these important facets of hedonic well-being. So this begs the question: Why are subjective indices of relationships robust predictors of happiness, but objective indicators show small and inconsistent correlations?

One possibility is that the correlation between satisfaction with one's relationships and satisfaction with life is simply a product of method invariance. In other words, the reason we get significant correlations between these two variables is because we are measuring them in a very similar way, and if you are prone to say you are satisfied with your life, you are also prone to say you are satisfied with your relationships—thus the link between these two variables is somewhat spurious. Moreover, it might be that genuinely happy people are going to evaluate their relationships positively, regardless of the objective aspects of their relationships. Surely method invariance explains part of this association; however, there is evidence to suggest that the correlation between subjective indicators of social support and happiness is not simply a product of common response biases. It appears that perception of social support is not simply the by-product of the traits of the one receiving the support (see Lakey, 2013).

In exploring this issue there is a critical question that must be answered: What are the factors that contribute to perceived social support? How I perceive the supportiveness of others in my life must result from three factors: (a) my own characteristics (i.e., my unique traits that contribute both to how I report social support and how others respond to me); (b) the objective characteristics of those providing me support; and (c) the unique relationship that I have with those providing me support (Lakey, 2013). Two studies used an ingenious methodology in an attempt to disentangle these influences (Branje, van Aken, & van Lieshout, 2002; Lakey, McCabe, Fisicaro, & Drew, 1996). These researchers identified sources of social support that were common to all of their participants (e.g., family members, professors, and sorority sisters). By determining these common sources of social support, they were able to disentangle the three factors that contribute to perceived social support. They found that characteristics of the support providers explained between 3% and 15% of the variance in perceived social support, and the traits of the recipient of social support explained between 13% and 34% of the variance. But, astonishingly, between 59% and 72% of the variance in perceived social support was explained by the unique relationships between the providers and the recipients. Thus the "subjective" report of social support is not simply reflective of the response bias or the taste preferences of the respondent. The evidence suggests that when you report on how supportive someone is of you, *this is largely reflective of your assessment of your unique interaction with that person*. In this sense, it is likely that your perceived social support is reflective of subtle and unique dynamics of your relationships that just can't be picked up by "objective" indicators such as frequency of contact and number of friends.

These studies drive home the point that when it comes to your happiness, the quality of your relationships is more important than quantity. But this brings up the issue of alternative relationships and, more specifically, how technology has now enabled electronic affiliations through social networking sites such as Facebook. Are electronic links a good proxy for more traditional face-to-face relationships? This is an important question for understanding happiness in modern times. After all, there are a number of advantages of electronic relationships over face-to-face interactions. You don't have to be in the same location as the persons you're communing with; you can relate to them at your own convenience; and you have a great deal more control over how you present yourself to them. So what is the relationship between your use of social media sites and your social well-being?

In a study published in 2009 (Jones & Fox), fully 95% of undergraduates said they spent at least 1 hour per day on the Internet, and much of that Internet time was spent on Facebook or other social networking sites (Hinsch & Sheldon, 2013). For most of us, social networking and the Internet consume a significant slice of our lives, so how do they impact our happiness? Is using Facebook good or bad for you? As with many things in life, the answer appears to be "yes"; in terms of your emotional and social life, the Internet can be both good and bad. Indeed, the jury is still out with regard to the overall impact of the Internet on your well-being, but it appears that there are a few reliable conclusions that can be drawn. First, Facebook can enhance your relationships if you are already well connected with others. Many people, however, resort to Facebook when they're feeling disconnected, and Facebook doesn't seem to do much to decrease your feelings of being disconnected from others (Sheldon, Abad, & Hinsch, 2011). These conclusions are derived from a series of studies that were born out of a pair of paradoxical findings: Facebook use was positively correlated both with reports of feeling connected with others and feeling disconnected from others. In an attempt to resolve this paradox, Sheldon and colleagues designed several studies to show that Facebook use encourages feelings of connectedness with others, and when people are feeling disconnected from others, they often use Facebook to cope with their loneliness.

The problem is that although Facebook use makes us feel as though we are becoming more connected with others as we're using it, in the long run the evidence suggests that it does not help with more essential social issues like loneliness and feelings of disconnection. This was perhaps best demonstrated by two studies that encouraged Facebook users to decrease their Facebook use (Hinsch & Sheldon, 2013). Although the results of both studies were similar, I show the results of Study 2 in Figure 5.1 because this best illustrates their findings. As can be seen from the trajectory of the dark solid line, those who took a *Facebook vacation* experienced a significant increase in life satisfaction, and this effect appeared to linger after the treatment period. Interestingly, the authors investigated both Facebook use and the use of connected online games, but found no differences between the two, supporting the idea that Facebook use and online gaming

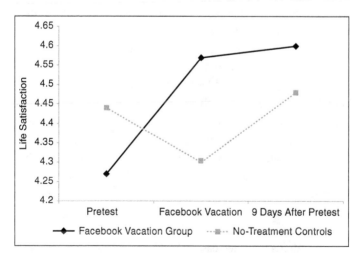

FIGURE 5.1 Results of a Facebook "vacation."
Source: Hinsch and Sheldon (2013).

provide similar functions. Moreover, the authors found that this increase in SWB for those on a Facebook vacation was largely due to a *decrease* in procrastination. In other words, taking time off from Facebook helped students to avoid procrastinating, which in turn increased their satisfaction with life. Interestingly, although life satisfaction increased, positive affect actually decreased somewhat during the Facebook deprivation period. This supports the idea that although Facebook may provide us with an immediate bump in pleasant feelings, over the long run extensive use of Facebook might actually decrease our satisfaction with life. Thus Facebook might provide some short-term gain but long-term pain for certain users. Although there are some problems with these studies (such as not randomly assigning participants to the treatment groups), the results of this research clearly support the conclusion of Sheldon et al. (2011, pp. 773, 774): "Overall, Facebook use appears to be a positive phenomenon, although perhaps not as positive as face-to-face sociality. However, Facebook may also offer an overly tempting coping device for the lonely, one that feels good but does not actually address underlying feelings of social disconnection in life."

So are Internet relationships a good replacement for face-to-face interactions when it comes to your happiness? Although social networking sites like Facebook may be a good tool to remain connected with others—particularly those who are far away geographically—investigations indicate that Internet relationships cannot fully meet your friendship needs. I should be quick to add, however, that a great deal more research is required in this area and, as the Internet changes, so might these conclusions. But studies that have tracked our social interaction over the last 20 years or so have shown that as our online social networks have increased, our face-to-face social networks and our confidants have decreased (McPherson, Brashears, & Smith-Lovin, 2006; Sigman, 2009). It only makes sense that as we spend more time on the Internet we have less time to spend face to face with others. Furthermore, there is evidence to suggest that decreases in American happiness over the last 30 years are largely associated with declines in social connections (Bartolini, Bilancini, & Pugno, 2013). In short, there is both good and bad in our use of social networking sites like Facebook. It can be a useful tool to connect with others, but it probably can't replace embodied relationships, and when it is used to cope with our loneliness and sense of being disconnected from others, it is likely to backfire.

The issue of Internet relationships also brings up another alternative form of relationships: our relationships with our pets. How does your dog or cat contribute to your happiness? Unfortunately, this is another question that defies a simple, clear answer. Despite the fact that the health benefits of pet ownership are so assumed in the media that the effect even has its own name—the *pet effect*—a dispassionate look at the research must conclude: "That empirical studies of the effects of pets on human health and well-being have produced a mishmash of conflicting results" (Herzog, 2011, p. 237). For example, one study showed that pet owners had higher self-esteem, more frequent positive moods, and greater life satisfaction—all variables that are important to SWB (El-Alayli, Lystad, Webb, Hollingsworth, & Ciolli, 2006). On the other hand, a Pew survey of 3,000 Americans found no differences in the percentage who rated themselves as "very happy" between those who owned pets and those who did not (see Herzog, 2010). Usually, if there were any meaningful differences in the happiness of people these would come out in a survey of that many people. Moreover, two studies of Scandinavian populations found that pet owners had higher rates of some psychological problems such as anxiety and depression (Koivusilta & Ojanlatva, 2006; Mullersdorf, Granstrom, Sahlqvist, & Tillgren, 2010). These conflicting results are complicated by the fact that very few studies in this area rise above the level of correlational designs.

I should be quick to point out that this ambiguity in the findings does not in any way suggest that pets make people unhappy; it's simply that the research does not unequivocally indicate that pets promote happiness. More than likely, the resolution to this confusion of results will possibly be similar to what we saw with Internet relationships. If pets do enhance SWB, it's likely to be because they fulfill social needs, but they're probably not a good substitute for human contact. Indeed, some research has suggested that pets do not compensate for relationship deficits; rather, they provide social benefits that are complementary to human relationships (McConnell, Brown, Shoda, Stayton, & Martin, 2011). McConnell and colleagues found that people who relate well to other people also seem to relate well to their pets. So, much like the Internet, pets may be able to contribute to your social well-being; nevertheless, they aren't very fulfilling if you don't have much in the way of quality human relationships.

In sum, what can we conclude about the importance of social support to your happiness? Although the case has probably been overstated in the past, the evidence suggests that social support is a clear and consistent predictor of happiness. But the important point to highlight here is that the quality of your relationships is more crucial to your happiness than the quantity of your social contacts.

FRIENDS WITH HAPPINESS BENEFITS

We have seen that quality relationships are important to your SWB. Now I would like to explore different types of relationships, and I begin with a discussion of how friendships impact happiness. Multiple studies have shown that friendship is a powerful predictor of happiness. Indeed, this finding extends across various age, ethnic, and cultural groups (for a review, see Demir, Orthel, & Andelin, 2013). As with relationships more generally, simply counting the number of friends one has doesn't tell us much about an individual's happiness; rather, the quality of the friendship is more important. When we use quantitative friendship variables like the number of friends, this typically correlates with happiness in the range of $r = .10$ to $.20$ (i.e., fairly small relationships). Qualitative variables, however, show much stronger relationships with SWB ($r = .20$ to $.50$; Demir et al., 2013). For instance, research shows that how you talk to your friends matters to your happiness (Mehl, Vazire, Holleran, & Clark, 2010). In this study, the researchers found that the proportion of people's substantive conversations was positively correlated with all of their SWB measures, but the proportion of "small talk" was actually negatively correlated with their happiness variables. Thus the quality of how you communicate with your friends matters. As you might expect, the quality of your relationship with your best friend is more important to your happiness than your interactions with other friends (Demir, Ozdemir, & Weitekamp, 2007). This may be due in part to the fact that you are more likely to engage in significant conversation rather than small talk with your best friend.

Some observations indicate that friends are more important to happiness at certain stages of life rather than others. To illustrate, for college students who are not involved in a romantic relationship, friendship is very predictive of happiness (Demir, 2010). It appears, however, that the importance of friendship to happiness declines as people enter the stage of life where they are more focused on their spouses and children (Bertera, 2005). Then, when we approach and enter our retirement years, friends again become more essential to our happiness (Antonucci & Akiyama, 1995). Although the findings seem to point to the significance of friendships in happiness, most of the studies in this area are cross-sectional and correlational, and therefore a host of alternative explanations are viable. Thus I believe that future research in this area should focus on prospective research designs and experimental designs that specifically investigate the mechanics and dynamics of successful friendships. In sum, the research favors the idea that friendships are crucial to your happiness. Now we turn to the relationship that is most likely to generate one's best friend—marriage.

LOVE, MARRIAGE, AND HAPPINESS

If you were to ask me who my best friend is, I would be quick to identify my wife. Now, let's explore the topic of marital bliss. Does marriage enhance one's happiness? Research has shown that marriage is one of the more robust demographic predictors of happiness: Across a number of studies, married people tend to be happier than the never married, divorced, or those cohabiting (for reviews, see Diener, Suh, Lucas, & Smith, 1999; Myers, 2000). Although it is sometimes claimed that marriage benefits the happiness of men more than women, the data show fairly clearly that the marriage happiness bump is very similar for men and women (Inglehart, 1990; Wood, Rhodes, & Whelan, 1989). Marriage is far from an automatic boost to one's happiness, however, because investigations show that those in unhappy marriages are often less happy than the unmarried (Myers, 2000).

Of course, just because married people tend to be happier does not necessarily mean that marriage promotes happiness. Some studies indicate that happy people are more likely to get and stay married (Mastekaasa, 1992). Furthermore, longitudinal research has shown that, on average, people experience a bump in happiness after marriage, but return to their premarital happiness levels within a few years (Lucas, Clark, Georgellis, &

Diener, 2003). This general finding, however, hides some intriguing patterns in the results. If people had a strong initial positive response to marriage, they remained significantly happier than their premarital SWB even 10 years after marriage. If, however, they had an initial negative response to marriage, this did not portend well for marital bliss. Assuredly, the happiness of these folks tended to get worse over the years. The moral of the story is perhaps best captured by Dan Gilbert's conclusion (Munsey, 2010, p. 20): "It's not marriage that makes you happy; it's a happy marriage that makes you happy."

So what makes for a happy marriage? Although this really requires a book-length answer in itself, let me offer four things that reliably characterize successful marriages. First—and perhaps foremost—marriages endure and thrive when the partners positively express their affection to each other 5 times more frequently than expressing anger or irritation. This has famously been called the *Gottman Ratio*, named after the researcher who has so carefully investigated the important dynamics of happy marriages (e.g., Gottman, 1994). Second, couples who share leisure activities typically have happier marriages. When couples start vacationing separately, that may not be a good sign. Third, those couples who share spiritual activities are more likely to thrive together (Greeley, 1991). Thus the old adage, "Couples who pray and play together, stay together," actually contains some empirical truth. Fourth, happy marriages are often characterized by an equitable sharing of the household tasks (Feeney, Peterson, & Noller, 1994; Schafer & Keith, 1980). Marital satisfaction suffers when one of the partners feels unfairly burdened with the household tasks. In sum, although married individuals tend to be happier than those not married, this very general relationship hides a great many important variables that are important to a happy marriage, and the research is clear: It is a happy marriage that most contributes to a happy life.

THE JOY OF PARENTING?

Perhaps one of the most contentious issues in the science of SWB has to do with the happiness of parents. For example, in one study the author found that fully 80% of parents said they got "great satisfaction" from interaction with their children the previous day (far more than any other activity; Robinson, 1977); nevertheless, in another oft-cited study that used the day reconstruction method, the researchers found that mothers garnered less joy from parenting than from watching television or preparing meals (Kahnemann, Krueger, Schkade, Schwartz, & Stone, 2004). An important review on this topic pointed out that the problem may lie in the question. Asking a broad question such as "Are parents happier than nonparents?" is destined to provide conflicting answers because it washes over so many critical variables including age of the parents, age of the children, gender of the parents, income of the parents, and so forth (Nelson, Kushlev, & Lyubomirsky, 2014). From their extensive review, Nelson and collaborators concluded that parents tend to be less happy when their parenting is associated with magnified financial problems, increased marital dysfunction, and increased sleep disturbance. On the other hand, they found that parents were inclined to be happier when their parenting was associated with increased meaning in life and the satisfaction of basic psychological needs.

One of the issues that may complicate this question is that recent research has suggested that our enjoyment of daily activities may consist of two relatively independent dimensions: *pleasure* and *reward* (White & Dolan, 2009). Pleasure more specifically involves the feelings that we experience during an activity, whereas reward involves more "nonhedonic" aspects of what makes an activity rewarding. White and Dolan's reward scale included items such as "focused," "competent," and "I feel the activities in this episode were worthwhile and meaningful."

Clearly, pleasure items related more to hedonic well-being, whereas the reward items were more relevant to eudaimonic well-being. It is easy to see how an activity such as parenting might not be overly pleasurable, yet still be rewarding, and this is exactly what the authors found. This study showed clearly that when it comes to our happiness, we need to consider how rewarding an activity is in addition to how pleasurable it is. And this issue is an important consideration when reflecting on the joy of parenting.

Recently a group of researchers conducted three studies in an attempt to resolve some of the ambiguities surrounding the benefits of parenting to SWB (Nelson, Kushlev, English, Dunn, & Lyubomirsky, 2013). In Study 1, they used a large representative sample of almost 7,000 U.S. residents to see how the happiness of parents compared with that of nonparents. In this large sample, they found that parents tended to have higher life satisfaction, more happiness, and greater meaning in life than did nonparents. In Study 2, the investigators randomly paged parents and nonparents to report their emotional status 5 times per day, over a 1-week period. As in Study 1, parents reported higher levels of positive emotion and greater meaning in life than did nonparents. In Study 3, they essentially replicated these findings using the day-reconstruction method and a within-subjects approach. These three studies provide compelling validation that far from being a miserable calling, parenting can be a great source of satisfaction—particularly if it brings meaning into one's life.

THE DYNAMICS OF HAPPY RELATIONSHIPS

Up to this point we have focused on how different types of relationships affect your happiness. But this approach has a tendency to ignore the common relationship dynamics that might impact happiness across relationships. In this section we focus on three dynamics of happy relationships: capitalization, gratitude, and forgiveness.

Capitalizing on the Good in Relationships

Shelly Gable and her colleagues have been able to identify an important characteristic of successful relationships: capitalizing on the good. Simply defined, *capitalization* is any type of response to a positive event that enhances your positive experience of that event (Langston, 1994). As such, capitalization is not specifically a relationship dynamic; however, one of the most common and effective ways of capitalizing on positive events is to share our good news with others. Gable's research has shown that this is one of the most significant dynamics of close relationships: When we have someone we're comfortable sharing our successes with, this enhances our SWB. Indeed, she has found that when we share good news with someone about a positive event, it enhances our SWB above and beyond the impact of the positive event itself (Gable, Reis, Impett, & Asher, 2004). Furthermore, she has shown that how your relationship partner responds to your good news is important. When your partner responds in an active and constructive way (e.g., "Wow, that is really good news."), it improves the well-being of the relationship (Gable et al., 2004; Gable, Gonzaga, & Strachman, 2006). Moreover, the researchers have found that it is easier to respond in a healthy way to positive events rather than negative events. When we respond to positive events in an active, constructive manner, this makes it easier for our partners to take our responses to negative events positively (Gable, Gosnell, Maisel, & Strachman, 2012). One of the best pieces of advice for your relationships is: When someone tells you good news, try to experience the person's pleasure and respond actively and enthusiastically to the news. On the other hand, if you respond passively ("Oh, that's nice.") or destructively ("How in the world did you get that raise?"), this inevitably mutes the impact of the good event. So make sure you don't respond with what I call the "cold-water response" to good news (a passive or destructive response). Rather, if you can experience your partner's good news in an enthusiastic way, this bodes well for your relationship.

Gratitude and Happy Relationships

One of the best ways to respond to positive events is with gratitude, and exciting new research has shown that happy relationships are grateful relationships. Gratitude is clearly important to your social well-being (for a review, see Watkins, 2014), and here we explore some of the specifics of this relationship.

How does gratitude enhance your relationships? In brief, I have argued that gratitude enhances social well-being because it amplifies the good in your relationships. Gratitude appears to amplify the good in your relationships in several ways. First, when you express gratitude, this amplifies the good that others see in you. Studies show very clearly that people like grateful people, and they tend to dislike ungrateful folks (e.g., McCullough, Emmons, & Tsang, 2002; Suls, Witenberg, & Gutkin, 1981; Watkins, Martin, & Faulkner, 2003). Second, gratitude enhances social well-being by helping people form and bond new relationships. For example, in a study of developing relationships in college sororities, Algoe, Haidt, and Gable (2008) found that gratitude in "little sisters" for gifts given by their "big sisters" predicted increased relationship quality later. Recent evidence suggests that gratitude might encourage the bonding of relationships through the release of oxytocin—a hormone that appears to be critical in the formation of human attachments (Algoe & Way, 2014).

How does gratitude assist in the formation of relationships? Several studies have determined that the action tendencies that are activated by gratitude are definitively prosocial (Algoe & Haidt, 2009; Watkins, Scheer, Ovnicek, & Kolts, 2006). In other words, when we feel grateful, we feel urges to approach and be kind to others. Demonstrating these prosocial inclinations, Bartlett, Condon, Cruz, Baumann, and Desteno (2012) showed that compared to those in their neutral conditions, those induced to feel grateful were almost twice as likely to choose to come back to the laboratory and work with their benefactors. Bartlett et al. (2012) also reported that gratitude promotes the inclusion of others, even when it is costly to do so. Taken together, data indicate that gratitude motivates us to affiliate with others, which enhances our ability to form relationships with others.

Furthermore, research has shown that gratitude helps *maintain* healthy relationships. To illustrate, in a 2-week daily diary study of married couples, Gordon, Arnette, and Smith (2011) found that both felt and expressed gratitude to one's spouse predicted satisfaction with the relationship. In another study of romantic relationships, Algoe, Gable, and Maisel (2010) found that gratitude prospectively predicted increased relationship satisfaction. Similarly, in couples in marriages of more than 4 years, Kubacka, Kinfenauer, Rusbult, and Keijsers (2011) determined that gratitude was often experienced when one saw a partner engaging in relationship maintenance behavior, and then gratitude predicted more relationship maintenance behaviors on the part of the spouse (see also Gordon, Impett, Kogan, Oveis, & Keltner, 2012). These studies demonstrate that when we feel appreciated this helps us appreciate others, which then encourages us to do things that support the relationship. Stated differently, expressing gratitude helps us to see the good in others, which encourages them to see the good in us. Here again we can see that gratitude amplifies the good in our relationships.

The correlational nature of these studies leaves some doubt about whether gratitude actually *causes* us to do things that encourage and maintain our relationships. Now, however, experimental evidence provides clearer support that gratitude enhances relationship maintenance behaviors (Lambert, Clark, Durtschi, Fincham, & Graham, 2010; Lambert & Fincham, 2011). For instance, in a compelling evaluation of romantic relationships, responses to gratitude expressions in the laboratory predicted improved relationship quality 6 months later (Algoe, Fredrickson, & Gable, 2013). Taken together, all of this research provides strong evidence that gratitude amplifies the good in relationships by.encouraging relationship maintenance.

To summarize, research provides strong support for the theory that gratitude enhances happiness by encouraging and supporting healthy relationships. Sara Algoe has been a leader in investigations on the impact of gratitude on close relationships, and I have found that her *Find-Bind-and-Remind theory of gratitude* is particularly useful in helping us understand the social consequences of gratitude (Algoe, 2012). She argues convincingly that gratitude functions to help us *find* new relationships, to *remind* us of ongoing relationships that are important to flourishing, and to *bind* our relationships into enduring and supportive social structures. As we have seen, research shows that relationships are important to SWB (e.g., Burt, 1986; Diener & Seligman, 2004), and gratitude might enhance happiness by amplifying the good in relationships. In short, experiencing and expressing gratitude to those who are important to you is an essential dynamic of happy relationships.

The Importance of Forgiveness to Happy Relationships

If you've never made any mistakes in your relationships, then you can skip reading this section. But if you're like me—and I strongly suspect that you are—you've made comments that have been hurtful to those you love, and you've forgotten to do things that would help those who are important to you. In other words, we seem to consistently screw up in those relationships that are most meaningful to us. Undoubtedly, partly because we feel secure with those to whom we are closest, we feel free to hurt those we love most. If we have any kind of regular close contact with other humans, we need to forgive them, and they need to forgive us. In short, none of us are perfect in our relationships, and this is why forgiveness is so crucial to happy relationships.

We learned in Chapter 2 that forgiveness is "not holding the wrongs from others against them and refraining from revenge." When someone makes a biting remark to me, my natural response is to bite back but, more often than not, this is not good for the relationship. Forgiveness allows me to overcome my natural instinct to "bite back," or to seek revenge. Not only is the tendency to forgive associated with SWB, there is also clear evidence that forgiveness is an important dynamic of healthy relationships (for reviews, see McCullough, 2000; McCullough, Root, Tabak, & Witvliet, 2009). Research has shown that people who are prone to forgive are also good at maintaining a positive relationship with those close to them (e.g., McCullough et al., 1998). Conversely, failure to forgive others close to us tends to lead to tension in the relationship (e.g., Karremans, Van Lange, Ouwerkerk, & Kluwer, 2003).

Clearly, forgiveness is essential in happy relationships but, almost by definition, forgiveness is not easy. Forgiveness is not just saying "That's okay." Rather, it is fully acknowledging the transgression, but then making the conscious decision to not hold it against the transgressor, and going beyond that to seek a mutual peace. So what promotes forgiveness? McCullough and colleagues (2009) argue that there are three critical antecedents for forgiveness: "careworthiness," "expected value," and "safety." First, when I see my transgressor as worthy of care, then I am more likely to forgive. Research demonstrates that you're more likely to forgive when you are close to the person who has hurt you, and when you're able to empathize with that person (e.g.,

McCullough et al., 1998). Here is where compassion becomes crucial, and perhaps I should add that as a fourth important dynamic for healthy relationships. Compassion, however, is more than just empathizing with my transgressor, it is also feeling motivated to help the person. Compassion is bound to be a critical antecedent for forgiveness, but research also indicates that forgiveness creates more compassion (Witvliet, Ludwig, & Vander Laan, 2001).

Second, McCullough et al. (2009) show that we're more likely to forgive when we see that the relationship with our transgressor has future value for us. If we don't see any use in the relationship—or even see it as destructive—then we aren't very likely to forgive. Third, they show that we're more likely to forgive our transgressor when we have some sense of safety. If we feel as though our transgressor is likely to hurt us again, we aren't likely to forgive.

To summarize, we have seen that there are at least three critical dynamics of happy relationships. First, people in happy relationships are good at capitalizing on the successes of their partners. Second, happy relationships tend to be grateful relationships. When the partners in a relationship are experiencing and expressing gratitude toward each other, their relationship is bound to flourish. Finally, we have seen that forgiveness is critical in healthy relationships. Because we all end up hurting those we love, forgiveness is the key to an ongoing positive relationship.

HOW GIVING TO OTHERS IS IMPORTANT TO HAPPINESS

Although we have known for years that happy people tend to be giving people (Myers, 1992, 2000), it was usually assumed that the causal direction was from happiness to giving. In other words, the supposition was that being in a good mood also puts you in a giving mood. Whereas the work of Isen has surely provided evidence for that theory (e.g., Isen, 1987), only recently we have seen that giving in itself produces a boost to happiness (for excellent reviews, see Dunn, Aknin, & Norton, 2014; Dunn & Norton, 2013).

Elizabeth Dunn and colleagues published the seminal group of studies demonstrating the giving happiness effect (Dunn, Aknin, & Norton, 2008). In the first study, they showed that *prosocial spending* (spending money on others and on charities) was more strongly correlated with happiness than personal spending (spending money on personal bills and on things for yourself). In the second study, they followed people who had received a substantial bonus at work, and tracked what they did with their "windfalls." They found that prosocial spending predicted future increases in happiness but that personal spending did not. In the conclusive third study, the researchers actually gave people money (either $5 or $20), and the individuals were told to either spend the money on themselves or on others. Figure 5.2 shows the results of this study. Clearly, people who spent their money on others ended up being happier than those who spent it on themselves. What's more, the amount of money didn't seem to matter—the pure act of giving was what was important. Furthermore, it appears that we're completely unaware—even mistaken—about the giving and happiness effect. When this study was described to another group of participants, people actually thought they would be happier if they spent the money on themselves rather than on others. Indeed, this mistaken belief might well be impeding our happiness.

New research has shown that the giving effect seems intrinsic to human nature—it's not simply a product of what our parents told us to believe. Studies have now determined that the effect of prosocial spending extends across countries both poor and rich (Aknin et al., 2013), and the giving effect even impacts the

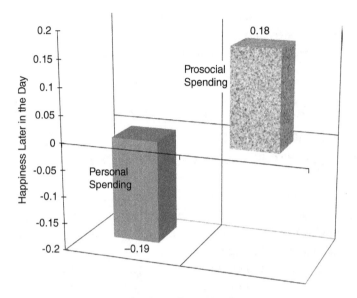

FIGURE 5.2 Happiness level as a function of spending instructions.

happiness of children younger than 2 years old (Aknin, Dunn, & Norton, 2012). There are a few boundary conditions to the giving effect. It appears that prosocial spending has greater impact on our happiness if we use it to enhance our relationship with others, rather than just giving to strangers (Aknin, Sandstrom, Dunn, & Norton, 2011). So don't just buy your friends cards from Starbucks, take them out for a mocha. Another important caveat is that if you freely choose to spend your money on others, you're more likely to see a boost in your happiness (Weinstein & Ryan, 2010). Therefore, don't start giving just because I told you to; give for the joy of giving in itself. Taken together, it appears that giving to others is more likely to enhance your happiness when it helps you fulfill the three fundamental psychological needs that were explored in Chapter 1: relatedness, competence, and autonomy. And now there is evidence that giving and happiness act in a cycle of virtue (Aknin et al., 2012). Giving enhances your happiness, but happiness in turn makes you more likely to give. Certainly, research seems to now affirm the declaration of Jesus: "It is more blessed to give than to receive" (Acts 20:35, New Revised Standard Version).

SUMMARY AND CONCLUSIONS: THE UPWARD SPIRAL OF RELATIONSHIPS AND HAPPINESS

This chapter concludes that your relationships are important to your happiness. The quality—but not so much the quantity—of our relationships enhances our SWB. We have seen that the quality of your friendships and your marriage is crucial to your happiness. But don't just get married to get happy; that's a proposition that's bound to backfire. Indeed, you may be better off single than in an unhappy marriage. It has also been demonstrated that there are at least three important dynamics to happy relationships: capitalization, gratitude, and forgiveness. Finally—and perhaps most significant—we have seen the importance of giving in our relationships. You actually have much to gain by giving in your relationships. In short, quality relationships boost our happiness. But research also shows that our happiness enhances our relationships, and depression tends to make our relationships worse. "Misery may love company," quipped David Myers, "but company doesn't love misery" (1992, p. 20). Thus the research paints a picture of an upward spiral: Quality relationships enhance happiness and, in turn, happiness promotes quality relationships. This is perhaps one of the most important cycles of virtue to maintaining our happiness.

We began this chapter by exploring an intriguing series of studies conducted by Epley and Schroeder (2014). In these exercises, people felt happier when they communed with strangers; nevertheless, for some reason they believed that they would be happier when they kept to themselves. Why are we so wrong about this? How can it be that we keep on believing that trying to talk to strangers will be an aversive experience, when in fact the opposite is true? Epley and Schroeder found that we maintain these mistaken beliefs because we think that strangers don't want us to talk to them, when in fact that's not true. In essence, we preserve these false beliefs because of a *lack* of experience. When I'm on the bus or on a plane, I think that you don't want me to talk to you and you think that I don't want you to speak with me. The result is that we rarely speak to each other and we don't get the chance to experience the joy of communing with someone new. As Epley and Schroeder noted in their title, we are "mistakenly seeking solitude." Investigations, however, have confirmed Aristotle's proclamation that we are "social animals," and our relationships contribute in an important way to our happiness.

REFERENCES

Aknin, L. B., Barrington-Leigh, C. P., Dunn, E. W., Helliwell, J. F., Burns, J., Biswas-Diener, R., . . . Norton, M. I. (2013). Prosocial spending and well-being: Cross-cultural evidence for a psychological universal. *Journal of Personality and Social Psychology, 104,* 635–652. doi:10.1037/a0031578

Aknin, L. B., Dunn, E. W., & Norton, M. I. (2012). Happiness runs in a circular motion: Evidence for a positive feedback loop between prosocial spending and happiness. *Journal of Happiness Studies, 13,* 347–355. doi:10.1007/s10902-011-9267-5

Aknin, L. B., Sandstrom, G. M., Dunn, E. W., & Norton, M. I. (2011). It's the recipient that counts: Spending money on strong social ties leads to greater happiness than spending on weak social ties. *PLoS ONE, 6*(2). doi:10.1371/journal.pone.0017018

Algoe, S. B. (2012). Find, remind, and bind: The functions of gratitude in everyday relationships. *Social and Personality Psychology Compass, 6,* 455–469.

Algoe, S. B., Fredrickson, B. L., & Gable, S. L. (2013). The social functions of the emotion of gratitude via expression. *Emotion, 13,* 605–609.

Algoe, S. B., Gable, S. L., & Maisel, N. C. (2010). It's the little things: Everyday gratitude as a booster shot for romantic relationships. *Personal Relationships, 17,* 217–233.

Algoe, S. B., & Haidt, J. (2009). Witnessing excellence in action: The "other praising" emotions of elevation, gratitude, and admiration. *Journal of Positive Psychology, 4,* 105–127.

Algoe, S. B., Haidt, J., & Gable, S. L. (2008). Beyond reciprocity: Gratitude and relationships in everyday life. *Emotion, 8,* 425–429.

Algoe, S. B., & Way, B. (2014). Evidence for a role of the oxytocin system, indexed by genetic variation in CD38, in the social bonding effects of expressed gratitude. *Social Cognitive and Affective Neuroscience, 9*(12). doi:10.1093/scan/nst182

Antonucci, T. C., & Akiyama, H. (1995). Convoys of social relations: Family and friendships within a life span context. In R. Blieszner & V. H. Bedford (Eds.), *Handbook of aging and the family* (pp. 355–372). Westport, CT: Greenwood Press.

Bartlett, M. Y., Condon, P., Cruz, J., Baumann, J., & Desteno, D. (2012). Gratitude: Prompting behaviours that build relationships. *Cognition and Emotion, 26,* 2–13.

Bartolini, S., Bilancini, E., & Pugno, M. (2013). Did the decline in social connections depress Americans' happiness? *Social Indicators Research, 110,* 1033–1059. doi:10.1007/s11205-011-9971-x

Bertera, E. M. (2005). Mental health in U.S.A. adults: The role of positive social support and social negativity in personal relationships. *Journal of Social and Personal Relationships, 22,* 3–48.

Branje, S. J. T., van Aken, M. A. G., & van Lieshout, C. F. M. (2002). Relational support in families with adolescents. *Journal of Family Psychology, 16,* 351–362.

Burt, R. S. (1986). *Strangers, friends and happiness* (GSS Technical Report No. 72). Chicago, IL: University of Chicago Press.

Cooper, H., Okamura, L., & Gurka, V. (1992). Social activity and subjective well-being. *Personality and Individual Differences, 13,* 573–583.

Demir, M. (2010). Close relationships and happiness among emerging adults. *Journal of Happiness Studies, 11,* 293–313.

Demir, M., Orthel, H., & Andelin, A. K. (2013). Friendships and happiness. In S. A. David, I. Boniwell, & A. Conley Ayers (Eds.), *The Oxford handbook of happiness* (pp. 860–870). Oxford, England: Oxford University Press.

Demir, M., Ozdemir, M., & Weitekamp, L. A. (2007). Looking to happy tomorrow with friends: Best and close friendships as they predict happiness. *Journal of Happiness Studies, 8,* 243–271.

Diener, E., & Seligman, M. E. P. (2004). Beyond money: Toward an economy of well-being. *Psychological Science in the Public Interest, 5,* 1–31.

Diener, E., Suh, E. M., Lucas, R. E., & Smith, H. L. (1999). Subjective well-being: Three decades of progress. *Psychological Bulletin, 125,* 276–302.

Dunn, E., & Norton, M. (2013). *Happy money: The science of happier spending.* New York, NY: Simon & Schuster.

Dunn, E. W., Aknin, L. B., & Norton, M. I. (2008). Spending money on others promotes happiness. *Science, 319,* 1687–1688.

Dunn, E. W., Aknin, L. B., & Norton, M. I. (2014). Prosocial spending and happiness: Using money to benefit others pays off. *Current Directions in Psychological Science, 23,* 41–47.

El-Alayli, A., Lystad, A. L., Webb, S. R., Hollingsworth, S. L., & Ciolli, J. L. (2006). Reigning cats and dogs: A pet-enhancement bias and its link to pet attachment, pet-self similarity, self-enhancement, and well-being. *Basic and Applied Social Psychology, 28,* 131–143.

Epley, N., & Schroeder, J. (2014). Mistakenly seeking solitude. *Journal of Experimental Psychology: General, 143,* 1980–1999.

Feeney, J., Peterson, C., & Noller, P. (1994). Equity and marital satisfaction over the family life cycle. *Personality Relationships, 1,* 83–99.

Gable, S. L., Gonzaga, G. C., & Strachman, A. (2006). Will you be there for me when things go right? Supportive responses to positive event disclosures. *Journal of Personality and Social Psychology, 91,* 904–917. doi:10.1037/0022-3514.91.5.904

Gable, S. L., Gosnell, C. L., Maisel, N. C., & Strachman, A. (2012). Safely testing the alarm: Close others' responses to personal positive events. *Journal of Personality and Social Psychology, 103,* 963–981. doi:10.1037/a0029488

Gable, S. L., Reis, H. T., Impett, E. A., & Asher, E. R. (2004). What do you do when things go right? The intrapersonal and interpersonal benefits of sharing positive events. *Journal of Personality and Social Psychology, 87,* 228–245. doi:10.1037/0022-3514.87.2.228

Gordon, C. L., Arnette, R. A. M., & Smith, R. E. (2011). Have you thanked your spouse today? Felt and expressed gratitude among married couples. *Personality and Individual Differences, 50,* 339–343.

Gordon, C. L., Impett, E. A., Kogan, A., Oveis, C., & Keltner, D. (2012). To have and to hold: Gratitude promotes relationship maintenance in intimate bonds. *Journal of Personality and Social Psychology, 103,* 257–274.

Gottman, J. M. (1994). *Why marriages succeed or fail and how you can make yours last.* New York, NY: Simon & Schuster.

Greeley, A. M. (1991). *Faithful attraction.* New York, NY: Tor Books.

Herzog, H. (2010). *Some we love, some we hate, some we eat: Why it's so hard to think straight about animals.* New York, NY: HarperCollins.

Herzog, H. (2011). The impact of pets on human health and psychological well-being: Fact, fiction, or hypothesis? *Current Directions in Psychological Science, 20,* 236–239.

Hinsch, C., & Sheldon, K. M. (2013). The impact of frequent social Internet consumption: Increased procrastination and lower life satisfaction. *Journal of Consumer Behaviour, 12,* 496–505.

Inglehart, R. (1990). *Culture shift in advanced industrial society.* Princeton, NJ: Princeton University Press.

Isen, A. M. (1987). Positive affect, cognitive processes, and social behavior. *Advances in Experimental Social Psychology, 20,* 203–253.

Jones, S., & Fox, S. (2009). *Generations online in 2009.* Washington, DC: Pew Internet and American life.

Kahnemann, D., Krueger, A. B., Schkade, D. A., Schwartz, N., & Stone, A. A. (2004). A survey method for characterizing daily life experience: The day reconstruction method. *Science, 306,* 1776–1780.

Koivusilta, L. K., & Ojanlatva, A. (2006). To have or not to have a pet for better health? *PLoS ONE, 1,* 1–9.

Kubacka, K. E., Kinfenauer, C., Rusbult, C. E., & Keijsers, L. (2011). Maintaining close relationships: Gratitude as a motivator and a detector of maintenance behavior. *Personality and Social Psychology Bulletin, 37,* 1362–1375.

Lakey, B. (2013). Perceived social support and happiness: The role of personality and relational processes. In S. A. David, I. Boniwell, & A. C. Ayers (Eds.), *The Oxford handbook of happiness* (pp. 847–859). Oxford, England: Oxford University Press.

Lakey, B., McCabe, K., Fisicaro, S., & Drew, J. (1996). Personal and environmental sources of social support: Three generalizability studies. *Journal of Personality and Social Psychology, 70,* 1270–1280.

Lambert, N. M., Clark, M. S., Durtschi, J., Fincham, F. D., & Graham, S. M. (2010). Benefits of expressing gratitude: Expressing gratitude to a partner changes one's view of the relationship. *Psychological Science, 21,* 574–580.

Lambert, N. M., & Fincham, F. D. (2011). Expressing gratitude to a partner leads to more relationship maintenance behavior. *Emotion, 11,* 52–60.

Langston, C. A. (1994). Capitalizing on and coping with daily-life events: Expressive responses to positive events. *Journal of Personality and Social Psychology, 67,* 1112–1125. doi:10.1037/0022-3514.67.6.1112

Lucas, R. E., Clark, A. E., Georgellis, Y., & Diener, E. (2003). Reexamining adaptation and the set point model of happiness: Reactions to changes in marital status. *Journal of Personality and Social Psychology, 84,* 527–539. doi:10.1037/0022-3514.84.3.527

Lucas, R. E., & Dyrenforth, P. S. (2006). Does the existence of social relationships matter for subjective well-being? In K. D. Vohs & E. J. Finkel (Eds.), *Self and relationships: Connecting intrapersonal and interpersonal processes* (pp. 254–273). New York, NY: Guilford Press.

Mastekaasa, A. (1992). Marriage and psychological well-being: Some evidence on selection into marriage. *Journal of Marriage and the Family, 54,* 901–911.

McConnell, A. R., Brown, C. M., Shoda, T. M., Stayton, L. E., & Martin, C. E. (2011). Friends with benefits: On the positive consequences of pet ownership. *Journal of Personality and Social Psychology, 101,* 1239–1252.

McCullough, M. E. (2000). Forgiveness as human strength: Theory, measurement, and links to well-being. *Journal of Social and Clinical Psychology, 19,* 43–55.

McCullough, M. E., Emmons, R. A., & Tsang, J. (2002). The grateful disposition: A conceptual and empirical topography. *Journal of Personality and Social Psychology, 82,* 112–127.

McCullough, M. E., Rachal, K. C., Sandage, S. J., Worthington, E. L., Brown, S. W., & Hight, T. L. (1998). Interpersonal forgiving in close relationships: II. Theoretical elaboration and measurement. *Journal of Personality and Social Psychology, 75,* 1586-1603.

McCullough, M. E., Root, L. M., Tabak, B. A., & Witvliet, C. (2009). Forgiveness. In S. J. Lopez & C. R. Snyder (Eds.), *Oxford handbook of positive psychology* (pp. 427–436). New York, NY: Oxford University Press.

McPherson, M., Brashears, M., & Smith-Lovin, L. (2006). Social isolation in America: Changes in core discussion networks over two decades. *American Sociological Review, 71,* 353–375.

Mehl, M. R., Vazire, S., Holleran, S. E., & Clark, C. S. (2010). Eavesdropping on happiness: Well-being is related to having less small talk and more substantive conversations. *Psychological Science, 21,* 539–541. doi:10.1177/0956797610362675

Mullersdorf, M., Granstrom, F., Sahlqvist, L., & Tillgren, P. (2010). Aspects of health, physical/leisure activities, work and sociodemographics associated with pet ownership in Sweden. *Scandinavian Journal of Public Health, 38,* 53–63.

Munsey, C. (2010). Does marriage make us happy? *APA Monitor, 41*(9), 20.

Myers, D. G. (1992). *The pursuit of happiness: Discovering the pathway to fulfillment, well-being, and enduring personal joy.* New York, NY: Avon Books.

Myers, D. G. (2000). The funds, friends, and faith of happy people. *American Psychologist, 55,* 56–67. doi:10.1037/0003-066X.55.1.56

Nelson, S. K., Kushlev, K., English, T., Dunn, E. W., & Lyubomirsky, S. (2013). In defense of parenthood: Children are associated with more joy than misery. *Psychological Science, 24,* 3–10. doi:10.1177/0956797612447798

Nelson, S. K., Kushlev, K., & Lyubomirsky, S. (2014). The pains and pleasures of parenting: When, why, and how is parenthood associated with more or less well-being? *Psychological Bulletin, 140,* 846–895.

Okun, M. A., Stock, W. A., Haring, M. J., & Witter, R. A. (1984). The social activity/subjective well-being relation: A quantitative synthesis. *Research on Aging, 6,* 45–65.

Robinson, J. P. (1977). *How Americans use time.* New York, NY: Praeger.

Saphire-Bernstein, S., & Taylor, S. E. (2013). Close relationships and happiness. In S. A. David, I. Boniwell, & A. C. Ayers (Eds.), *The Oxford handbook of happiness* (pp. 821–833). Oxford, England: Oxford University Press.

Schafer, R. B., & Keith, P. M. (1980). Equity and depression among married couples. *Social Psychology Quarterly, 43,* 430–435.

Sheldon, K. M., Abad, N., & Hinsch, C. (2011). A two-process view of Facebook use and relatedness need-satisfaction: Disconnection drives use, and connection rewards it. *Journal of Personality and Social Psychology, 100,* 766–775.

Sigman, A. (2009). Well connected? The biological implications of 'social networking.' *Biologist, 56,* 14–21.

Suls, J., Witenberg, S., & Gutkin, D. (1981). Evaluating reciprocal and nonreciprocal prosocial behavior: Developmental trends. *Personality and Social Psychology Bulletin, 7,* 225–231.

Watkins, P. C. (2014). *Gratitude and the good life: Toward a psychology of appreciation.* Dordrecht, The Netherlands: Springer.

Watkins, P. C., Martin, B. D., & Faulkner, G. (2003, May). *Are grateful people happy people? Informant judgments of grateful acquaintances.* Paper presented at the 83rd Annual Convention of the Western Psychological Association, Vancouver, BC, Canada.

Watkins, P. C., Scheer, J., Ovnicek, M., & Kolts, R. (2006). The debt of gratitude: Dissociating gratitude from indebtedness. *Cognition and Emotion, 20,* 217–241.

Weinstein, N., & Ryan, R. M. (2010). When helping helps: Autonomous motivation for prosocial behavior and its influence on the well-being for the helper and the recipient. *Journal of Personality and Social Psychology, 98,* 222–244.

White, M. P., & Dolan, P. (2009). Accounting for the richness of daily activities. *Psychological Science, 20,* 1000–1008. doi:10.1111/ j.1467-9280.2009.02392.x

Witvliet, C. V. O., Ludwig, T. E., & Vander Laan, K. L. (2001). Granting forgiveness or harboring grudges: Implications for emotion, physiology, and health. *Psychological Science, 12,* 117–123.

Wood, W., Rhodes, N., & Whelan, M. (1989). Sex differences in positive well-being: A consideration of emotional style and marital status. *Psychological Bulletin, 106,* 249–264.

How Do Happy People Think? The Mind-Set of Happiness

ost of us are familiar with the "glass half empty or half full" example. When two children are each given a glass of juice, one may focus on the fact that it is half empty, and complain that more is wanted. The other child, however, may see the same glass and is happy to be getting that much juice. This book demonstrates that objective circumstances such as your income predict very little of your happiness. Why? It is not so much your circumstances that are important to your happiness. Rather, what is important to your happiness is *how you see* your circumstances. As Abraham Lincoln said, "Most folks are about as happy as they make up their minds to be." Indeed, how we think is critical to our happiness.

Even before the positive psychology movement got off the ground, Chris Peterson conducted a study that detailed the significance of positive thinking to well-being (Peterson, Seligman, & Vaillant, 1988). To accomplish his investigation, Peterson was able to gain access to an amazing data set. A select group of men from Harvard University in the 1930s and 1940s were initially subjected to comprehensive evaluation, and they have been followed since that time. Most of these men served in World War II and in 1945 they were asked to describe their difficult wartime experiences. Peterson realized that the responses of the men to this question were a gold mine to understanding how people think about life, and how their thinking impacts their well-being later. How would they describe these events? Would they paint them in a pessimistic way, blaming themselves or other chronic and global problems? Or would they report on them in a more optimistic manner, explaining their wartime experiences in a specific way, with causes that were not likely to continue to affect them in the present? The researchers of this study have been assessing a number of different variables in these men, including health status. Figure 6.1 shows how their optimistic positive thinking in 1945 correlated with good health later. These associations were carried out after controlling for their initial health status, so we can't say that they were simply in better health to begin with, which then created more optimism. Astonishingly, the positive thinking of these young men back in 1945 predicted better health after they were 45 years old. Note that the relationship keeps climbing until it reaches its apex at age 45, but the prediction is still significant after that age. Clearly, how we think about our lives is crucial to our well-being, and this chapter explores the connection between cognition and happiness.

As we survey this topic, I follow the helpful AIM acronym suggested by Diener (e.g., Diener & Biswas-Diener, 2008). AIM

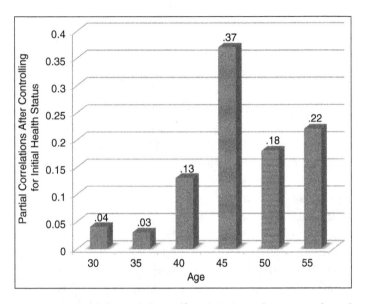

FIGURE 6.1 Partial correlations of optimistic explanatory style and health by age.

stands for three stages of cognition that help us to grasp how we think about things: attention, interpretation, and memory. Thus we examine each of these stages of cognition in turn, and discuss how they relate to happiness. I follow this discussion with research on affective forecasting, and how inaccurately forecasting our emotional future might inhibit our happiness.

ATTENTION: WHAT GRABS THE ATTENTION OF HAPPY PEOPLE?

Because we cannot simultaneously attend to everything within our sphere of awareness, we must prioritize some things over others. In cognitive science, this is referred to as *attention allocation*, and in this section we explore how happy people allocate their attention to different things in their environment. In this portion of the book we see that some things immediately grab our attention, and other things hold our attention ("I just can't seem to take my eyes off that."), and both of these forms of attention allocation bear on our happiness. So what do happy people pay attention to?

First, it is important to note that consistent with the "bad is stronger than good" principle, in general, negative and threatening things are more likely to capture our attention, regardless of how happy we are (Baumeister, Bratslavsky, Finkenauer, & Vohs, 2001). This is consistent with evolutionary theory; in order to escape danger our attention system needs to quickly identify threat in the environment. Going beyond this general principle, however, it is probably safe to conclude that happy people tend to allocate more of their attention to positive information (and away from threatening things), than do unhappy folks. I am somewhat cautious in this suggestion because most of the relevant research compares clinical subjects such as depressed and anxious people with controls (Mathews, 1997). Presuming that the nonclinical control subjects in these studies were happier than those with depression or anxiety, happiness would be associated with an allocation of attention to the positive.

It is somewhat surprising to me that researchers have not yet systematically investigated attention biases in happiness. Fortunately a few recent studies have shown that, indeed, happiness and positive emotion are associated with a positive attention bias (Sanchez & Vasquez, 2014; Sanchez, Vazquez, Gomez, & Joormann, 2014; Tamir & Robinson, 2007). There are many issues left to be resolved here, such as the time sequence of this happy attention bias. Is it that happy people are quicker to notice the good in their lives? Or is it that they are more likely to remain focused on the positive once it has grabbed their attention? Perhaps both of these things characterize the attention biases of happy people, but I look forward to more systematic research that will help resolve these issues related to the allocation of attention and subjective well-being (SWB).

Recent studies have suggested that allocation of attention to positive information is not simply a result of being happy; it has consequences for future emotional well-being as well. Sanchez and colleagues (2014) found that when subjects turned their attention to happy faces following a negative mood induction, they recovered more quickly from their unpleasant mood. Similarly, Beevers and Carver (2003) found that if their participants did not shift their attention toward negative information following a negative mood induction, they showed less depressed mood in response to life stressors 7 weeks later. In sum, happy people seem to direct their attention to positive things in their lives, and paying attention to the positive things in life is likely to improve your mood.

So what if you just naturally seem to notice the bad things in your life? Is there any way of dealing with this negative attention bias? Exciting new research suggests that indeed there might be exercises that can help you learn to direct your attention to the good. Led by Colin MacLeod and associates, researchers have developed *attention bias training* procedures that actually train positive attention biases, and it appears that this training can also impact mood (for reviews, see Hertel & Mathews, 2011; MacLeod & Clarke, 2015). Researchers have argued that this attention bias training could be an important treatment component for treating those with anxiety disorders; however, I believe that this treatment has great potential for happiness interventions as well.

Not only is SWB associated with a positive attention bias, it is also associated with *broadened attention*. In one review, Fredrickson and Branigan (2005) randomly assigned their participants to be induced into one of several different emotional states (amusement, contentment, neutral, anger, or fear). These emotions were encouraged with film clips (such as Sylvester Stallone's film

Cliffhanger), which have been shown to reliably induce particular emotional states. Then they had their subjects judge various figure arrays in a way that allowed them to determine if their subjects were paying attention to the details of the array, or to the global shape of the figure. As predicted, participants in the positive emotion conditions tended to see the figures more globally than those in the neutral and negative emotional conditions. Thus, this exercise showed that positive emotion (the hallmark of happy people) broadened the scope of their attention (see also Johnson, Waugh, & Fredrickson, 2010).

Sometimes it's better for us to attend to the details of a situation, but sometimes it's more adaptive for us to pay more attention to "the big picture." The classes that I teach are inclined to be content rich (my students would say "content heavy"), and so it is easy for my students to get lost in the details of the class, and lose sight of the main themes or the big picture. Periodically, I try to help my students see the big picture themes of the class so that they don't lose sight of the forest because they're lost in the details of the trees. I think this is true in everyday life as well. Sometimes it's easy to get lost in the details of life—the daily tasks and things on our "to-do" lists—and lose sight of the bigger picture of what we're trying to do or be in life. Positive emotion and happiness may help us to take that bird's-eye view that helps us see the big picture. In fact, across a series of studies, Labroo and Patrick (2009) showed that positive emotions help us psychologically distance ourselves from situations and decisions in such a way that allows us to see the big picture. In short, positive emotion broadens the scope of our attention so that we can better see the more global features of our lives.

Research also suggests that happiness might help us get out of the shackles of self-preoccupation so that we can see beyond ourselves. Studies show that there is a strong relationship between negative affect and self-focused attention, particularly the ruminative style of self-focus. *Ruminative self-focus* is essentially a preoccupation with your negative mood states and their causes and consequences (Mor & Winquist, 2002). Moreover, the relationship between negative emotion and self-preoccupation appears to be reciprocal: When you're in a negative mood you tend to be more self-preoccupied, but when you're focused on yourself this tends to promote negative moods. Thus if positive affect indeed has the ability to "undo" negative emotional states (Fredrickson, Mancuso, Branigan, & Tugade, 2000), positive emotional states may have the unique ability to help us break out of the vicious cycle of self-preoccupation and negative emotions (see also Robinson & Compton, 2008).

How do happy people allocate their attention? In sum, happy people have a tendency to allocate their attention to the positive aspects of both their environment and themselves. They are more likely to take notice of the global features of a situation (and thus look at the big picture), and they are less likely to get trapped in self-preoccupation. The good news here is that recent work in cognitive bias modification has shown that this positive attention bias can be trained. In other words, we may be able to train ourselves to take better notice of the positive in our lives.

INTERPRETATION: HOW DO HAPPY PEOPLE INTERPRET THE EVENTS IN THEIR LIVES?

How Do Happy People Interpret Positive Events?

Imagine yourself in the following scenario:

> You are studying for a difficult examination and you feel that you have a pretty good handle on the material. While studying, you receive an e-mail from a friend listing a number of questions your friend thinks will be on the test. As you're reading the list of

questions, you wonder how helpful these will be to your study-ing. You find yourself interested in your emotional response to this e-mail.

How would you respond to this situation? If you think that your friend contacted you because of the feeling that you can't study effectively on your own, you're likely to feel a little irritated at this e-mail. If, on the other hand, you think your friend genuinely wants to help you do well on your test, you're likely to be glad you got the e-mail. Clearly, your emotional response to this e-mail depends on how you *interpret* the situation. If you think about it, just about all situations require some interpretation—particularly those that are social in nature. And thus our emo-tional responses to life situations invariably depend on how we interpret those situations. In the following section, we explore the interpretation style of happy people.

The first stage of cognition involves attention: We have to attend to information in our environment before we process that information. The second stage then is interpretation. Once some-thing has entered our sphere of awareness, we then start inter-preting the event—filling in the missing information and giving the event some meaning to us. As the earlier example shows, each event is open to several different ways we can interpret the situ-ation. If we chronically interpret events in a cynical or negative way (e.g., "She sent me those questions because she thinks I'm stupid."), we're likely to end up pretty unhappy. If, on the other hand, we are inclined to interpret events in a positive manner (e.g., "That was so thoughtful that she wanted to help me do well on that test."), we're likely to be much happier. Clearly, our interpretation style should impact our happiness.

Given the importance of interpretation style to SWB, I am again a bit surprised that more systematic research has not been conducted on the interpretation styles that are characteristic of happiness. As with attention bias, most of the studies that have been conducted with interpretation tendencies have been carried out with people who suffer from emotional disorders. Here again, we see that anxious and depressed people tend to exhibit negative interpretation styles, whereas nondisordered people show benign tendencies (Hertel & Mathews, 2011). In other words, when there is something ambiguous about a situation, anxious and depressed people tend to interpret the situation negatively but those who do not have emotional disorders interpret it in a neutral or positive manner. We have found that positive biases such as these can be found in happy people (Watkins, McCurrach, & Timbrook, 2015). In response to benefit scenarios, happy people tended to make more positive interpretations of the value and the intentionality of the benefit. Interestingly, these associations were stronger with eudaimonic than hedonic well-being.

Additional evidence points to the positive interpretation biases of happy people. One study showed that those high in life satisfaction had stronger and longer emotional reactions to positive events (Seidlitz, Wyer, & Diener, 1997). This implies that happy people were interpreting positive events more positively. Another study showed that happy people were more likely to categorize life events as positive (Seidlitz & Diener, 1993). In this study, people listed positive events from their lives. Independent judges then went back and rated the positivity of these events. Somewhat surprisingly, the positive events that were listed by the unhappy people were rated more positively than those listed by happy folks. What this means is that events that many people would judge as neutral, happy people categorized as positive. This might be a meaningful factor that keeps happy people happy. If we consistently see life events as positive, then we are much more likely to have "the pervasive sense that life is good."

The good news here is that like attention, investigations indicate that positive interpretation biases can be trained (Hertel &

Mathews, 2011). Researchers have developed tasks that train individuals to interpret ambiguous situations in a positive manner. Moreover, studies show that changing one's interpretation tendencies also changes one's mood. Ambiguous events are everywhere, and how you interpret situations in your life is bound to impact your happiness. Happy people are inclined to make positive interpretations of the various circumstances in their lives, and some studies suggest that your interpretation tendencies can be trained to be more positive, which might be consequential to your happiness.

In one of the classic studies in positive psychology, Sonja Lyubomirsky and Lee Ross (1997) showed that happy people are much less impacted by social comparison than unhappy folks. Briefly, *social comparison* is when you are comparing yourself to someone else. *Upward social comparison* is when you're comparing yourself to someone who has done better or has more than you, and *downward social comparison* refers to when you're comparing yourself to someone who has less or has performed more poorly than you. In one study, Lyubomirsky and Ross had their subjects give a speech. Respondents then received various forms of feedback for their performances. Another participant—who was actually an associate of the researchers—also received feedback for speech performance. Some subjects were told they did well with their speeches, whereas others were told they did poorly. If they were told they did well, however, their peers who also gave speeches were either not given any feedback, or they were told that they actually did better than the real subjects. So if the respondents got positive feedback on their speech performances, they were randomly assigned to a no social comparison or an upward social comparison condition. Interestingly, there was virtually no difference between the two social comparison conditions for happy people: If they got positive feedback on their speeches, their positive affect improved regardless of how their peers did. The results for unhappy students, however, were very different. Like the happy subjects, if they were told that they did well and no feedback was provided for their peers, their positive affect increased. But if their peers were told that they did better in the speeches, this completely wiped out the effect of doing well. The implication from this study is that if happy people do well on a task, they feel better about it regardless of how other people do. For unhappy folks, however, they can do well but have their experience ruined because someone else did better. If happy individuals get 94% on a test, they'll feel good about it even if another person gets a 99%. But for unhappy people, another person's excellent score could ruin the joy they should be experiencing for their good performance. The upshot of these studies is that happy people don't let the performance of others affect their interpretation of a good performance.

Savoring is another important interpretation style of happy people. Cognitive *savoring* is any way you might think about a positive event that maintains or increases your positive emotional response to that event (also referred to as *capitalization*). Fred Bryant made the provocative observation that although psychology has literally tens of thousands of articles on how people think about negative events, very few studies have investigated how people think about positive events (Bryant, 1989). Let's return again to the example of an excellent test grade. There are a number of ways you could think about this event. You might say to yourself, "Gee, a lot of other people did better than I, it must have been an easy test" or "Because I got a good grade, I just know I'll bomb the next test." Clearly, in both of these cases thinking in this way would decrease your enjoyment of your success. If, however, you said to yourself, "I really can do well on Dr. Watkins's tests" or "Araceli really helped me to study well," these statements would help you savor your good grade. Indeed, research shows that happy people tend to savor positive events more than unhappy folks, and savoring positive events encourages SWB (Bryant, 2003; Bryant, Smart, & King, 2005; Bryant & Veroff, 2007; Jose, Lim, & Bryant, 2012).

Another vital interpretation issue deals with how well we understand benefits in our lives. Do you think that you would enjoy a benefit more if you understood why you received the favor? If you're like most folks, you might think that the more you comprehend a positive event, the happier you will be about it, but actually research indicates the opposite (Wilson, Centerbar, Kermer, & Gilbert, 2005). Wilson and colleagues conducted an exercise where they handed out silver dollars to students. These coins were attached to one of two different cards. Each card contained the exact same words, but on one card the words were arranged so that it made sense to people as to why they received the silver dollar, and on the other card the words were arranged so that people would be uncertain as to why they received this gift. Independent researchers came by 5 minutes later and surveyed the students' happiness. They found that students who were uncertain about why they received the dollar were happier than those who did understand the gift. When it comes to benefits in our lives, perhaps "ignorance is bliss."

Earlier in this section, we explored how happy people tend to interpret positive events, and let me now summarize these findings. First, although there could be more research done in this area, happy people are inclined to interpret ambiguous events in a positive way. Ambiguous events are everywhere, and how we interpret them is critical to our emotional responses to these situations. Indeed, people can learn to interpret events in a more positive fashion, and this has been shown to improve their emotional well-being. Second, we see that happy people don't let upward social comparisons ruin the joy of their success. When happy people do well on a task, even if they see that someone else has done better, they interpret their performance in a positive manner, and thus they still can enjoy their success. Third, we have seen that happy people are good at savoring positive events. When something good happens to happy individuals, they think about it in a way that maintains and even increases their positive emotional response. And finally, we saw that being certain about what causes good things in our lives might not be conducive to happiness. This might imply that happy people don't spend a lot of time trying to figure out why good things happen to them.

How Do Happy People Interpret Negative Events?

To misquote a crass euphemism: "Bad stuff happens." As much as we might want our lives to be filled with the good and be devoid of the bad, things that we don't like happen to all of us. There are even findings suggesting that people who have a tendency to avoid activities that might have unpleasant consequences are inclined to be less happy than most. Avoiding that job application, because you're afraid of how you'll feel if you don't get it, will guarantee that you won't get the job. Hesitating asking that special person out—because of the anxiety of the invitation and the pain of the potential rejection—could mean that you've bypassed being with someone who would offer wonderful companionship. Here, Abraham Maslow (1964/1996, pp. 21, 22) offers sage advice, "It is time to jettison the conventional, hedonistic definition of happiness as simply a state of pleasure without pain . . . It is a privilege to have children to weep over because of their troubles, rather than to have no children at all." Because unpleasant events in our lives are inevitable, how we deal with life's trials without avoiding them is critical for our happiness. In the following part of this chapter, I explore how happy people interpret the negative events in their lives.

Although some bad events exert their influence on us because they continue to impact our physical well-being (e.g., a car accident

229

that permanently impairs us in some way, or a chronic illness), most unpleasant occurrences impact us through our memories of the event. As I now write, many of us in Washington State are still ruing the Seattle Seahawks' decision to pass on the 1-yard line on their last play of the 2015 Super Bowl, a call that probably cost them the game. As I think about that event, it does not have continuing physical consequences that impact my well-being; it is only the memory of the play that upsets me. Romantic rejection, a poor test grade, a social faux pas at a party—all are occurrences that probably don't have any enduring physical impact on our lives; however, it is our memories of these bad events that continue to impact our emotional well-being. How can we best interpret these events so that we can put these memories to bed? Recent research shows that positive reappraisal is one of the most effective ways of interpreting troubling events in our lives.

We engage in *positive reappraisal* (also known as *positive reframing*) when we think about a negative situation in such a way as to identify what might be the positive consequences of the event. For example, one of the ways that I positively reappraised the Seahawks' big game loss was by looking at how this might be an important growth experience for quarterback Russell Wilson. "Too much success early in his career might make him arrogant and complacent," I reasoned, "and thus this loss might be a good way for him to remain humble and continue to work hard." Only time will tell whether my conjectures will come true, but thinking this way about the loss did make me feel a little better.

A number of studies have shown the benefits of positive reappraisal (e.g., King & Miner, 2000), but I attempt to show its usefulness by describing a study in which we investigated one form of positive reappraisal that we termed *grateful reappraisal* (Watkins, Cruz, Holben, & Kolts, 2008). In this exercise, all of our participants were asked to recall an unpleasant "open memory." An *open memory* is a disagreeable memory from your past that you still feel is connected with some unfinished business. You don't understand the event well, it remains as an "open book" for you, and it continues to trouble you and intrude into your consciousness. If a romantic partner breaks up with you out of the blue, and you really don't grasp why you were dumped, this may well be an open memory for you (indeed, this seemed to be our students' most common open memory).

After recalling this open memory, our subjects described it in various ways and completed other outcome measures. For the next 3 days, all of our respondents wrote for 20 minutes each day. In our control condition they wrote about neutral things (such as their plans for the next day) that were completely unrelated to their open memory. In the emotional disclosure condition, students wrote about the event involving their emotional memory, including all their emotions and thoughts about the event. This form of writing has been shown to have a number of psychological and physical benefits (Pennebaker, 1997). In the *grateful reappraisal* writing condition (our intervention of interest), participants wrote about the beneficial consequences of this event for which they might be grateful. In this writing condition, we made sure that as the students wrote about their painful memories, we were not asking them to call their bad events good. Rather, we were simply asking them to identify consequences or benefits of this disturbing situation for which they might now be grateful. For instance, after a difficult romantic breakup, students might see how they have grown in their relationships with others, and how they could be better partners in their next relationship.

So how did grateful reappraisal impact our participants' unpleasant open memories? We found that compared to the two comparison writing treatments, those students who gratefully reappraised their painful memories experienced more psychological closure, less unpleasant affect when recalling the memories, and the memories became less intrusive. All of these findings implied that grateful reappraisal helped people

231

"take care of the emotional business" of their unpleasant open memories, and thus helped them put troubling occurrences from their past to bed, so to speak. In short, research suggests that a very effective way of interpreting negative events is with positive reappraisal.

So, positive reappraisal is an effective way of dealing with negative events in your life. But is this really a happy interpretation style? Are happy people more likely to use positive reappraisal? Furthermore, does the use of positive reappraisal keep happy people happy? Although there does not seem to be a great deal of research in this area, studies support the conclusion that happy people are more likely to use positive reframing than unhappy folks (Balzarotti, Biassoni, Villani, Prunas, & Velotti, 2014; Barber, 2011; Etezadi & Pushkar, 2013; Haga, Kraft, & Corby, 2009). Because most of these evaluations are cross-sectional and correlational, however, the question remains: Is positive reappraisal the coping style that helps happy people maintain their high SWB? In this respect, we are in need of prospective and experimental studies that can help bring clearer answers. But for now we can safely conclude that, in general, positive reappraisal is an effective means of dealing with negative events, and happy people seem prone to use this style of coping.

In summary, what can we conclude about the interpretation styles of happy people? First, happy people tend to interpret events in their lives in a positive manner. Happy people are inclined to interpret ambiguous aspects of a situation in a positive direction, and research indicates that interpreting situations in this manner has positive emotional consequences. Second, research suggests that we need not be stuck in our negative interpretation style; positive interpretation biases can be trained. Third, we saw that happy people interpret success in their lives as simply that: success. Contrasting with unhappy folks, happy people don't let upward social comparisons ruin their interpretation and experience of success. Fourth, we learned that happy people interpret the good things in their lives in a way that allows them to savor those events, and thus they have a tendency to enjoy benefits in their lives more than less happy individuals. Finally, we have seen that positive reappraisal is an effective way of interpreting negative events in our lives, and happy people are inclined to use this coping style when dealing with difficult situations in their lives.

MEMORY: HOW DO HAPPY PEOPLE REFLECT ON THEIR PAST?

Thus far, we have covered the "A" and the "I" of our AIM approach to the thinking styles of happy people; we have explored how happy people *attend* to things and *interpret* events in their lives. But how we remember our past ("M") is important to our happiness as well.

There are several ways in which being able to easily recall positive things from our past should enhance our happiness (see Watkins, 2014, for a full account of these effects). First, if we can easily bring to mind good things from our past, this should have a direct and positive impact on our mood. Although there are a few exceptions, typically, it feels good to bring pleasant memories from our past to mind. Indeed, this is such an effective way of boosting your mood that researchers often use this technique to induce positive emotion in the laboratory. Second, not only does it boost your mood, recalling of positive events also enhances your satisfaction with life (Strack, Schwarz, & Gschneidinger, 1985). Third, when positive things from your past come easily to mind, this should encourage your optimism about the future. When we feel good about our past, we're likely to feel good about our future as well.

Fourth, when positive events easily come to mind this should give us more confidence to engage in happiness-supporting activities. Let's say someone invites you to a party this Friday night. If past positive experiences of parties easily come to mind, you're likely to feel that this party will be enjoyable as well, and so you'll probably decide to go. If, however, you can't think of fun parties that you've been to (or worse yet, you recall bad parties), then you're likely to conclude that the party won't be much fun and you'll end up avoiding it.

Fifth and finally, when you can easily think of good things from your past you'll probably cope better with disappointments. To illustrate, let's say you get what you consider to be a bad test grade. If, as you're thinking about the test, you can easily recall good performances on tests, then you're likely to conclude that this is something you can fix and the bad grade isn't a permanent indication of your stupidity. Recalling good grades from your past should give you the confidence to continue to study hard for the next test, and thus you have dealt with your disappointing grade successfully. In short, how we remember our past is crucial to our happiness.

Happiness and Dwelling on the Past

Before we explore what happy people tend to remember, let's look first at how happiness is related to focusing on our past. In one study in my laboratory, we had happy and unhappy people process different types of stimuli (Watkins, Grimm, Whitney, & Brown, 2005). Our participants were exposed to pleasant and unpleasant scents, saw positive and negative pictures, and listened to different types of music. As they were exposed to these stimuli we simply asked them to *think aloud*—to verbalize their thoughts. The experimenter listened to their verbalized thoughts and wrote down anytime it was thought the subjects were talking about a life event from their past (an *autobiographical memory*). After the think-aloud phase, the experimenter went back over the memories with the respondents and confirmed whether or not

these were indeed occurrences from their past; then the participants judged whether the events were positive or negative. One
of the most interesting findings from this study was that our
unhappy respondents verbalized significantly more memories
than did our happy subjects. Thus happy people do not seem
to dwell in the past as much as unhappy people. This supports
Michael Robinson's characterization of happy thinking: Happy
people appear to be focused on the present—on what is going on
right now—whereas unhappy people spend more time dwelling
on the past (Robinson & Compton, 2008).

A Happy Memory Bias

So happy people don't seem to be as focused on the past as
unhappy folks are; however, when they do remember events
from the past, what do happy people tend to remember?
Stated differently, what do the memory biases of happy people
resemble? Let's return to the think-aloud study I described earlier (Watkins et al., 2005). In that study we found that positive
events were more likely to come to mind for happy people, but
unhappy individuals did not show this bias. Similarly, when
Seidlitz and Diener (1993) asked their participants to recall positive and negative events from their lives, they also discovered
a positive memory bias in happier folks. We have also shown
that this memory bias extends to grateful people (Watkins,
Grimm, & Kolts, 2004).

So we see that positive memories come to mind more easily
for happy than unhappy folks. But is this really a memory bias?
Couldn't it be an encoding bias in that happy people are more
likely to get positive events into their memory banks in the first
place? Couldn't it just be a frequency bias? Perhaps it's not so
much that happy people have a positive recall bias, rather they
actually have more positive events in their lives to recall. Indeed,
research shows that the "memory bias" in happy people is not a

retrieval bias, but rather is due to the fact that they actually have more positive things happen to them, and they are more likely to interpret events in a positive fashion (Seidlitz & Diener, 1993; Seidlitz et al., 1997). Given the same number of positive events to recall, happy people are no more likely to remember them than unhappy folks.

How can it be that there is a positive memory bias associated with happiness, but no retrieval bias? Although positive memories come to mind more readily for happy than unhappy people, it's not because they're better at retrieving those memories; it appears that it's because they simply have more positive life events stored in memory that are available to recall. Although the memory bias in happiness does not appear to be due to a retrieval bias, nonetheless research shows that in both intentional and unintentional life-event memory recall, positive events more easily come to mind for happy people, and this probably has significant advantages for their SWB.

Although there does not appear to be a happy retrieval bias, it does seem that positive concepts and events are organized in memory in such a way as to be beneficial for happy people. Investigations have found that if a positive event or concept is activated in memory, this is more likely to activate other positive concepts for happy rather than for unhappy people (Robinson & von Hippel, 2006). This implies that happy people have more developed networks of positive memories than do unhappy folks. This presents significant advantages for happy people because they're likely to experience more happy reminiscences, and when they do recall something positive, this is more likely to activate other positive concepts and memories. Thus, when these positive memory networks are activated in happy people, they should have more confidence about the future and more confidence to approach activities that enhance their happiness. Conversely, research has demonstrated that depressed people tend to have a more developed network of negative memories (e.g., Teasdale & Dent, 1987;

Watkins, Hurst, Keenan, & Mathews, 1993), which might be an important maintenance factor in depression. The implication of these findings is that there may be a significant advantage for people to develop their positive memory networks, and in Chapter 7 we explore happiness-promoting treatments that might accomplish this goal. In short, the positive memory networks of happy people appear to be more organized and more developed, and this might be a crucial cognitive mechanism that maintains their SWB.

How Do Happy People Remember Emotional Events?

Up to this point, we see that positive memories come to mind more easily for happy people, and their positive memory networks seem to be more extensive and organized. But research also shows that people high in SWB recall emotional events from their past in a very different way from less happy folks. Observations have determined that, generally, people display what has been called a *fading affect bias* in memory (Gibbons, Lee, & Walker, 2011; Walker, Skowronski, & Thompson, 2003; Walker, Vogl, & Thompson, 1997). It probably won't be surprising to you that emotional memories become less emotional with time. As time passes, positive memories lose some of their joy and negative memories lose some of their bite. Figure 6.2 illustrates this *fading affect* effect. As you can see, both positive and negative memories become less emotional with time. But the surprise comes with the bias: Note that positive memories retain more of their pleasantness and negative memories lose more of their unpleasant affect. In other words, there is less fading affect for positive than for negative memories. This is good news: Over time, our pleasant memories still feel good when we remember them, but our negative memories tend to lose much of their emotional pain.

Intriguingly, happiness appears to play an important role in the fading affect bias. Research has found that happy people

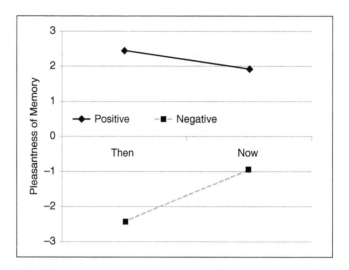

FIGURE 6.2 Fading affect bias.
Source: Walker, Skowronski, and Thompson (2003).

have a stronger fading affect bias than do unhappy individuals (Walker, Skowronski, Gibbons, Vogl, & Thompson, 2003). In other words, positive memories retain more of their joy for happy than for unhappy folks, and negative memories lose more of their bite for happy people. Figure 6.3 shows this effect with positive memories. Clearly, Walker and colleagues have suggested that a strong fading affect bias might be important to supporting SWB (Walker, Skowronski, Gibbons, Vogl, & Thompson, 2003).

The Life Stories of Happy People

An important aspect of the "M" of the AIM of cognition is how we tell our life stories. How we remember our past and tell it in story form is significant. Dan McAdams has argued convincingly that our *narrative identity*—our ever-evolving life story—contributes in an essential way to our well-being (McAdams, 1985, 2001,

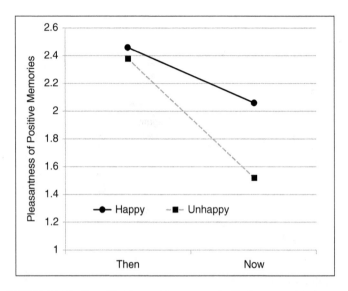

FIGURE 6.3 Fading affect in positive memories for happy and unhappy people.

2006/2013; McAdams & McLean, 2013). The stories that we tell about our lives provide some coherence and purpose to our lives. As you might expect, happy people tend to have positive life stories, but a more interesting characteristic of their life stories emerges: *redemptive sequences*. A redemptive sequence in your life story is when a bad event becomes good. For example, perhaps a difficult romantic breakup resulted in becoming involved in a much better relationship. For me, one of the more significant redemptive sequences in my life story was when I lost the election for another term as chair of the psychology department. This "loss" allowed me to return to teaching and scholarship; it was at that point that I could launch myself into gratitude research, which has become a very fulfilling pursuit for me. Interestingly, McAdams's work has shown that redemptive sequences in one's life story are even more predictive of happiness than positive events.

A reasonable objection to this research might propose that it's being happy that produces positive and redemptive life stories, and thus these happy narrative identities are not consequential to our SWB. Recent investigations, however, suggest that we can edit and rewrite our life stories, and that this has beneficial effects on our happiness (Wilson, 2011). Thus, how you tell your life story may be important to your happiness in that it provides your life with purpose and meaning.

We are now at a place where we can characterize memory in happy people. First, research suggests that happy people tend to dwell in the present rather than the past. They are unlikely to ruminate on past events, and they are particularly less likely to ruminate on negative events from their past. Second, there appears to be a happy memory bias, in that positive memories are more likely to come to mind for those high in SWB. Moreover, we have seen that the positive memory networks of happy people are more organized and more extensive. When a happy person recalls a pleasant memory, more pleasant memories are likely to come to mind. Third, we find that happy people have a strong fading affect bias. One way that memory might maintain our happiness is that positive memories tend to retain their joy, whereas negative memories lose their bite. Fourth, we see that happy people are prone to tell positive—and redemptive—life stories. How we see our past seems to be vital to our present happiness. Now let's turn to how forecasting the future might be important to SWB.

FORECASTING—AND MISFORECASTING—YOUR EMOTIONAL FUTURE

One of the distinct differences between humans and other animals is that we can think about our future. For all other animals, their reality is what they perceive right now, but as humans, we can look into and predict our future. We may get it wrong, but often we get it right, and we can also predict our future emotional reactions. When we think about asking someone out for a date, inevitably we find ourselves musing on how we'll feel if we're accepted or if we're rejected. When you think about applying for a job, a promotion, or graduate school, you probably find yourself thinking about the possible outcomes of your application and your consequent emotional reactions and these emotional forecasts could be important to what you decide to do. Predicting how we emotionally respond to a situation is what we call *affective forecasting* (Wilson & Gilbert, 2003, 2005), and *affective forecasting errors* are typical mistakes that people make in predicting their emotional responses. How accurate we are about our emotional future is likely to be a crucial determinant of our happiness.

As it turns out, we're pretty good at predicting whether we're going to respond positively or negatively to a situation. If our team wins an important game, we can accurately predict that we'll feel good about it. If they lose, we know that we'll be disappointed. As Wilson and Gilbert so cleverly quipped, "People know that a root beer will be more pleasant than a root canal" (2005, p. 131). What we're not so good at forecasting is the intensity and the duration of our emotional responses, and this leads us to our first affective forecasting error.

Impact Bias: The King of Forecasting Errors

Perhaps the "king" of forecasting errors—the overarching mistake that summarizes most of the errors that we discuss here—is referred to as impact bias. This pertains to the fact that we tend to overestimate both the intensity and duration of our emotional reactions (Wilson & Gilbert, 2005). Although the intensity and duration of emotional responses are theoretically distinct constructs, because they are difficult to disentangle Wilson and Gilbert refer to these collectively under the term *impact bias* (2005). Students are inclined to overestimate how pleased they'll be if they get the dormitory that they want, and overestimate their displeasure at being put into the dormitory they want to avoid (Dunn, Wilson, & Gilbert, 2003). Professors have a tendency to think that they're going to be happier when they get tenure than the happiness that actually ensues, and although they predict that being denied tenure will destroy their happiness, it turns out that this disappointment doesn't impact their long-term SWB all that much. Likewise, our emotional reactions to romantic acceptance and romantic rejection are overestimated (for reviews, see Wilson & Gilbert, 2003, 2005, 2013).

So how does overestimating our emotional reactions impact our happiness? Well, many people live with a philosophy that happiness is made up of all pleasure and no pain, and because they anticipate that certain activities might result in pain, they never attempt them, hence they miss out on many enjoyable experiences and accomplishments. I remember the anticipation—and the anxiety—of thinking about asking my future wife for our first date. If I had anticipated too intense and lengthy unhappiness if she rejected my invitation, I might never have asked her out, and might never have been able to enjoy the beautiful relationship we have now. Now let's explore some of the more specific forms of impact bias.

Immune Neglect

One of the foremost reasons that we overestimate the impact and duration of our negative emotional responses is because of *immune neglect*—we underestimate how powerful our psychological defenses are for dealing with unpleasant events (Gilbert, Pinel, Wilson, Blumberg, & Wheatley, 1998). Just as there exists a very effective immune system for warding off and dealing with invasions to our body, so too research has found that our mind has an effective immune system for dealing with disappointments in life. For example, one of the things that we start doing immediately after a bad event is try to make sense of that event. The more we can understand an unwanted event, the better we feel about it. After learning that I lost the election for my second term as chair of the psychology department, I immediately started thinking about some of the advantages of not being chair. I thought about my original goals for becoming a professor (teaching and research, not making a lot of money), and I began imagining new research ventures. Within a day or so, I really wasn't too bothered about my "loss."

So why do we so easily neglect our psychological immune system? One reason is that these psychological defenses tend to operate at an unconscious level, so we are inclined to ignore their operation—and their effectiveness. How might recognizing the effectiveness of our psychological immune system be important to our happiness? At times we refrain from doing things because we're afraid of our disappointment if we don't get the results that we want. We might avoid applying for that job, or asking that person out, or submitting that article to that journal because we're afraid of how it might feel if we're rejected. But if we can remember how effective our psychological immune system really is, then we might not be so avoidant of potential rejection, and as the saying goes, "nothing ventured, nothing gained."

The Focusing Illusion

Another reason that we tend to overestimate both positive and negative emotional responses is because of the so-called *focusing illusion* (also known as *focalism*). With this error, people attend to more salient features of a choice and they ignore other important aspects that will undoubtedly influence their future happiness. Many people, for example, make the choice to move into a bigger, more expensive house. When making the choice, they are inclined to focus on the added space and the new view; however, they ignore other significant aspects of the decision, such as bigger monthly mortgage payments, the pain and hassles of the move, and added driving time to work. Often in situations such as this, several months after the move they're no happier than they were in their old house. However, they're now stuck with a bigger mortgage payment for a longer period of time.

Many of my students are convinced that they would be so much happier living in Seattle than in Spokane. They cite the beautiful Puget Sound, the vibrant music scene, the warmer (if not wetter) weather, and major league sports teams such as the Mariners, Sounders, and the Seahawks. But in thinking about this decision, they typically forget about things like a greatly increased cost of living, traffic, crowds, and all the other headaches that come with living in a major city. Would they actually be happier if they moved to Seattle? Well, remember the study that's explored in Chapter 3 comparing midwestern students to Southern California students (Schkade & Kahneman, 1998)? Although students from both regions thought that students in Southern California would be happier, in fact, students living in the Midwest were just as happy as their fellow students in California. Why were they mistaken? Evidence from this study suggests that it was most likely because of the focusing illusion. In making their decision as to who was happier, people focused on the most prominent features of Southern California: sunny beaches, warm weather, outdoor activities, shorts and sandals all year long. What they failed to consider were the other things that come with a place where a great many people want to live: a much higher cost of living, traffic, and the constant hassle of crowds. So can the focusing illusion cost you some of your happiness? Indeed it can. If you make a major decision such as moving to a new location, taking a higher paying job, or moving into a more expensive house, it's likely that the focusing illusion will come into play. You'll tend to focus on those salient (and positive) aspects of the new choice, and ignore the other critical aspects of your decision that might actually lower your happiness. Fortunately, this is one of the affective forecasting errors that can most easily be corrected. Studies have shown that if you direct people to think about more than just the most noticeable features of a choice, then they won't ignore the other factors that are likely to impact their happiness, and they'll be inclined to make a more intelligent decision for their future happiness (Wilson, Wheatley, Meyers, Gilbert, & Axsom, 2000).

The Want-for-Like Confusion

Sometimes we make a bad decision about our emotional future because we confuse how much we want something with how much we're going to like it (Diener & Biswas-Diener, 2008). As I now write, my wife and I are thinking about buying a travel trailer. Although there are many things that recommend this purchase, it is very easy right now for us to automatically assume that how much we want this trailer is going to translate into how much we'll enjoy using it. How might the *want-for-like confusion* diminish our happiness? Often we may want an expensive item very badly—usually because we're convinced we have to have it for our happiness. But when we assume that our want will equate to our like, after we purchase it, we might be sadly mistaken and end up purchasing something expensive that does nothing to enhance our happiness.

Diener and Biswas-Diener (2008) suggest several ways of combating the want-for-like confusion. First, it is important to recognize the want/like dichotomy, and realize that we all tend to naturally assume that if we want something badly, then we'll end up liking it a great deal. When we recognize this natural tendency, then we can assess how badly we want something and this should help us combat the want-for-like confusion. As you're assessing how much you want something, think carefully about *why* you want that thing, and determine if those reasons will translate into enjoyment in the future. Remember that the rush of getting something will wear off fairly quickly, and then your liking of that thing might not be what you thought it would be. I'm sure that buying a new trailer will be an exciting thing for us, but if we only use it once a year, it's not likely to enhance our SWB in the long run. This leads to the final consideration for combatting the want-for-like confusion: Think carefully about how this purchase will enhance your life several months *after* the purchase. And as you're doing this, remember the impact bias and the principle of adaptation: You're going to get used to that extra 10 inches of television screen fairly quickly. It's not that want never translates into like; it's just that we usually assume that it does, and often in important decisions and purchases in our life, it doesn't. In short, if you carefully and intentionally think about the things you really want, you should be able to counteract the want-for-like confusion.

The Maximizing Fallacy

Another forecasting error that is easy to fall into is the *maximizing fallacy*: the tendency to think that the best decisions for our happiness are those that maximize all of our possible options. Researchers have found that some of us tend to be *maximizers* in our decision making—we seek the best possible option, which requires an exhaustive search of all possible choices—and some of us are *satisficers*—we simply seek the "good enough" choice (Schwartz et al., 2002). Different from maximizers, satisficers tend to choose the first "good enough" decision they come across. So when parking at their favorite big-box store, satisficers pick the first good parking spot they come across, whereas maximizers tend to cruise the lot hoping to find that ideal spot close to the entrance. As it turns out, the satisficing strategy tends to be better for your happiness (Schwartz et al., 2002). For example, although maximizers tend to make more money after college (presumably because they've made a more comprehensive job search and decision), satisficers are happier with their jobs (Iyengar, Wells, & Schwartz, 2006).

Social Neglect

Recently, another affective forecasting error has been revealed: *social neglect*. Research has found that we tend to underestimate the positive impact of our interaction with others, and so we avoid others when in fact this might be an important boost to our happiness. Recall the study in Chapter 5 where some people were instructed to commute to work in their usual fashion (typically in solitude) and others were told to interact with a stranger (Epley & Schroeder, 2014). Contrary to our affective forecasts, people were significantly happier when they interacted with others. As seen in Chapter 5, happy people are social people, and our contact and communion with others is essential to our happiness. Interestingly, however, we often underestimate the importance of others to our future happiness.

Relatedly, we also underestimate how giving to others will positively impact our future well-being. Recall from Chapter 5 that even though we think spending money on ourselves will make us happier than spending money on others, in fact, Dunn, Aknin, and Norton (2008, 2014) found that the opposite was true. Therefore, one of the most important affective forecasting errors to be aware of appears to be social neglect: the tendency to underestimate how vital others are to our happiness, and to not realize how giving to others can enhance our SWB. To quote Chris Peterson again, when it comes to our happiness, "Others matter."

Neglecting Nearby Nature

Just as we underestimate the contribution of others to our happiness, so we also underestimate the pleasures of spending time in nature. In Chapter 3, we explored leisure activities that enhance your SWB and we found that spending time in nature enhances our well-being, even though we often do not realize how valuable walking in the woods might be (Nisbet & Zelenski, 2011). So when considering your leisure activities, one important affective forecasting error to remember is that we often underestimate the joy we might experience with a simple walk in the park.

Affective Forecasting Errors and Happiness Intelligence

Emotional intelligence has been shown to be crucial to well-being; might there also be a *happiness intelligence* that is conducive to SWB? Wouldn't accurate knowledge about what makes you happy and what doesn't be essential to your SWB? Although I am not aware of any research in this area, if a construct such as happiness intelligence does exist, one would think that knowing about affective forecasting errors would be a vital component of happiness intelligence. Shouldn't people high in happiness intelligence understand that we are inclined to overestimate the intensity and duration of our emotional reactions? Shouldn't they grasp how effective our psychological immune system is and thus not fear occasional disappointments? When individuals understand the focusing illusion, they should be able to make intelligent decisions about their future happiness, and they'll also understand that, in most circumstances, we're better off with a satisficing decision strategy rather than a maximizing approach. Finally, people high in happiness intelligence will grasp the importance of communing with and giving to others, and they'll comprehend the joy of communing with nature. Perhaps people do differ in their happiness intelligence, and perhaps happiness intelligence is an important characteristic of happy people. In short, people with "happiness smarts" should understand affective forecasting errors, and they will be able to use this knowledge to make informed decisions about their future happiness.

SUMMARY AND CONCLUSIONS ABOUT HAPPY THINKING

In this chapter I attempted to describe the cognitive character-istics of happy people. In brief, we saw that happy people tend to pay more attention to positive information, tend to interpret events in a positive manner, and easily recall positive events from their past. Moreover, happy people are able to retain more of the joy from their positive memories, and they rethink their negative memories in such a way so that these recollections lose much of their emotional pain. We also learned that happy people have coherent, meaningful, and positive life stories that are charac-terized by redemptive events. Finally, we explored how affective forecasting errors can impact your happiness. Unsuccessfully forecasting your emotional future can have unwanted conse-quences for your happiness. In sum, probably one of the main reasons that external circumstances have so little impact on our happiness is because people think so differently about the same circumstances. For one person, a train ride to work is only some-thing to endure; for another it is an opportunity to meet new people and have new experiences. How we think about our lives is eminently important to our happiness.

REFERENCES

Balzarotti, S., Biassoni, F., Villani, D., Prunas, A., & Velotti, P. (2014). Individual differences in cognitive emotion regulation: Implications for subjective and psychological well-being. *Journal of Happiness Studies*. doi:10.1007/s10902-014-9587-3

Barber, J. E. (2011). An examination of happiness and its relationship to community college students' coping strategies and aca-demic performance. *Dissertation Abstracts International, Section A: Humanities and Social Sciences, 71*(10-A), 3512.

Baumeister, R. F., Bratslavsky, E., Finkenauer, C., & Vohs, K. D. (2001). Bad is stronger than good. *Review of General Psychology, 5*, 323–370.

Beevers, C. G., & Carver, C. S. (2003). Attentional bias and mood persistence as prospective predictors of dysphoria. *Cognitive Therapy and Research, 27*, 619–637. doi:10.1023/A:1026347610928

Bryant, F. B. (1989). A four-factor model of perceived control: Avoiding, coping, obtaining, and savoring. *Journal of Personality, 57*, 773–797. doi:10.1111/j.1467-6494.1989.tb00494.x

Bryant, F. B. (2003). Savoring Beliefs Inventory (SBI): A scale for measuring beliefs about savouring. *Journal of Mental Health, 12*, 175–196. doi:10.1080/0963823031000103489

Bryant, F. B., Smart, C. M., & King, S. P. (2005). Using the past to enhance the present: Boosting happiness through positive reminiscence. *Journal of Happiness Studies, 6*, 227–260. doi:10.1007/s10902-005-3889-4

Bryant, F. B., & Veroff, J. (2007). *Savoring: A new model of positive experience.* Mahwah, NJ: Lawrence Erlbaum.

Diener, E., & Biswas-Diener, R. (2008). *Happiness: Unlocking the mysteries of psychological wealth.* Malden, MA: Blackwell.

Dunn, E. W., Aknin, L. B., & Norton, M. I. (2008). Spending money on others promotes happiness. *Science, 319*, 1687–1688.

Dunn, E. W., Aknin, L. B., & Norton, M. I. (2014). Prosocial spending and happiness: Using money to benefit others pays off. *Current Directions in Psychological Science, 23*, 41–47.

Dunn, E. W., Wilson, T. D., & Gilbert, D. T. (2003). Location, location, location: The misprediction of satisfaction in housing lotteries. *Personality and Social Psychology Bulletin, 29*, 1421–1432. doi:10.1177/0146167203256867

Epley, N., & Schroeder, J. (2014). Mistakenly seeking solitude. *Journal of Experimental Psychology: General, 143*, 1980–1999.

Etezadi, S., & Pushkar, D. (2013). Why are wise people happier? An explanatory model of wisdom and emotional well-being in older adults. *Journal of Happiness Studies, 14*, 929–950. doi:1-.1007/s10902-012-9362-2

Fredrickson, B. L., & Branigan, C. (2005). Positive emotions broaden the scope of attention and thought-action repertoires. *Cognition and Emotion, 19,* 313–332. doi:10.1080/02699930441000238

Fredrickson, B. L., Mancuso, R. A., Branigan, C., & Tugade, M. M. (2000). The undoing effect of positive emotions. *Motivation and Emotion, 24,* 237–258. doi:10.1023/A:1010796329158

Gibbons, J. A., Lee, S. A., & Walker, W. R. (2011). The fading affect bias begins within 12 hours and persists for 3 months. *Applied Cognitive Psychology, 25,* 663–672. doi:10.1002/acp.1738

Gilbert, D. T., Pinel, E. C., Wilson, T. D., Blumberg, S. J., & Wheatley, T. P. (1998). Immune neglect: A source of durability bias in affective forecasting. *Journal of Personality and Social Psychology, 75,* 617–638. doi:10.1037/0022-3514.75.3.617

Haga, S. M., Kraft, P., & Corby, E. (2009). Emotion regulation: Antecedents and well-being outcomes of cognitive reappraisal and expressive suppression in cross-cultural samples. *Journal of Happiness Studies, 10,* 271–291. doi:10.1007/s10902-007-9080-3

Hertel, P. T., & Mathews, A. (2011). Cognitive bias modification: Past perspectives, current findings, and future applications. *Perspectives on Psychological Science, 6,* 521–536.

Iyengar, S. S., Wells, R. E., & Schwartz, B. (2006). Doing better but feeling worse: Looking for the "best" job undermines satisfaction. *Psychological Science, 17,* 143–150. doi:10.1111/j.1467-9280.2006.01677.x

Johnson, K. J., Waugh, C. E., & Fredrickson, B. L. (2010). Smile to see the forest: Facially expressed emotions broaden cognition. *Cognition and Emotion, 24,* 299–321.

Jose, P. E., Lim, B. T., & Bryant, F. B. (2012). Does savoring increase happiness? A daily diary study. *Journal of Positive Psychology, 7,* 176–187. doi:10.1080/17439760.2012.671345

King, L. A., & Miner, K. N. (2000). Writing about the perceived benefits of traumatic events: Implications for physical health. *Personality and Social Psychology Bulletin, 26,* 220–230.

Labroo, A. A., & Patrick, V. M. (2009). Psychological distancing: Why happiness helps you see the big picture. *Journal of Consumer Research, 35,* 800–809. doi:10.1086/593683

Lyubomirsky, S., & Ross, L. (1997). Hedonic consequences of social comparison: A contrast of happy and unhappy people. *Journal of Personality and Social Psychology, 73,* 1141–1157.

MacLeod, C., & Clarke, P. J. F. (2015). The attention bias modification approach to anxiety intervention. *Clinical Psychological Science, 3,* 58–78.

Maslow, A. (1996). The psychology of happiness. In E. Hoffman (Ed.), *Future visions: The unpublished papers of Abraham Maslow* (pp. 21–25). Thousand Oaks, CA: Sage. (Original work published 1964)

Mathews, A. (1997). Information-processing biases in emotional disorders. In D. M. Clark & C. G. Fairburn (Eds.), *Science and practice of cognitive behaviour therapy* (pp. 47–66). New York, NY: Oxford University Press.

McAdams, D. P. (1985). *Power, intimacy, and the life story: Personological inquiries into identity.* Homewood, IL: Dorsey Press.

McAdams, D. P. (2001). The psychology of life stories. *Review of General Psychology, 5,* 100–122.

McAdams, D. P. (2013). *The redemptive self: Stories Americans live by* (Rev. and expanded ed.). New York, NY: Oxford University Press. (Original work published 2006)

McAdams, D. P., & McLean, K. C. (2013). Narrative identity. *Current Directions in Psychological Science, 22,* 233–238.

Mor, N., & Winquist, J. (2002). Self-focused attention and negative affect: A meta-analysis. *Psychological Bulletin, 128,* 638–662. doi:10.1037/0033-2909.128.4.638

Nisbet, E. K., & Zelenski, J. M. (2011). Understanding nearby nature: Affective forecasting errors obscure the happy path to sustainability. *Psychological Science, 22,* 1101–1106.

Pennebaker, J. W. (1997). *Opening up: The healing power of expressing emotions* (Rev. ed.). New York, NY: Guilford Press.

Peterson, C., Seligman, M. E., & Vaillant, G. E. (1988). Pessimistic explanatory style is a risk factor for physical illness: A thirty-five-year longitudinal study. *Journal of Personality and Social Psychology, 55,* 23–27. doi:10.1037/0022-3514.55.1.23

Robinson, M. D., & Compton, R. J. (2008). The happy mind in action: The cognitive basis of subjective well-being. In M. Eid & R. J.

Larsen (Eds.), *The science of subjective well-being* (pp. 220–238). New York, NY: Guilford Press.

Robinson, M. D., & von Hippel, W. (2006). Rose-colored priming effects: Life satisfaction and affective priming. *Journal of Positive Psychology, 1,* 187–197. doi:10.1080/17439760 600885705

Sanchez, A., & Vazquez, C. (2014). Looking at the eyes of happiness: Positive emotions mediate the influence of life satisfaction on attention to happy faces. *Journal of Positive Psychology, 9,* 435–448. doi:10.1080/17439760.2014.910827

Sanchez, A., Vazquez, C., Gomez, D., & Joormann, J. (2014). Gaze-fixation to happy faces predicts mood repair after a negative mood induction. *Emotion, 14,* 85–94. doi:10.1037/a0034500

Schkade, D. A., & Kahneman, D. (1998). Does living in California make people happy? A focusing illusion in judgments of life satisfaction. *Psychological Science, 9,* 340–346.

Schwartz, B., Ward, A., Monterosso, J., Lyubomirsky, S., White, K., & Lehman, D. R. (2002). Maximizing versus satisficing: Happiness is a matter of choice. *Journal of Personality and Social Psychology, 83*(5), 1178–1197. doi:10.1037/0022-3514.83.5.1178

Seidlitz, L., & Diener, E. (1993). Memory for positive versus negative life events: Theories for the differences between happy and unhappy persons. *Journal of Personality and Social Psychology, 64,* 654–664. doi:10.1037/0022-3514.64.4.654

Seidlitz, L. J., Wyer, R. S., & Diener, E. (1997). Cognitive correlates of subjective well-being: The processing of valenced life events by happy and unhappy persons. *Journal of Research in Personality, 31,* 240–256. doi:10.1006/jrpe.1997.2184

Strack, F., Schwarz, N., & Gschneidinger, E. (1985). Happiness and reminiscing: The role of time perspective, affect, and mode of thinking. *Journal of Personality and Social Psychology, 49,* 1460–1469. doi:10.1037/0022-3514.49.6.1460

Tamir, M., & Robinson, M. D. (2007). The happy spotlight: Positive mood and selective attention to rewarding information. *Personality and Social Psychology Bulletin, 33,* 1124–1136. doi:10.1177/0146167207301030

Teasdale, J. D., & Dent, J. (1987). Cognitive vulnerability to depression: An investigation of two hypotheses. *British Journal of*

Clinical Psychology, 26, 113–126. doi:10.1111/j.2044-8260.1987
.tb00737.x

Walker, W. R., Skowronski, J. J., Gibbons, J. A., Vogl, R. J., & Thompson,
C. P. (2003). On the emotions that accompany autobiographical
memories: Dysphoria disrupts the fading affect bias. Cognition and
Emotion, 17, 703–723. doi:10.1080/02699930302287

Walker, W. R., Skowronski, J. J., & Thompson, C. P. (2003). Life is
pleasant—and memory helps to keep it that way! Review of General
Psychology, 7, 203–210. doi:10.1037/1089-2680.7.2.203

Walker, W. R., Vogl, R. J., & Thompson, C. P. (1997). Autobiographical memory: Unpleasantness fades faster than pleasantness over
time. Applied Cognitive Psychology, 11, 399–413.

Watkins, P. C. (2014). Gratitude and the good life: Toward a psychology of
appreciation. Dordrecht, The Netherlands: Springer.

Watkins, P. C., Cruz, L., Holben, H., & Kolts, R. L. (2008). Taking care
of business? Grateful processing of unpleasant memories. Journal
of Positive Psychology, 3, 87–99.

Watkins, P. C., Grimm, D. L., & Kolts, R. (2004). Counting your
blessings: Positive memories among grateful persons. Current
Psychology, 23, 52–67.

Watkins, P. C., Grimm, D. L., Whitney, A., & Brown, A. (2005). Unintentional memory bias in depression. In A. V. Clark (Ed.), Mood
state and health (pp. 59–86). Hauppage, NY: Nova Science.

Watkins, P. C., McCurrach, D., & Timbrook, T. (2015). Happy people
show positive interpretation biases. Manuscript in preparation.

Wilson, T. D. (2011). Redirect: The surprising new science of psychological
change. New York, NY: Little Brown/Hachette Book Group.

Wilson, T. D., Centerbar, D. B., Kermer, D. A., & Gilbert, D. T. (2005).
The pleasures of uncertainty: Prolonging positive moods in ways
people do not anticipate. Journal of Personality and Social Psychology,
88, 5–21. doi:10.1037/0022-3514.88.1.5

Wilson, T. D., & Gilbert, D. T. (2003). Affective forecasting. In M. P.
Zanna (Ed.), Advances in experimental social psychology (Vol. 35,
pp. 345–411). San Diego, CA: Elsevier Academic Press. doi:10.1016/
S0065-2601(03)01006-2

Wilson, T. D., & Gilbert, D. T. (2005). Affective forecasting: Knowing what to want. *Current Directions in Psychological Science, 14,* 131–134. doi:10.1111/j.0963-7214.2005.00355.x

Wilson, T. D., & Gilbert, D. T. (2013). The impact bias is alive and well. *Journal of Personality and Social Psychology, 105,* 740–748. doi:10.1037/a0032662

Wilson, T. D., Wheatley, T., Meyers, J. M., Gilbert, D. T., & Axsom, D. (2000). Focalism: A source of durability bias in affective forecasting. *Journal of Personality and Social Psychology, 78,* 821–836. doi:10.1037/0022-3514.78.5.821

Can You Change
Your Happiness?

urveys show that people value happiness across cultures (Diener, 2000). In short, virtually everyone wants to be happy. I suspect that most students who take my positive psychology course—and many of the people who purchased this book—have a desire to improve their happiness. In this chapter we explore whether it is possible to improve your happiness. If boosting your happiness is achievable, this begs the question of *how*: How can you change your happiness? In this chapter I explain some of the most effective techniques found by psychological science to increase happiness. But before we examine successful treatments for happiness, we must face an important issue: Is it even possible to change your happiness?

CHALLENGES TO CHANGING YOUR HAPPINESS

There are several good reasons to suspect that it may be very difficult—if not impossible—to change your happiness. First, as we saw in Chapter 4, there is a strong genetic contribution to happiness, leading some researchers to conclude that it is about as realistic to adjust your happiness as it is to alter your eye color (Lykken & Tellegen, 1996). Second, we know that subjective well-being (SWB) measures such as satisfaction with life operate much like a trait. In other words, satisfaction with life is very stable over time and thus doesn't show a great deal of change.

But perhaps the most serious challenge to the effectiveness of pursuing your own happiness is recent evidence suggesting that if you overvalue your happiness, this actually leads to less happiness. Research by Iris Mauss and collaborators has shown that people vulnerable to depressive disorders tend to value happiness more highly (Ford, Mauss, & Gruber, 2015; Ford, Shallcross, Mauss, Floerke, & Gruber, 2014), lonely people show a higher valuing of happiness than those less lonely (Mauss et al., 2012), and those who are under considerable stress and who highly value happiness are actually less happy (Mauss, Tamir, Anderson, & Savino, 2011). Thus people who are more likely to endorse statements such as "How happy I am at any given moment says a lot about how worthwhile my life is" might actually be *less* happy.

Of course, because of the correlational nature of these results, it might be that those who are less happy (people vulnerable to depression, lonely people, individuals under stress) desire happiness more than those who are already happy. Hence valuing happiness might be more of a consequence of unhappiness rather than the cause. As C. S. Lewis observed (1966/1993, p. 405): "Indeed the best thing about happiness itself is that it liberates you from thinking about happiness—as the greatest pleasure that money can give us is to make it unnecessary to think about money." But these results cannot be dismissed so easily. In several studies Mauss and colleagues have experimentally manipulated the value of happiness, and have demonstrated that those encouraged to value happiness showed less happiness in response to a positive mood induction than those not encouraged to value happiness (Mauss et al., 2011).

So is it fruitless to pursue your own happiness? Contrasting with the studies already noted, Catalino, Algoe, and Fredrickson (2014) found that those who "prioritized positivity" to achieve happiness were happier than those who did not. This appears to be contradictory to the results of Mauss and colleagues, so how can we make sense of these apparently conflicting findings? First, it is important to acknowledge that the pursuit of happiness *can* backfire. If people obsessively pursue happiness (Catalino et al., 2014), expecting and demanding an unrealistic happiness in their lives, this is bound to result in disappointment, and hence unhappiness. Moreover, focusing on some things that are associated with happiness might paradoxically lead to unhappiness. We saw in Chapter 4 that positive self-regard is crucial to happiness; however, if you just focus on your own self-esteem and your own positive emotions, you're not likely to be able to accept yourself or experience positive emotions frequently. When you're only concentrating on yourself, you can't very well focus on others and, as we've seen, happy people tend to be other-oriented.

The resolution to this dilemma might be found in "going back to the future," if you will. Recall that in Chapter 1 of this text I emphasized several "takeaways" from the history of happiness. One of the important themes stressed by Aristotle and also by J. S. Mill (1972) is that happiness is more likely to be the result of pursuing such things as relationships and growth of character, and that a direct pursuit of happiness is doomed to failure. The findings of Catalino et al. (2014) point out that we can prioritize the search for happiness, but that this is only successful when we prioritize certain positive activities in our daily lives that are likely to result in our happiness. When we are obsessive about our happiness—when we view it as an entitlement or we demand an unrealistic level of happiness or think that positive emotions are something that we must experience at all times—then our pursuit of happiness is likely to backfire. When we prioritize certain happiness-related activities, however, research suggests that our search for happiness can be successful (Lyubomirsky & Layous, 2013). What are these positive activities that we can prioritize in our lives? In the next section of this chapter, we investigate the types of positive activities that treatment outcome studies have shown to be successful in promoting SWB.

SUCCESSFUL HAPPINESS TREATMENTS

Now, let's evaluate various treatments that studies have found to be successful in enhancing SWB. As I review these interventions, it is helpful to think about the things that they are changing that in turn promote happiness. Another way of phrasing this is: What are the psychological mechanisms that explain why these treatments are effective? We return to this question at the end of the section. I believe that this question should guide future research in positive psychology, and it may also be informative as to the happiness treatments that will be most effective for you.

I have chosen to divide the treatments into five categories. First, we explore procedures that focus on understanding and using your personal strengths. Then we turn to more forward-looking methods: interventions that focus on improving your feelings and attitudes about the future. Third, we examine contemplative and meditation approaches to encouraging your happiness, and in particular concentrate on a treatment called *loving-kindness meditation* (LKM). We then look at interventions that focus on giving. Here, we see that showing kindness to others does indeed support SWB. Finally, we investigate some of the most successful happiness interventions: strategies oriented around gratitude. After discussing the five different types of happiness interventions, we delve into more comprehensive treatments that incorporate a number of different interventions. Finally, I describe an important issue for understanding current happiness treatments that I believe also provides direction for future research: moderators and mediators of happiness treatments. What are the variables that have an impact on whether or not happiness treatments will work?

Know Thyself—and Use It: Capitalizing on Your Strengths

The first class of treatments focuses on understanding your psychological strengths, and using them in your everyday life. In Chapter 1 we discussed how Aristotle felt that happiness is the result of being true to yourself (i.e., living in a way that is consistent with your true nature). For Aristotle, being true to yourself meant an accurate understanding of who you are, and the ability to live your life in a way that is consistent with your true self. An accurate understanding of who I am is important here. If I think that at 58 years old and at a height of 5 ft. 8 in. I have the ability to be an NBA basketball player, that's bound to be a sure-fire formula for unhappiness. On the other hand, understanding that I love to learn, I appreciate beauty, and that the transcendent is important to me, can help me organize my life in a way that will support my SWB. Happiness interventions that help people identify and use their strengths attempt to follow Aristotle's understanding of eudaimonic well-being, and there is now good empirical support for this intervention (Duan, Ho, Tang, Li, & Zhang, 2014; Govindji & Linley, 2007; Page & Vella-Brodrick, 2013; Seligman, Steen, Park, & Peterson, 2005).

The first test of using your strengths was conducted by Seligman and colleagues (2005), and because this was an important study for the exploration of positive psychology interventions, I describe it in some detail here. This exercise was conducted online, meaning that both the outcome assessment and the treatments were administered online to people who were seeking to improve their happiness. The research was a randomized controlled trial (RCT); participants were randomly assigned to one of five active positive psychology procedures, or to a placebo condition. In the placebo exercise people were asked to "write about your early memories." Participants were to complete this task every night for a week and, indeed, a placebo effect was demonstrated: Subjects showed a significant increase in their happiness after the active treatment phase. This is crucial because in order to demonstrate that positive psychology techniques have specific effects on happiness that extend beyond demand and placebo effects, we must be able to compare the active treatments to an effective placebo condition. Emotional well-being was assessed with the Steen Happiness Index (SHI; Seligman et al., 2005), and the Center for Epidemiological Studies Depression Scale (CES-D; Radloff, 1977). Assessments were made before and after treatment, as well as 1 week, 1 month, 3 months, and 6 months following the treatment phase. This was an important study for not only did it use the gold star of medical and psychological treatment outcome studies (the RCT), it also included a significant follow-up assessment of SWB.

One of the positive psychology interventions used by Seligman et al. (2005) was called using "signature strengths." Participants who were assigned to this treatment first took the inventory of strengths developed by Peterson, Park, and Seligman (2005). After completing this measure, respondents were told their top five strengths that were identified by this questionnaire (i.e., their signature strengths). For the next week, subjects in this treatment were asked to choose one of their signature strengths each day and to use it "in a new and different way" (p. 416). The results from this treatment are shown in Figure 7.1. There are a couple of things to highlight from this graph. First, note the significant placebo effect from those in the placebo treatment. This is a fairly typical result: an increase in well-being immediately after the treatment phase, but happiness returned to baseline fairly quickly. Second, the happiness of those in the signature strengths procedure exceeded the placebo control group at 1-month follow-up, and remained significantly above the controls at 3 months and 6 months following treatment. Third, notice the happiness trajectory of those in the signature strengths group. Although they did not experience a large immediate bump in happiness following treatment, their happiness continued to climb after the treatment phase. Depression

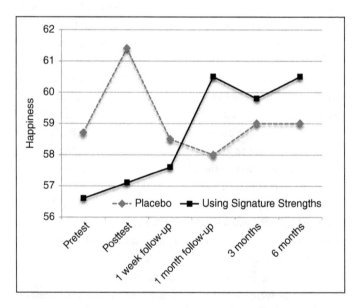

FIGURE 7.1 Using signature strengths treatment outcome results.
Source: Seligman et al. (2005).

results were consistent with the happiness findings. This is a pattern of results almost unheard of in clinical psychology. In clinical psychology outcome studies, usually the beneficial treatment effects begin to wear off immediately after the intervention has concluded. But I highlight this pattern of results here because, as we'll see later, it's not unusual to see continued improvement after the treatment phase with positive psychology interventions.

In short, this study and others show that knowing and using your signature strengths have real potential to enhance your happiness. There are a couple of caveats that need to be discussed, however. First, results using this treatment are not overwhelming. Although some studies used active control groups, others simply used wait-list control conditions, and I am quite frankly a bit surprised that more studies have not tested this method. Furthermore, two signature strengths techniques that were tested in Seligman et al. (2005) failed to outperform the placebo treatment. Both of these procedures just emphasized identifying one's signature strengths. In the "you at your best" treatment, participants wrote about a time where they felt that they were at their best, and they also identified the personal strengths that were revealed through this time. In the "identifying signature strengths" treatment, people simply took the strengths' survey and were asked to use them more often in the upcoming week. Neither of these methods showed enhanced SWB compared to the placebo condition. It may be that simply "knowing thyself" isn't enough; we also need to know how to use our strengths and we need to be creative about how we can use them in "new and different ways."

Imagining a Better Future: Goals and Optimism Treatments

Thus far we have seen that knowing and using your signature strengths are effective ways of enhancing your happiness, but *how* does this treatment work? Recent evidence supports the idea that when we understand and use are strengths, we are aided in successfully pursuing goals that are conducive to our SWB (Linley, Nielsen, Gillett, & Biswas-Diener, 2010). Throughout this book it has been demonstrated that two prominent characteristics of happy people are that they are goal-oriented and optimistic. In short, happy people have a healthy future outlook. So it makes sense that interventions designed to enhance these qualities would heighten happiness as well.

Being oriented toward a positive future should mean that you have goals to pursue that will actually enhance your happiness. Here, we consider procedures that have attempted to help people establish and pursue healthy goals. Indeed, there is evidence that encouraging people to write about and pursue their goals can boost SWB (Coote & MacLeod, 2012; Farquharson & MacLeod, 2014; MacLeod, Coates, & Hetherton, 2008; Sheldon et al., 2010). I describe here the research conducted by Sheldon and colleagues (2010) because they used a rigorous design and their treatment illustrates goal-based interventions well. This study emphasized healthy goal pursuit. Recall that although happy people are goal-oriented people, not all goals are created equal when it comes to our happiness. Whereas intrinsic goals are conducive to happiness, extrinsic goals have the potential to degrade our well-being. To review, intrinsic goals focus on the fulfillment of our basic psychological needs as proposed by Ryan and Deci (2000). Thus goals related to your autonomy (owning and taking responsibility for your direction in life), competence (feeling that you do things well and are improving in your abilities), and relatedness (feeling that you have meaningful connections with others in your life) should be conducive to your happiness; however, goals related to circumstances such as more money and a better place to live should not enhance your happiness. Sheldon et al. randomly assigned their participants to one of four different goal-related treatments: goals related to improving your circumstances (such as a higher paying job or a larger house), and goals related to one of our three psychological needs (autonomy, competence, or relatedness).

Participants in this study were first directed to the specific "psychological need" that they had been assigned: autonomy, competence, relatedness, or changing their circumstances. They were told "to give special attention" to this specific need during the next 6 months. Respondents then were engaged in a brainstorming activity where they were encouraged to think about how their need was not being met right now. In the circumstances condition they were told to brainstorm about the life circumstances they could change. Following the brainstorming session, they were encouraged to write down four goals that they could pursue over the next 6 months that might help satisfy their need. Note how this fairly simple strategy could be used in your own life. Indeed, only participants assigned to pursue intrinsic goals and who invested effort in seeking those goals showed improvements in happiness. Those pursuing circumstantial goals, however, showed no improvements in happiness.

Given the apparent importance of goals to happiness, it is perhaps surprising that there has not been more research demonstrating the success of goal treatments in enhancing happiness. One of the more successful goal-oriented methods, however, has been the so-called "best possible selves" intervention. In this approach, participants are first asked to write for 10 minutes about their best possible lives. For example, in the seminal King (2001) study that investigated this technique, Dr. King gave her subjects the following instructions:

> Think about your life in the future. Imagine that everything has gone as well as it possibly could. You have worked hard and succeeded at accomplishing all of your life goals. Think of this as the realization of all of your life dreams. Now, write about what you imagined.

Some studies using the best possible selves technique ask their subjects to focus on a particular life domain. For instance, students may be asked to write about their "best possible academic life" (Layous, Nelson, & Lyubomirsky, 2013, p. 641). Researchers may then ask their respondentts to write down the goals that would help them achieve this best possible self. A number of studies have shown that using this strategy results in increases in several different well-being variables (Boehm, Lyubomirsky, & Sheldon, 2011; King, 2001; Layous et al., 2013; Lyubomirsky, Dickerhoof, Boehm, & Sheldon, 2011; Peters, Flink, Boersma, & Linton, 2010; Sheldon & Lyubomirsky, 2006).

Some of these investigations found that when imagining your best possible self, optimism was enhanced, and as we have seen, being optimistic about your future is important to your SWB. Other approaches have been developed to directly impact optimism and thus boost SWB (Cheavens, Feldman, Gum, Michael, & Snyder, 2006; Shapira & Mongrain, 2010). Sergeant and Mongrain's (2014) examination of an online optimism intervention provides a good example of these treatments. In this study, participants were randomly assigned to either a placebo or the optimism treatment. Each technique took place every other day over a 3-week period. The optimism treatment had two components that were administered on alternating sessions. On one day, participants listed five things "that made them feel their life was enjoyable, enriching, and/or worthwhile" (p. 265). After listing these good things, they then were to "list three things that could help them see the bright side of a difficult situation" (p. 265). Positive psychology researchers commonly classify listing good things as a gratitude intervention, which we'll discuss later, but the rationale was that by recalling good things from one's past, this should brighten one's view of the future. Indeed, research has shown that counting one's blessings does enhance one's view of the upcoming week (Emmons & McCullough, 2003). At alternating exercise sessions, participants were to describe a goal they would like to accomplish within the next few days, and then they were encouraged to write down the steps they would need to take to achieve this goal. This method succeeded in improving some emotional well-being variables, but not all measures showed success. Given the significance of optimism to SWB, I am again surprised that there are not more published studies on optimism treatments, and I look forward to more research in this realm.

The Contemplative Way to Happiness

Religious traditions from both the East and the West have emphasized meditation and contemplation as paths to spiritual well-being. Most mindfulness meditation studies have been directed to repairing dysfunctional negative emotional states. Only a few trials have investigated the impact of mindfulness on SWB, and not all have found significant treatment effects (Sin & Lyubomirsky, 2009). One meditation practice has shown great promise, however, for enhancing happiness: Loving-kindness meditation (LKM; Salzberg, 1995). Rather than having a person focus on the current moment in an accepting and nonevaluative manner as in mindfulness meditation, in LKM the individual is encouraged to meditate and concentrate on warm and tender feelings in an open-hearted way. Note that LKM is a meditation approach that focuses more on positive emotions than other contemplative practices. First, individuals are directed to focus the region of their hearts on a person for whom they already have warm feelings. They are then asked to extend this "loving-kindness" to the self, and then to an "ever widening circle of others." Indeed, Fredrickson, Cohn, Coffey, Pek, and Finkel (2008) found that a 7-week LKM treatment produced significantly more daily positive emotions than a wait-list control group, and this in turn resulted in higher life satisfaction and lower depression. In other words, it appeared that the positive emotions produced by LKM enhanced important personal resources that in turn boosted emotional well-being. This is an encouraging finding, for it suggests that positive psychology interventions may be able to produce upward spirals that have healthy, long-term effects on SWB. Indeed, a 15-month, long-term, follow-up study showed that LKM continued to have positive effects on well-being (Cohn & Fredrickson, 2010).

Random Acts of Kindness

The treatments we have covered thus far have been more self-focused, but we now turn to other-focused interventions. We have seen that cultivating kind thoughts toward yourself and others enhances happiness, but research shows that kind acts toward others are also effective at boosting your well-being. Recall from Chapter 5 that happy people are giving people, and Elizabeth Dunn's research has determined that spending money on others tends to make us happier than spending money on ourselves (Dunn, Aknin, & Norton, 2008; Dunn, Aknin, & Norton, 2014; Dunn & Norton, 2013). Other studies show that simply instructing people to engage in kind acts toward others also improves SWB (e.g., Lyubomirsky, King, & Diener, 2005; Mongrain, Chin, & Shapira, 2011). In the Lyubomirsky study, they compared no-treatment controls to two different acts of kindness interventions: either five acts of kindness in 1 day, or five acts spread out over the week. You might think that spreading your kindness out would be more conducive to your happiness, but the authors actually found that people gained more SWB when they performed all of their kindness on 1 day of the week. More about this pattern of results later, but for now it's important to note that how you do your positive activities matters. In sum, it does appear that "It is more blessed to give than to receive"; when you give kindness to others, you may be the one who benefits most.

Amplifying the Good: Gratitude and Appreciation Treatments

Perhaps the most successful class of happiness interventions has been that involving gratitude. I say this not so much because of the treatment effect size of these interventions, but more because of the sheer number of gratitude treatment experiments that have shown significant short-term and long-term benefits (for reviews, see Watkins, 2014; Watkins & McCurrach, in press). As I often mention in this text, when it comes to psychology: "Bad is stronger than good" (Baumeister, Bratslavsky, Finkenauer, & Vohs, 2001). Even though we are inclined to have more pleasant than unpleasant experiences, bad information, bad memories, bad feedback, and bad interactions tend to exert more psychological power over us than the good in our lives. It is easy to let the "bad" in our lives drown out the good. Thus we need something that can help us amplify the good, and I believe that exercises of gratitude do just that (Watkins, 2014). In this part of the chapter, I have broken gratitude treatments into four categories: grateful recounting (exercises that involve recalling good things from our past), grateful reflection (techniques that encourage you to reflect on someone you're grateful for), grateful expression (treatments that encourage some type of expression of gratitude), and grateful reappraisal (treatments that encourage you to gratefully rethink unpleasant experiences). All of these techniques have been shown to have positive effects on your well-being, and they are fairly easy to incorporate into your life.

Grateful Recounting

"Count your blessings, name them one by one," goes the old hymn. Counting blessings as a path to happiness has been encouraged across time, religion, and culture. In this section of the chapter we explore the effectiveness of *grateful recounting* for enhancing SWB. Grateful recounting exercises involve some type of listing of benefits, also referred to as "gratitude lists" (Wood, Froh, &

Geraghty, 2010), and they have been one of the most tested of positive psychology interventions. The instructions from the Emmons and McCullough seminal test of this exercise characterize this class of gratitude interventions (2003, p. 379): "There are many things, both large and small, that we might be grateful about. Think back over the past week and write down . . . up to five things in your life you are grateful or thankful for." Indeed, Emmons and McCullough discovered that doing this just once per week for 9 weeks significantly increased SWB. There have been a number of studies that have used variations of this approach, apparently to good effect. One interesting version of grateful recounting has people recall experiences of beauty, and the preliminary outcomes from this intervention are encouraging (Diessner, Rust, Solom, Frost, & Parsons, 2006).

Although there are now a number of replications of grateful recounting, Wood et al. (2010) pointed out a critical problem with these findings. Many of these investigations used a control group where subjects counted hassles in their lives, and it could be reasonably argued that this "control" condition might have *decreased* SWB. Thus it is difficult to conclude from these studies that counting blessings actually increased SWB; it might be that compared to the "control" treatment, counting your blessings just didn't decrease your happiness. This brings up a crucial point regarding positive psychology intervention outcome studies: An active control treatment condition may not be a good control comparison. Fortunately, there are now several investigations that have shown grateful recounting to be superior to wait-list, no treatment, and placebo treatments (for a review, see Watkins, 2014).

The ideal comparison condition would be a placebo control condition that shows a significant placebo effect, and to date only a few studies have met that criterion. One such effort was the Seligman et al. (2005) online RCT that I describe earlier. As we have seen, their placebo treatment produced a significant boost in happiness, so active treatment comparisons to this treatment group are very informative. One of the active treatments in this study was the so-called "three-blessings" treatment. In this intervention, participants recall "three good things" (three things that have gone well), within the last 24 hours. As originally conceived, subjects completed this exercise every evening for 1 week. The results from this study are illustrated in Figure 7.2. The dotted gray line is the same placebo treatment I explained earlier (recalling early memories). Once again, note that there was a placebo bump in happiness, but the happiness of these respondents quickly returned to baseline. But remarkably, the SWB of those in the three-blessings treatment kept rising, even after the active treatment phase had ceased. Indeed, happiness still appears to be going up fully 6 months after the treatment phase. This isn't just a fortunate blip in the data, we found the same results using a

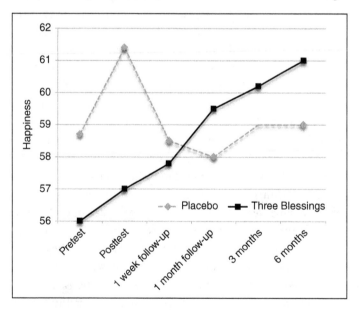

FIGURE 7.2 Three-blessings treatment outcome results.
Source: Seligman et al. (2005).

similar three-blessings intervention; the SWB of those in the grateful recounting treatment kept going up after treatment (Watkins, Uhder, & Pichinevskiy, 2015). Later, I'll talk a little more about why I think we're getting this effect. One of the problems with the Seligman et al. study was that we could not be sure whether or not the subjects were actually completing the gratitude exercises. In our study, they responded to our e-mails each day during the treatment period so we could ensure treatment integrity.

Another issue with grateful recounting exercises is whether or not gratitude is actually required. After all, it could be that listing any positive things about our lives—whether or not we're actually grateful for them—is the critical mechanism that explains why this treatment is effective. But in our study we showed that gratitude is a crucial aspect of counting your blessings (Watkins et al., 2015). Our participants were randomly assigned to one of three treatment conditions: placebo control that did show a significant placebo effect, pride three-blessings, or gratitude three-blessings. In both of the three-blessings treatments people listed three good things that had happened to them within the last 2 days. With the gratitude three-blessings treatment we had them write about how each thing made them feel grateful, but with the pride three-blessings treatment we asked them to write about "how this thing makes you feel better than others or better than average." You might rightly complain that this is a pathological form of pride, as indeed I argued in earlier chapters. But we were concerned with isolating grateful processing between our two three-blessings treatments. If we had simply asked our subjects in the pride three-blessings exercise to write about "how this thing makes you feel good about yourself," it is likely that they would have been processing many of these benefits with gratitude. We felt that with our pride three-blessings instructions, however, grateful processing would largely be limited to the gratitude treatment condition. Indeed, although the pride three-blessings test did not outperform our placebo condition, those in the gratitude three-blessings exercise showed a greater increase of happiness than respondents in both of the other treatments. This means that it's not just the recalling of good things that makes this technique effective; gratitude appears to be a crucial component of "counting your blessings."

Grateful Reflection

Grateful reflection, also known as *grateful contemplation,* simply refers to a practice of thinking about people you are grateful for, and considering how they have benefited you. Research has found that grateful reflection significantly increases positive emotion (Watkins, Woodward, Stone, & Kolts, 2003). Although writing has sometimes been used with this activity, some research suggests that writing may invoke cognitive processes that actually interfere with positive emotions (Lyubomirsky, Sousa, & Dickerhoof, 2006). In fact, in our study of grateful reflection we found that thinking about individuals you're grateful for produced more positive affect than writing about them (Watkins et al., 2003). It should be pointed out that, as far as I am aware, this intervention has yet to be tested regarding long-term impact on SWB. Because it does appear to be a reliable method of immediately boosting positive emotions, I predict that a regular practice of this technique should improve long-term happiness as well. It might be that this approach is best incorporated with other gratitude exercises such as grateful recounting (Watkins, 2014).

Grateful Expression

The hallmark of any emotional state is that it changes our action tendencies or our thought/action readiness. When we're afraid, we want to run. When we're angry, we're ready to fight. And when we feel grateful, we're prepared to express our gratitude in some way, sometimes in word ("thanks"), and sometimes in deed. The point is that the feeling of gratitude is preparing us for some expression of gratitude; however, many gratitude exercises do not necessarily encourage grateful expression. Activities that foster some type of expression of thankfulness may be referred to as *grateful expression*. These exercises, most notably the so-called *gratitude visit*, have been shown to produce large increases in happiness (e.g., Froh, Kashdan, Ozimkowski, & Miller, 2009; Seligman et al., 2005). In the gratitude visit, individuals are encouraged to write letters of gratitude to people they believe they have not properly thanked. Then they are to actually deliver and read the letters to their benefactors. Some versions of this treatment allow individuals to read their letters over the telephone if they can't deliver them in person; however, the important aspect of this technique is that it is an *embodied form of gratitude*—a very personal expression of thanks. In other words, just texting your thanks to someone is not likely to have much of an impact.

Seligman and colleagues (2005) report that this is a very powerful and moving exercise, and Figure 7.3 details the results. This graph illustrates the large boost in happiness that results from a gratitude visit. In fact, the gratitude visit was by far the most successful treatment that Seligman tested for enhancing happiness. Note the pattern of results from the follow-up assessments, however. By the time 6 months rolled around, the happiness of those who did their gratitude visits had returned to baseline. Whereas this might seem to be a discouraging result, we really shouldn't expect that one expression of gratitude would make us permanently happier. Indeed, I am quite impressed that the happiness of those in the gratitude visit treatment was still significantly above the placebo controls at 1-month follow-up. And who's to say that you can only express your gratitude once? More than likely, a consistent practice of expressing your gratitude will result in more permanent increases in your happiness. How often should you express your gratitude? How should you express your gratitude? To whom should you express your gratitude? These are all questions awaiting future research.

275

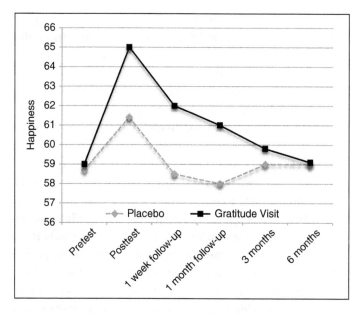

FIGURE 7.3 Gratitude visit treatment outcome results.
Source: Seligman et al. (2005).

Grateful Reappraisal

The final class of gratitude interventions I call *grateful reappraisal* (also called *positive reappraisal*), and this technique basically involves finding positive consequences from bad events that you can now be thankful for. One of the most salient characteristics of grateful people is that they appear to be very good at dealing with difficult and unpleasant situations (Watkins, 2014; Wood, Maltby, Gillett, Linley, & Joseph, 2008). Researchers have posited that this may be because grateful people are good at reframing negative occurrences in their lives. Put simply, they may be very good at "finding the silver lining" in the dark clouds of their lives. Indeed, studies have demonstrated that grateful reappraisal does foster well-being and the healing of painful memories (King & Miner, 2000; Watkins, Cruz, Holben, & Kolts, 2008). In our study, we first asked all of our participants to recall an unpleasant open memory. An *open memory* is an emotional memory that you feel you don't understand well, and you've had difficulty putting the memory behind you, so to speak. It's a memory that tends to be intrusive, and seems to be somewhat of an "open book" with "unfinished business" for you. After recalling and reporting on this memory, we randomly assigned our respondents to one of three writing conditions. In each condition, people wrote for 20 minutes on 3 consecutive days. In the control condition they simply wrote about their upcoming day. In the emotional disclosure condition, they wrote in a free-form manner about all of their thoughts and feelings surrounding the event that was the subject of their open memory. In the condition of interest, our grateful reappraisal treatment, we asked our participants to try and identify positive consequences of this difficult and painful event. We were quick to make sure that we were not asking them to call this bad event good. Rather, we asked them to consider, "As the result of this event, what kinds of things do you now feel thankful or grateful for?" (For the complete wording of this intervention, see Watkins, 2014; Watkins et al., 2008.) We found that those in the grateful reappraisal writing condition showed more closure of the memory, less unpleasant emotion associated with the memory, and the memory proved to be less intrusive. In order to be happy, you can't just avoid bad things in your life. Happy people deal with the unpleasant circumstances in their lives in a healthy way, and one effective way to deal with the bad stuff in your life appears to be grateful reappraisal.

Comprehensive Happiness Treatments

Thus far we have explored specific happiness treatments, techniques that are specific positive activities designed to boost SWB. Initially, however, happiness treatments were more comprehensive in nature, and they involved a number of different components. Sometimes called "shotgun" treatments, these interventions were designed to target a number of different areas related to happiness. The pioneering work of Fordyce (1977, 1983) illustrates comprehensive happiness treatments well. Fordyce developed his program based on what was known about happiness at the time, and he applied it, in several studies, to students in his psychology courses. Through his pilot work, he proposed "14 fundamentals of happiness" that could be applied in daily life. These fundamentals of happiness (1977, p. 517) are:

1. Spend more time socializing
2. Strengthen your closest relationships
3. Develop an outgoing, social personality
4. Be a better friend
5. Work on a healthy personality
6. Lower expectations and aspirations
7. Develop positive, optimistic thinking
8. Value happiness
9. Become more active
10. Become involved with meaningful work
11. Get organized and plan things out
12. Develop your present orientation (being in the moment)
13. Reduce negative feelings
14. Stop worrying

In one study (1977, Study 2), participants were given instruction as to how they could incorporate these principles into their daily lives, and they were urged to select one principle to focus on in each day of the treatment phase to apply to their lives. Throughout these studies Fordyce compared the active treatment condition to various control groups, including placebo controls. Despite the quasi-experimental designs used in his studies (he randomly assigned his different classes to the treatment conditions), the evidence for the effectiveness of his program was promising. As you can see from the list of the "fundamentals," many of these principles are based on the findings we have discussed in this book. For example, we have seen that your social life is important to your happiness, and fundamentals 1 through 4 clearly attempt to speak to this issue. Other principles, however, may be somewhat surprising to you. For instance, fundamental 6, "lower expectations and aspirations," may seem at least curious, and it appears to be contradictory to the following fundamental that advises people to be optimistic. This principle is based on goals research and the fact that if you have unrealistic or unreachable goals, this is bound to create dissatisfaction in your life. Another concern might be that these principles are too general to be effectively applied in your daily life. To illustrate, *how* can you "strengthen your closest relationships" and what does it mean to "be a better friend"? Although Fordyce apparently gave more specific instructions as to how his students could incorporate these principles into their lives, these details were not provided in his articles. Sometimes a general, vague positive encouragement can be more frustrating than helpful. A coach who tells the players, "Just go out there and win" without providing them with specific instruction as to how to score more points than the other team, isn't likely to be very effective.

I also have concerns about some of the avoidance-oriented principles, such as "reduce negative feelings" and "stop worrying." Not only are these goals lacking in the specifics that a person would need to accomplish these things, but some evidence suggests that trying to stop doing these things might paradoxically increase them. Admittedly, these findings were not available at the time Fordyce developed his program; however, the research program of Wegner demonstrated that by trying to suppress certain thoughts, this could lead to a paradoxical rebound effect where you actually experience more of those thoughts (Wegner, 1989). Nonetheless, the treatment outcome results from Fordyce's studies are very encouraging, and offered the hopeful suggestion that we could indeed enhance people's happiness.

More recently, happiness treatment packages have been developed based on our current knowledge of SWB, and here we consider two of these approaches: *well-being therapy* (WBT) and *positive psychotherapy* (PPT). WBT was developed by Fava and associates (e.g., Fava & Ruini, 2013). This treatment package focuses on the six domains of well-being posited by Ryff (1989): environmental mastery, personal growth, purpose in life, autonomy, self-acceptance, and positive relations with others. The goals of this approach are to identify impairments in each of these areas, and then to facilitate growth in the domains of need. This program emphasizes the importance of self-observations, and early sessions are devoted to identifying each individual's "episodes of well-being" (Fava & Ruini, 2013, p. 1038). The aim here is to help people gain insight into the circumstances of their happiness. In the next phase of therapy, individuals are encouraged through self-monitoring to identify those cognitions that interrupt their experiences of well-being. In the final stage of treatment, a person is urged to pursue "optimal experiences" (p. 1041). This program has been used in clinical psychology settings, and the initial outcome results are encouraging (see Fava & Ruini, 2013, for a review).

Another promising treatment package was developed by Seligman and colleagues (Rashid, 2013; Seligman, Rashid, & Parks, 2006). PPT is a program that uses many of the successful positive psychology interventions that we discussed earlier in this chapter. As with WBT, this approach was developed for use in clinical psychology settings. Rather than focusing on intervening with excess negative thoughts and affect, it attempts to enhance individuals' positive emotional experiences, and their engagement and meaning in life. Thus PPT strives to encourage these areas of well-being by incorporating positive activities such as using your strengths, best possible selves, the three-blessing exercise, and the gratitude visit. It also utilizes more experimental techniques such as an exercise designed to boost people's ability to savor positive experiences. Like WBT, the treatment outcome findings of PPT are encouraging, and offer more evidence that people can improve their happiness.

In this section of the chapter we have considered comprehensive treatment packages, also referred to as "shotgun" treatments, designed to improve one's happiness. I think the picture of a shotgun might be illuminating here. If you're out hunting wild turkeys (a difficult task, I'm told), you might fire your shotgun into a bush where you think a turkey resides. A shotgun shoots a number of projectiles that spread over the general area at which you're pointing the gun, and the hope is that one of these projectiles might hit what you're more generally aiming at. Similarly, shotgun treatments shoot in the general direction of increasing one's happiness with a variety of techniques, hoping that several of the exercises will hit their target and thus improve one's happiness. Although these strategies have been found to have better effect than specific positive psychology interventions (Sin & Lyubomirsky, 2009), I think we can do better than that. If we can specifically identify individuals' needs in relation to their happiness (a happiness formulation, if you will), then we can definitively target those needs with precise happiness treatment interventions. In essence, this is what is covered in the next part of this chapter: How can happiness treatments be used most effectively?

What Works Best, When, and for Whom? The Optimal Application of Happiness Treatments

Research on happiness treatments has now progressed to the point where investigators are looking at the moderators and mediators of happiness techniques. In other words, we are now looking at the conditions (such as personality and gender) that impact the success of positive psychology interventions (moderators), and we are beginning to investigate the *how* of these treatments (mediators). For example, how does the gratitude three-blessings exercise increase happiness? Often, these mediators are referred to as the *mechanisms* of happiness treatments. In this section, I argue that it is crucial to understand the mechanisms of the different positive psychology interventions, for only then can we comprehend how to optimally apply these methods.

Who benefits most from happiness treatments? Some research suggests that there are some cultural differences here; for example, gratitude and optimism approaches seem to enhance happiness more for Western students than for Eastern students (Boehm et al., 2011; Layous, Lee, Choi, & Lyubomirsky, 2013). Other studies indicate that positive psychology interventions work somewhat better with older populations (Sin & Lyubomirsky, 2009), and this might be because this age group is more motivated and has more time to commit to improving their SWB (Lyubomirsky et al., 2011; Sin & Lyubomirsky, 2009). Sin and Lyubomirsky's meta-analysis also proposes that those who are moderately depressed appear to benefit more from positive activities than those not depressed. Other investigations, however, argue that depression may prevent individuals from fully using positive psychology interventions (Sin, Della Porta, & Lyubomirsky, 2011), so more research is needed to resolve this question. But how can we use this research to optimally deliver happiness treatments? How can we make sense of these varying conclusions to understand how and when positive psychology interventions work?

A simple interpretation of these findings is that *happiness treatments work best for those who need them most*. This follows from Lyubomirsky's model of the importance of a person/activity fit in explaining the effectiveness of positive activities for enhancing SWB (Layous & Lyubomirsky, 2014; Lyubomirsky & Layous, 2013). Dr. Lyubomirsky argues that happiness treatments work best when there is a fit between the activity and the person engaging in the activity. What determines person/activity fit? Lyubomirsky seems to propose that those activities that best fit a person's particular needs will provide the greatest improvement in SWB. Here I think it is helpful to return to Ryan and Deci's theory of well-being (2000). Recall that there are three fundamental psychological needs that should be met in order for people to feel fulfilled and satisfied with their lives: autonomy, competence, and relatedness. Thus, if people seeking to improve their happiness have significant deficits in the need area of relatedness, positive psychology interventions that enhance relatedness should provide the best "person/activity" fit for these individuals.

What determines whether a positive activity "fits" a person? It seems that most assume that people's preferences and their enjoyment of an activity best determine whether a specific activity fits a particular person. I remember walking behind a couple of students after I had my class engage in a gratitude three-blessings exercise. One student was quite enthusiastic about the process, "Wasn't that great?" she asked her fellow student. But the second student responded, "Well, it really wasn't me; I didn't enjoy it all that much." So should we conclude that a gratitude three-blessings intervention would not be the best fit for the second student, and that it would be ideal for the first? I submit that it depends on whether or not the intervention is meeting a need in a person's life, and even when it is meeting a need, the exercise might not always "feel good." Indeed, some evidence suggests that people are not always the best judges in determining the best positive activities for improving their SWB. For example, Parks, Della Porta, Pierce, Zilca, and Lyubomirsky (2012) found that the type of activities that "online happiness seekers" chose to practice in their lives (Study 2) were not always the techniques that were most effective for them (Study 3).

Consider my recent investigation of grateful recounting, for instance (Watkins et al., 2015). This was a study where the students in the active treatment condition had to recall three good things every day for 1 week, and write about how each thing made them feel grateful. I would have thought that those who enjoyed the exercise the most would gain most in terms of happiness, but that was not the case. In fact, my students' reports of their enjoyment of the activity did not predict improvement in SWB at all. Indeed, although it was only a statistically marginal finding, enjoyment of the three-blessings exercise was negatively correlated with improved happiness 5 weeks after the treatment phase ($r = -.18$). Thus, those who enjoyed the treatment least showed the greatest long-term gain in happiness. Also surprising to me was the fact that even though women enjoyed the gratitude exercise more than men, men gained significantly more from grateful recounting than did women. Moreover, we found that those who were least grateful at the start of the study gained the most from the gratitude procedure. Although all of these findings were somewhat surprising to me, they actually make a great deal of sense and they seem to tell a consistent story. If you're already fairly grateful, it's probably easier for you to recall good things from your day—and it's also easy for you to write about how they make you feel grateful—and you will probably enjoy the activity more. If, however, you're not a very grateful person, recalling good things from your day may be difficult and you might find writing about how they make you feel grateful to be even more frustrating. This likely results in less enjoyment of the activity. But does that mean it's not contributing to your future happiness? If you're already grateful, you'll probably choose a gratitude positive activity to improve your happiness and you'll enjoy it too, but do you have much to gain from the activity? If, as I argue later, this activity improves your SWB by developing more positive thinking habits, but you already have those positive thinking tendencies, then it makes sense that you won't gain a great deal from the treatment. On the other hand, if you're not grateful, you're not likely to have habitual patterns of positive thinking about your life and others. Although this might make an exercise like grateful recounting less enjoyable for you and you may not choose to engage in this activity, this might be the very activity that your happiness needs. This example points out that sometimes the very fact that an activity is not enjoyable for us may be the indication that this is the very activity we need. If we are out of shape, starting to exercise won't feel very good; nevertheless, that may be the indication that it is the very thing that we need to do for our health. Indeed, the road to happiness may not be the easy road—the path of least resistance. Some of the things we find most difficult to do may be the very things we need to do to enhance our long-term SWB.

In short, happiness treatments work best for those who need them most. This is where it is important to understand our psychological needs and what may be getting in the way of fulfilling our needs. I submit that the optimal positive psychology exercise for you is the activity that best meets the psychological needs that are not being met. But in order to complete this equation, we need to comprehend the *how* of happiness treatments, to use Lyubomirsky's phrase (2007). We must grasp the psychological mechanisms that different treatments are impacting. If I am right that grateful recounting increases happiness because it trains people to notice the positive in their lives and it also teaches them to interpret events in a more positive manner, then it makes sense that this intervention might work best on cynics—those individuals who have trouble trusting others, dwell on the negative, and make negative interpretations of situations in their lives. If on the other hand, people's happiness is impeded because they are plagued by a troubling event from their past that keeps intruding into their consciousness, then grateful reappraisal might be the best exercise for them. If, however, individuals do not have any of these unpleasant open memories that are troubling them, it doesn't make much sense to encourage them to engage in grateful reappraisal. In my mind, this is where research needs to be directed in positive psychology: understanding how positive psychology interventions work. For me, if we can answer the question "How do happiness treatments work?" we will be on our way to understanding how they can best be applied to improve people's happiness. In short, happiness treatments work best when they serve to help meet the psychological needs that are not being met.

POSITIVE CLINICAL PSYCHOLOGY

The encouraging findings of positive psychology interventions have led some to wonder if they might be effective adjuncts to more traditional clinical psychology treatments. Indeed, some of the previously mentioned studies have discovered that positive psychology interventions not only increase happiness, they significantly decrease depression symptoms as well (e.g., Seligman et al., 2005; Watkins et al., 2015). Moreover, in the Sin and Lyubomirsky meta-analysis (2009), they concluded that positive interventions had a slightly larger treatment effect with depression symptoms than with happiness. To be fair, most of the studies reviewed earlier were conducted with nonclinical populations, so it is something of a leap to conclude that they should actually help ameliorate clinical conditions. Two of the multicomponent treatments that I discuss earlier however, WBT and PPT, have been tested on people with diagnosed mental disorders, and the results have been encouraging. Moreover, a transdiagnostic model for incorporating positive activities into clinical interventions has been developed, and I have found this approach to be very helpful (Layous, Chancellor, & Lyubomirsky, 2014; see also Layous, Chancellor, Lyubomirsky, Wang, & Doraiswamy, 2011). Thus in a sense, positive psychology has come full circle; it might be that the people who most benefit from positive psychology research are those who are typically treated by those of us who focus on negative psychology: clinical and counseling psychologists.

Out of these promising data has emerged a movement somewhat distinct from positive psychology, so-called "positive clinical psychology" (Wood & Johnson, in press; Wood & Tarrier, 2010). This approach attempts to answer some of the critics of the positive psychology movement in that while attempting to integrate the development of strengths such as gratitude and other positive emotions into the treatment of psychological disorders, positive clinical psychology attempts to give equal weight to so-called "negative" aspects of disorders. Indeed, Wood and colleagues argue that "positive" and "negative" characteristics cannot be studied separately; they must be studied together. For example, encouraging enhanced happiness in a depressed individual should necessarily entail the alleviation of depression. It seems to me that both WBT and PPT would fit nicely into this vision, and although the positive clinical psychology movement is in its infancy, I believe it has great potential to enhance the standard treatment approaches of psychology.

SUMMARY AND CONCLUSIONS

In this chapter we explored two questions: Can you improve your happiness? If so, how can you improve your happiness? When I first began reading about the positive psychology movement in 1998 I was obviously excited about this new undertaking; however, I must confess that I was very skeptical about one of its goals. I just didn't see how interventions could actually make much of a lasting impact on an individual's happiness. Contrary to my cynicism, however, I have been pleasantly surprised with how effective positive psychology interventions have been. To be fair, we still have a long way to go and, most importantly, I believe that it is essential that we understand *how* happiness treatments work. But despite the many unresolved issues, multiple studies now lead us to the conclusion that people can change their happiness, and we now have a pretty good understanding of the treatments that are most effective. Knowing and using your personal strengths, imagining and planning for a better future, giving to others, meditating in a way that enhances warm and compassionate feelings toward yourself and others, and improving your gratitude all seem to be reliable paths to increasing your happiness. Can you improve your happiness? The encouraging answer appears to be that indeed, you can.

REFERENCES

Baumeister, R. F., Bratslavsky, E., Finkenauer, C., & Vohs, K. D. (2001). Bad is stronger than good. *Review of General Psychology, 5,* 323–370.

Boehm, J. K., Lyubomirsky, S., & Sheldon, K. M. (2011). A longitudinal experimental study comparing the effectiveness of happiness-enhancing strategies in Anglo Americans and Asian Americans. *Cognition and Emotion, 25,* 1263–1272. doi:10.1080/02699931.2010.541227

Catalino, L. I., Algoe, S. B., & Fredrickson, B. L. (2014). Prioritizing positivity: An effective approach to pursuing happiness? *Emotion, 14,* 1155–1161. doi:10.1037/a0038029

Cheavens, J. S., Feldman, D. B., Gum, A., Michael, S. T., & Snyder, C. R. (2006). Hope therapy in a community sample: A pilot investigation. *Social Indicators Research, 77,* 61–78. doi:10.1007/s11205-005-5553-0

Cohn, M. A., & Fredrickson, B. L. (2010). In search of durable positive psychology interventions: Predictors and consequences of long-term positive behavior change. *Journal of Positive Psychology, 5,* 355–366. doi:10.1080/17439760.2010.508883

Coote, H. J., & MacLeod, A. K. (2012). A self-help, positive goal-focused intervention to increase well-being in people with depression. *Clinical Psychology & Psychotherapy, 19,* 305–315. doi:10.1002/cpp.1797

Diener, E. (2000). Subjective well-being: The science of happiness and a proposal for a national index. *American Psychologist, 55,* 34–43.

Diessner, R., Rust, T., Solom, R. C., Frost, N., & Parsons, L. (2006). Beauty and hope: A moral beauty intervention. *Journal of Moral Education, 35,* 301–317. doi:10.1080/03057240600874430

Duan, W., Ho, S. Y., Tang, X., Li, T., & Zhang, Y. (2014). Character strength-based intervention to promote satisfaction with life in the Chinese university context. *Journal of Happiness Studies, 15,* 1347–1361. doi:10.1007/s10902-013-9479-y

Dunn, E., & Norton, M. (2013). *Happy money: The science of happier spending.* New York, NY: Simon & Schuster.

Dunn, E. W., Aknin, L. B., & Norton, M. I. (2008). Spending money on others promotes happiness. *Science, 319,* 1687–1688.

Dunn, E. W., Aknin, L. B., & Norton, M. I. (2014). Prosocial spending and happiness: Using money to benefit others pays off. *Current Directions in Psychological Science, 23,* 41–47.

Emmons, R. A., & McCullough, M. E. (2003). Counting blessings versus burdens: An experimental investigation of gratitude and subjective well-being in daily life. *Journal of Personality and Social Psychology, 84,* 377–389. doi:10.1037/0022-3514.84.2.377

Farquharson, L., & MacLeod, A. K. (2014). A brief goal-setting and planning intervention to improve well-being for people with psychiatric disorders. *Psychotherapy and Psychosomatics, 83*(2), 122–124. doi:10.1159/000356332

Fava, G. A., & Ruini, C. (2013). Well-being therapy: Theoretical background, clinical implications, and future directions. In S. A. David, I. Boniwell, & A. Conley Ayers (Eds.), *The Oxford handbook of happiness* (pp. 1037–1049). New York, NY: Oxford University Press.

Ford, B. Q., Mauss, I. B., & Gruber, J. (2015). Valuing happiness is associated with bipolar disorder. *Emotion, 15*(2), 211–222. doi:10.1037/emo0000048

Ford, B. Q., Shallcross, A. J., Mauss, I. B., Floerke, V. A., & Gruber, J. (2014). Desperately seeking happiness: Valuing happiness is associated with symptoms and diagnosis of depression. *Journal of Social and Clinical Psychology, 33,* 890–905. doi:10.1521/jscp.2014.33.10.890

Fordyce, M. W. (1977). Development of a program to increase personal happiness. *Journal of Counseling Psychology, 24,* 511–521. doi:10.1037/0022-0167.24.6.511

Fordyce, M. W. (1983). A program to increase happiness: Further studies. *Journal of Counseling Psychology, 30,* 483–498. doi:10.1037/0022-0167.30.4.483

Fredrickson, B. L., Cohn, M. A., Coffey, K. A., Pek, J., & Finkel, S. M. (2008). Open hearts build lives: Positive emotions, induced through loving-kindness meditation, build consequential personal resources. *Journal of Personality and Social Psychology, 95,* 1045–1062.

Froh, J. J., Kashdan, T. B., Ozimkowski, K. M., & Miller, N. (2009). Who benefits the most from a gratitude intervention in children and adolescents? Examining positive affect as a moderator. *Journal of Positive Psychology, 4,* 408–422. doi:10.1080/17439760902992464

Govindji, R., & Linley, P. A. (2007). Strengths use, self-concordance and well-being: Implications for strengths coaching and coaching psychologists. *International Coaching Psychology Review, 2*(2), 143–153.

King, L. A. (2001). The health benefits of writing about life goals. *Personality and Social Psychology Bulletin, 27,* 798–807. doi: 10.1177/0146167201277003

King, L. A., & Miner, K. N. (2000). Writing about the perceived benefits of traumatic events: Implications for physical health. *Personality and Social Psychology Bulletin, 26,* 220–230.

Layous, K., Chancellor, J., & Lyubomirsky, S. (2014). Positive activities as protective factors against mental health conditions. *Journal of Abnormal Psychology, 123,* 3–12. doi:10.1037/a0034709

Layous, K., Chancellor, J., Lyubomirsky, S., Wang, L., & Doraiswamy, P. M. (2011). Delivering happiness: Translating positive psychology intervention research for treating major and minor depressive disorders. *Journal of Alternative and Complementary Medicine, 17,* 675–683. doi:10.1089/acm.2011.0139

Layous, K., Lee, H., Choi, I., & Lyubomirsky, S. (2013). Culture matters when designing a successful happiness-increasing activity: A comparison of the United States and South Korea. *Journal of Cross-Cultural Psychology, 44*, 1294–1303. doi:10.1177/002202 2113487591

Layous, K., & Lyubomirsky, S. (2014). The how, why, what, when, and who of happiness: Mechanisms underlying the success of positive activity interventions. In J. Gruber & J. T. Moskowitz (Eds.), *Positive emotion: Integrating the light sides and dark sides* (pp. 473–495). New York, NY: Oxford University Press.

Layous, K., Nelson, S. K., & Lyubomirsky, S. (2013). What is the optimal way to deliver a positive activity intervention? The case of writing about one's best possible selves. *Journal of Happiness Studies, 14*, 635–654. doi:10.1007/s10902-012-9346-2

Lewis, C. S. (1993). *Letters of C. S. Lewis.* Orlando, FL: Harcourt Brace. (Original work published 1966)

Linley, P. A., Nielsen, K. M., Gillett, R., & Biswas-Diener, R. (2010). Using signature strengths in pursuit of goals: Effects on goal progress, need satisfaction, and well-being, and implications for coaching psychologists. *International Coaching Psychology Review, 5*(1), 6–15.

Lykken, D., & Tellegen, A. (1996). Happiness is a stochastic phenomenon. *Psychological Science, 7*, 186–189.

Lyubomirsky, S. (2007). *The how of happiness: A scientific approach to getting the life you want.* New York, NY: Penguin Press.

Lyubomirsky, S., Dickerhoof, R., Boehm, J. K., & Sheldon, K. M. (2011). Becoming happier takes both a will and a proper way: An experimental longitudinal intervention to boost well-being. *Emotion, 11*, 391–402. doi:10.1037/a0022575

Lyubomirsky, S., King, L., & Diener, E. (2005). The benefits of frequent positive affect: Does happiness lead to success? *Psychological Bulletin, 131*, 803–855.

Lyubomirsky, S., & Layous, K. (2013). How do simple activities increase well-being? *Current Directions in Psychological Science, 22*, 57–62.

Lyubomirsky, S., Sousa, L., & Dickerhoof, R. (2006). The costs and benefits of writing, talking, and thinking about life's triumphs and defeats. *Journal of Personality and Social Psychology, 90*, 692–708. doi:10.1037/0022-3514.90.4.692

MacLeod, A. K., Coates, E., & Hetherton, J. (2008). Increasing well-being through teaching goal-setting and planning skills: Results of a brief intervention. *Journal of Happiness Studies, 9,* 185–196. doi:10.1007/s10902-007-9057-2

Mauss, I. B., Savino, N. S., Anderson, C. L., Weisbuch, M., Tamir, M., & Laudenslager, M. L. (2012). The pursuit of happiness can be lonely. *Emotion, 12,* 908–912. doi:10.1037/a0025299

Mauss, I. B., Tamir, M., Anderson, C. L., & Savino, N. S. (2011). Can seeking happiness make people unhappy? Paradoxical effects of valuing happiness. *Emotion, 11,* 807–815. doi:10.1037/a0022010

Mill, J. S. (1972). *Utilitarianism, liberty, representative government.* New York, NY: E. P. Dutton.

Mongrain, M., Chin, J. M., & Shapira, L. B. (2011). Practicing compassion increases happiness and self-esteem. *Journal of Happiness Studies, 12,* 963–981. doi:10.1007/s10902-010-9239-1

Page, K. M., & Vella-Brodrick, D. A. (2013). The working for wellness program: RCT of an employee well-being intervention. *Journal of Happiness Studies, 14,* 1007–1031. doi:10.1007/s10902-012-9366-y

Parks, A. C., Della Porta, M. D., Pierce, R. S., Zilca, R., & Lyubomirsky, S. (2012). Pursuing happiness in everyday life: The characteristics and behaviors of online happiness seekers. *Emotion, 12,* 1222–1234. doi:10.1037/a0028587

Peters, M. L., Flink, I. K., Boersma, K., & Linton, S. J. (2010). Manipulating optimism: Can imagining a best possible self be used to increase positive future expectancies? *Journal of Positive Psychology, 5,* 204–211. doi:10.1080/17439761003790963

Peterson, C., Park, N., & Seligman, M. E. P. (2005). Assessment of character strengths. In G. P. Koocher, J. C. Norcross, & S. S. Hill III (Eds.), *Psychologists' desk reference* (2nd ed., pp. 93–98). New York, NY: Oxford University Press.

Radloff, L. S. (1977). The CES-D scale: A self-report depression scale for research in the general population. *Applied Psychological Measurement, 1,* 385–401. doi:10.1177/014662167700100306

Rashid, T. (2013). Positive psychology in practice: Positive psychotherapy. In S. A. David, I. Boniwell, & A. Conley Ayers (Eds.), *The*

Oxford handbook of happiness (pp. 978–993). New York, NY: Oxford University Press.

Ryan, R. M., & Deci, E. L. (2000). Self-determination theory and the facilitations of intrinsic motivation, social development, and well-being. *American Psychologist, 55,* 68–78.

Ryff, C. D. (1989). Happiness is everything, or is it? Explorations on the meaning of psychological well-being. *Journal of Personality and Social Psychology, 57,* 1069–1081. doi:10.1037/0022-3514.57.6.1069

Salzberg, S. (1995). *Loving-kindness: The revolutionary art of happiness.* Boston, MA: Shambhala.

Seligman, M. E. P., Rashid, T., & Parks, A. C. (2006). Positive psychotherapy. *American Psychologist, 61,* 774–788. doi:10.1037/0003-066X.61.8.774

Seligman, M. E. P., Steen, T. A., Park, N., & Peterson, C. (2005). Positive psychology progress: Empirical validation of interventions. *American Psychologist, 60,* 410–421.

Sergeant, S., & Mongrain, M. (2014). An online optimism intervention reduces depression in pessimistic individuals. *Journal of Consulting and Clinical Psychology, 82,* 263–274. doi:10.1037/a0035536

Shapira, L. B., & Mongrain, M. (2010). The benefits of self-compassion and optimism exercises for individuals vulnerable to depression. *Journal of Positive Psychology, 5*(5), 377–389. doi:10.1080/17439760.2010.516763

Sheldon, K. M., Abad, N., Ferguson, Y., Gunz, A., Houser-Marko, L., Nichols, C. P., & Lyubomirsky, S. (2010). Persistent pursuit of need-satisfying goals leads to increased happiness: A 6-month experimental longitudinal study. *Motivation and Emotion, 34,* 39–48. doi:10.1007/s11031-009-9153-1

Sheldon, K. M., & Lyubomirsky, S. (2006). How to increase and sustain positive emotion: The effects of expressing gratitude and visualizing best possible selves. *Journal of Positive Psychology, 1,* 73–82. doi:10.1080/17439760500510676

Sin, N. L., Della Porta, M. D., & Lyubomirsky, S. (2011). Tailoring positive psychology interventions to treat depressed individuals. In S. I. Donaldson, M. Csikszentmihalyi, & J. Nakamura (Eds.), *Applied positive psychology: Improving everyday life, health, schools, work, and society* (pp. 79–96). New York, NY: Routledge/Taylor & Francis Group.

Sin, N. L., & Lyubomirsky, S. (2009). Enhancing well-being and alleviating depressive symptoms with positive psychology interventions: A practice-friendly meta-analysis. *Journal of Clinical Psychology, 65,* 467–487. doi:10.1002/jclp.20593

Watkins, P. C. (2014). *Gratitude and the good life: Toward a psychology of appreciation.* Dordrecht, The Netherlands: Springer.

Watkins, P. C., Cruz, L., Holben, H., & Kolts, R. L. (2008). Taking care of business? Grateful processing of unpleasant memories. *Journal of Positive Psychology, 3,* 87–99.

Watkins, P. C., & McCurrach, D. (in press). Progress in the science of gratitude. In S. Lopez, L. Edwards, & S. Marques (Eds.), *The Oxford handbook of positive psychology* (3rd ed.). New York, NY: Oxford University Press.

Watkins, P. C., Uhder, J., & Pichinevskiy, S. (2015). Grateful recounting enhances subjective well-being: The importance of grateful processing. *Journal of Positive Psychology, 2,* 91–98.

Watkins, P. C., Woodward, K., Stone, T., & Kolts, R. (2003). Gratitude and happiness: Development of a measure of gratitude, and relationships with subjective well-being. *Social Behavior and Personality, 31,* 431–452.

Wegner, D. M. (1989). *White bears and other unwanted thoughts: Suppression, obsession, and the psychology of mental control.* New York, NY: Penguin Press.

Wood, A. M., Froh, J. J., & Geraghty, A. W. A. (2010). Gratitude and well-being: A review and theoretical integration. *Clinical Psychology Review, 30,* 890–905.

Wood, A. M., & Johnson, J. (Eds.). (in press). *The Wiley handbook of positive clinical psychology.* Chichester, England: Wiley.

Wood, A. M., Joseph, S., & Maltby, J. (2008). Gratitude uniquely predicts satisfaction with life: Incremental validity above the domains and facets of the five factor model. *Personality and Individual Differences, 45,* 49–54.

Wood, A. M., Maltby, J., Gillett, R., Linley, P. A., & Joseph, S. (2008). The role of gratitude in the development of social support, stress, and depression: Two longitudinal studies. *Journal of Research in Personality, 42,* 854–871.

Wood, A. M., & Tarrier, N. (2010). Positive clinical psychology: A new vision and strategy for integrated research and practice. *Clinical Psychology Review, 30,* 819–829.

Conclusions About Positive Psychology: Matters of Happiness

don't always make New Year's resolutions, unless I see something that I really want to change. This past year, however, I did think that there was something that needed modification. I had noticed that as I was getting older, I was getting a bit grumpier, and so I thought that my resolution would be: "I want to be less grumpy this year." But as I reflected on my potential resolution, I thought: "What does it mean to be less grumpy?" When you think about it, what do you do to be less grumpy? It isn't immediately obvious as to what I would need to do to decrease my grumpiness. But it was here that my involvement with positive psychology came to my aid. I realized that my goal was an avoidance goal and, as such, was not likely to be very successful. How could I change my "less grumpy" resolution to a positive, approach-oriented goal? I thought: "What about joyful play?" Wouldn't authentic play be the perfect antidote to the age-old problem of grumpiness? And so my New Year's resolution became one of play. I wanted to play more with my children, play more with my wife, play with my students and my friends, and even—if I may be so bold— play more with my God. I believe this example is a good illustration of the perspective that positive psychology has to offer us. Rather than being less grumpy, positive psychologists might recommend for us to engage in more joyful play.

In this chapter my goal is to package the contents of this book so that it is easy for you to remember its most important themes. I highlight here what I feel to be the most essential "take-aways" from the text. The thrust here is "matters of happiness," or "happiness matters," if you will. What I want you to take away from this chapter (and this book) are the most crucial things that matter to your happiness.

HAPPINESS MATTERS

If there is anything that I want you to learn from reading this book, it is that happiness matters. Happiness is not simply a nice consequence of a successful life. Indeed, happiness itself is consequential. Research has shown that there are a number of beneficial by-products to experiencing positive emotions frequently: better relationships, better health, and better occupational success, just to name a few (Lyubomirsky, King, & Diener, 2005). Happy people are not "contented cows"; for the most part they are productive members of society. To be sure, happiness matters.

But here I must be quick to issue a warning. It is also very possible that you could value happiness too much, in a way that actually inhibits your well-being (Mauss, Tamir, Anderson,

& Savino, 2011). If you obsessively seek happiness, if you feel entitled to happiness, if you must have happiness at all costs, if you base your value as a person on your happiness, if you must "feel good" at all times, or if you seek an unrealistic level of happiness, paradoxically, you may end up unhappy. As Diener and Biswas-Diener remind us (2008, p. 208), "Might all the well-intentioned meddlers be making you unhappier . . . by insisting that you need more happiness?" Happiness really does matter, but you can make it matter so much that it actually prevents you from flourishing.

SCIENCE MATTERS

As positive psychology and the study of happiness come more and more into the public eye, I increasingly see the need for science to be at the heart of positive psychology. This was the original intention of positive psychology and, in my view, we must be careful to keep our scientific orientation. It's not that science is the only knowledge base that has anything to contribute to our understanding of the good life. Indeed, I believe that as scientists of positive psychology it is of utmost importance that we attend to the contributions of philosophy, history, literature, theology, music, and other humanities. But as we seek to translate and apply our findings to the general public, there will always be the temptation to step out of science and into the realm of pop psychology. I have certainly seen this trend in my own research area of gratitude. Although the studies supporting the significance of gratitude to the good life are compelling, it is so tempting to argue that gratitude is the all-encompassing good that everyone must pursue. I am so easily lured into arguing that gratitude is "the secret" to the good life. Research has shown that there are a number of benefits to gratitude; however, when we make it the elixir to permanent happiness, we end up redefining everything that is good as gratitude. Then, gratitude unfortunately loses its meaning—and its power. I fear that we may be in danger of overstating the good of other virtues as well, virtues such as mindfulness, compassion, and forgiveness.

If we keep science at the heart of the positive psychology movement, however, I believe that for the most part we will be protected from these excesses. Chris Peterson, commenting on the future of positive psychology, wisely observed, "The endeavor will swim or sink in accordance with the science it produces over the next decade" (2006, p. 305). Certainly, the science that has emerged since his prediction has been impressive, but this success has the potential to spoil us. I feel that it is vital to keep Peterson's encouragement in mind as we seek to advance positive psychology. Despite my excitement about the potential of positive psychology, my passion for truth must remain paramount. And here, David Myers's sage advice is still relevant today (1992, p. 137): "Seek truth first and you may eventually find comfort. Seek comfort at the expense of truth and you may be a patsy for those who are all too willing to leave your wallet, and your heart, empty." As we envision the future of positive psychology, clearly, science matters.

NEEDS MATTER

When it comes to comprehending the causes of happiness, your genuine human needs matter. When your needs are satisfied, then you'll probably feel satisfied with life. Perhaps that principle is only too obvious, but it is a critical principle nonetheless when it comes to explaining happiness. First, we can see that when people's biological needs are met, they tend to be happy. Remember how this helps us grasp the relationship between income and subjective well-being (SWB). When people have enough money to pay for adequate food and shelter, they are inclined to be happy; however, after these basics in life have been purchased, there's not much happiness left to be bought.

Because most of us have enough financial resources to provide for our biological needs, the importance of fulfilling our psychological needs becomes paramount. As I have considered the science of happiness in writing this book, I have become increasingly impressed with Ryan and Deci's Self-Determination Theory (SDT) of happiness and how it very efficiently helps us understand psychological well-being (2000). When we say that in order to be happy we need to have our psychological needs met, this is fairly straightforward until we begin to discuss what our psychological needs really are. Ryan and Deci argue that we have three basic psychological needs that must be fulfilled in order to feel satisfied in life. First, when our *competence* need is fulfilled we feel that we are in control of the significant outcomes in our lives, and we have mastery over the critical tasks in our lives. Second, we also need to feel *autonomous* in order to feel satisfied with life. When the need for autonomy is met, we feel that what we are doing in life is self-determined; we don't feel forced by others to perform life tasks, and we believe that we have chosen our course in life. Finally, Ryan and Deci argue that *relatedness* is a fundamental and universal human need. In order to be happy we must feel that others accept us and that we have meaningful connections with people we deem important to us. In essence, relatedness connects to our feeling of belonging. When we do not feel accepted by others or that we belong to others, our need of relatedness will not be satisfied and consequently we won't be very happy.

So, when we feel competent, autonomous, and related, we will probably feel happy as well, and this is an important consideration when evaluating what you might want to change to improve your happiness. Remember that many people seek to enhance their happiness by improving their lives in ways that don't directly relate to these needs (called extrinsic goals). And so some pursue happiness through riches, beauty, and social status, and research shows that these goals are not conducive to happiness. A crucial consideration in improving your happiness is to carefully evaluate whether your three fundamental psychological needs are being met. If one or more of these needs are not being met, then ask yourself how you can change your life in order to meet those needs. For example, if you're not really feeling a sense of belonging to others, how can you change your life to fulfill this need? How can you change your leisure life to enhance relatedness? How can you relate to others at work differently? How can you change the way you relate to significant others in your life? Although SDT may seem like an obvious notion, as it turns out, this theory helps us explain much of the literature in the science of happiness. Indeed, needs matter.

HOW YOU THINK MATTERS

Why is it that your external circumstances end up explaining very little of your happiness? More than likely, it's because it's not your circumstances, but how you *think* about your circumstances that really matters when it comes to your happiness. For example, in Chapter 5 we learned that how you think about your relationships appears to be much more essential to your happiness than the objective circumstances of your relationships. In Chapter 6 we explored how happy people tend to think. We saw that happy people are inclined to attend to the good in their lives, they have a tendency to make positive interpretations of the various situations in their lives, and they easily recall pleasant experiences from their past. Not only are positive memories readily available for happy people to use, they tend to feel better about these memories when they do recall them.

But I submit that happy people have an additional important thinking characteristic. Happy people are open to seeing the good in their lives (see also Fredrickson, 2008). Happy people are not narrow in their views of what makes their lives good; they are creative enough thinkers to see many consequences as being good, even though they may not have expected that result. Sometimes my expectations of events get in the way of actually enjoying them. I may expect to really enjoy Renaissance art on my holiday in Italy, but perhaps the real benefit is in growing closer to my best traveling companion, my wife. I may expect to gain from sharing my research at an academic conference, but perhaps the real advantage of going to the conference is learning about someone else's research. I may expect that losing an election will be a humiliating experience for me, but perhaps the real boon is helping me see—once again—what is really important in my life. In the words of C. S. Lewis (1963, p. 26), "It seems to me that we often, almost sulkily, reject the good that God offers us because, at that moment, we expected some other good." Research shows that thinking in a broader, less expectation-driven manner enhances the experience of positive emotions, and positive emotions help us think in a more open way about the good in our lives (Fredrickson, 2008). This is an upward spiral that happy people make use of in their lives, and this is another reason why, when it comes to your happiness, how you think matters.

MEANING MATTERS

In a nutshell, the good life is a meaningful life. As Chapter 4 demonstrates, happy people are able to find purpose and meaning in their lives. When our lives are infused with meaning, there is a strong tendency for us to be happy. One way our lives can be more purpose-driven is by being more goal-oriented. But even here, the aims that seem to be most conducive to our happiness are aims that are meaningful to us. Intrinsic goals—that are relevant to our fundamental psychological needs—promote our SWB. When it comes to your happiness, goals matter.

Another way that people infuse meaning into their lives is through spirituality and religiosity. When people look to something sacred that transcends their self, their lives seem to be more meaningful, and this may be one reason why religious people are inclined to be happy people. Spirituality matters when it comes to your happiness, but a quick warning is in order. Any attempt to "get religion" in order to "get happiness" is bound to backfire. It is primarily when religion is a meaningful pursuit—an ultimate motive in your life—that it is conducive to well-being. In short, a life infused with meaning is bound to be a good life.

CHARACTER MATTERS

In Chapter 2 we examined an important pillar of positive psychology: the study of psychological strengths and virtues. The positive psychology movement has identified six primary virtues that are essential to the good life: *wisdom, courage, love, justice, temperance,* and *transcendence.* Although these virtues vary somewhat in their relationships to SWB, they all may be seen as critical to the life well lived. In our consideration of the good life, character matters.

In emphasizing psychological strengths and virtues, I have argued that it is imperative that you know your "signature strengths." But research shows that mere knowledge of your virtues is not enough; unquestionably, using your strengths is critical to enhancing your happiness (see Chapter 7).

If character matters to your happiness, then it is vital that we comprehend how psychological strengths develop, and I believe that this is the most crucial challenge for future research in positive psychology. How does gratitude develop? How does humility develop? How does humor develop? How does courage develop? All of these are important questions for grasping how character matters. As we think about the development of character, it is important to consider not only what enhances character development, but also what might inhibit the growth of psychological strengths. This was a valuable point emphasized by Peterson (2006). It may be that because these virtues are universal, there is a natural tendency for them to develop. If that is true, then the more important consideration is why don't they develop? For example, I have stressed that it is vital to know how gratitude develops (2014), but perhaps that's not the most crucial question. Maybe it's more important to understand what inhibits the growth of gratitude. Why doesn't gratitude develop in some people? Recently, for example, we have found that cynicism and narcissism both inhibit the growth of gratitude (Watkins, Solom, McCurrach, & Hutchison, 2014). Many have argued that secure attachment is important for the development of the psychological strengths, and we too have taken this approach in our investigations on the development of gratitude. But perhaps secure attachment is the default in development, and it is really more imperative to understand how *insecure attachment* prevents gratitude. Indeed, in a recent experimental attachment priming study, it appeared that it was more insecure attachment priming decreasing gratitude rather than secure attachment priming increasing gratitude (Konkler, Nienhuis, Hutchinson, Vance, & Watkins, 2015).

Before we leave the discussion about psychological strengths and virtues, I want to reemphasize a point I brought up in Chapter 2. Although each one of us has our own signature strengths that we need to understand and use, I believe that in our society and in psychology we need to stress a balance of the virtues. It is all too easy to fall prey to the "virtue of the moment" and celebrate some virtues while neglecting others. It is all too easy for us to hop on the gratitude bandwagon, while ignoring the study of the other strengths. All of the strengths are essential for an adequate understanding of the good life, and thus my plea as we go forward in positive psychology is to emphasize a balance of the virtues (cf. Lewis, 1944/2001). Even in our individual lives, I believe, we can neglect some virtues, with the result being that we lead an unbalanced life. In other words, balancing the strengths matters. Nonetheless, this discussion highlights the fact that the study of character is important to the study of the good life.

THE FUTURE MATTERS

How you think about the future matters to your happiness. People who feel that the future looks bright tend to be happy. People who have hope for tomorrow are inclined to be happy today. We have seen that happy people are more likely to be goal-oriented; nevertheless, unless you have hope about the future, you probably aren't going to put the effort into achieving those goals. If you're convinced that "I'll never get into graduate school anyway," it's unlikely that you'll even fill out an application. And if you don't apply, there's no way that you can achieve your goal of graduate school. "Nothing ventured, nothing gained," as they say, and feeling optimistic about your chances is crucial to any kind of venture.

More than likely, your feelings about your future are closely related to your feelings about locus of control. If you believe that you have control of the significant outcomes in your life (an *internal locus of control*), then you're probably going to feel pretty good about your future. If, however, you believe that what happens to you is merely the consequence of luck and fate, you'll probably feel pretty unsure about your future. Happy people take responsibility for their lives; they generally believe that they are in control of the important events of their lives; and thus they have a positive view of their future. In short, optimism and hope matter to your happiness.

GRATITUDE MATTERS

Why do people feel good about their future? More than likely, it's because they feel good about their past. And it is here where gratitude matters to your happiness. Grateful people tend to be happy people, and gratitude treatments have been some of the most successful interventions for improving people's happiness. Why is gratitude so important for your happiness? Research supports the theory that gratitude amplifies the good in your life (Watkins, 2014). Just as an amplifier boosts the sound going into a microphone, so gratitude amplifies the good that it focuses on. Gratitude tells us—very loudly and clearly—who and what are good in our lives. We see that because, psychologically speaking, "Bad is stronger than good" (Baumeister, Bratslavsky, Finkenauer, & Vohs, 2001); it is all too easy to let the bad in our lives drown out the good. But gratitude helps amplify the good, and in so doing improves our happiness.

SELF-ACCEPTANCE MATTERS

In this book we have seen that when you're satisfied with your self, you're very likely to be satisfied with your life. Self-esteem is one of the strongest correlates of happiness. But the problem is that self-esteem comes in many forms, some conducive to happiness, some not. People with high but unstable self-esteem are not particularly happy. Moreover, self-compassion is more strongly associated with happiness than self-esteem. For these reasons, self-acceptance—acknowledging and accepting who you really are—is more important to your enduring happiness than self-esteem.

One of the reasons that I think it's important to emphasize self-acceptance over self-esteem is because of the well-known *self-serving bias* in psychology. We say that we need to feel better about ourselves, we need to have more confidence in ourselves, and we need to have more compassion for ourselves; however, the research suggests that we are all too good at looking out for ourselves and our own self-esteem. If something goes wrong, my first response is to blame it on someone else. If I'm late for work, I can't believe how everyone else is driving so slow. But if I have plenty of time to get to work, I can't believe how fast everyone else is driving. If I feel down on myself, my natural response is "give yourself a break," to be a bit more selfish because "I need it." But it is here where our emphasis on self-esteem may backfire when it comes to our happiness. In the words of Chesterton (1905/1986, p. 165): "We do not merely love ourselves more than we love duty; we actually love ourselves more than we love joy." There is a way that we can be so focused on ourselves, that it actually undermines our happiness.

So, it's not just feeling good about yourself but accepting yourself that really matters to your happiness. This is why concentrating on yourself to improve your self-esteem and your happiness is likely to backfire. One consistent characteristic of unhappy people is that they tend to be preoccupied with themselves, whereas happy people seem to be somewhat self-forgetful. Here is where a healthy humility can help us accept ourselves and become less self-preoccupied. Indeed, humble people are more concerned with the needs of others than with their own needs, and this brings us to one of the most important matters of happiness.

OTHERS MATTER

Aristotle was right, we are social animals, and time and again studies show that rewarding relationships are vital to happiness. Although the research indicates that your relationships matter for your happiness, it appears it's more the quality than the quantity of your social life that counts. Research demonstrates that your perception of social support is more important to your happiness than objective indicators of social support. This is probably because our perceptions of our relationships are more finely tuned to unique interactions with others, and this is more critical to our SWB than objective indicators of relationships.

The pattern of results also suggests a cycle of virtue that is vital to your happiness: Happy people think about others in a more positive manner, which probably enhances the quality of their relationships, and this in turn heightens their happiness. We also saw that giving has an important—and likely reciprocal—relationship with happiness. Happy people tend to give more to others, and giving boosts your happiness in turn. And this takes us to another significant observation about happiness: Happy people are inclined to be other-focused, whereas unhappy people have a tendency to be self-focused. In short, the quality of your relationships matters to your happiness, but happy people don't just have relationships, they are *engaged* with their relationships.

ENGAGEMENT MATTERS

In this book we have seen that the happy life is an active life. Happy people are inclined to be more active in their work and in their play. Even in their leisure hours, happy people have a tendency to choose more active than passive leisure activities. Folk dancing produces more joy than watching television. Gardening is more fulfilling than playing solitaire on your computer. In these findings we are reminded of Sonja Lyubomirsky's theory of how *positive activities* are important to SWB. Positive activities are "simple, intentional, and regular practices" that improve positive affect, increase positive thinking, or help satisfy your psychological needs (Lyubomirsky & Layous, 2013, p. 57). Much of your happiness is under your control and, in life, what you intentionally choose to participate in is bound to affect your happiness.

Lyubomirsky's theory highlights the importance of the intentionality of positive activities and this brings up an important point about happy people's pursuits. Happy people are not simply busy people; they're not just going from one activity to another. Happy people are actively *engaged* in life. Happy people are not just doing life; they're living life. When we are engaged with something, we are committed to it and we are actively involved with it, cognitively, emotionally, and behaviorally. When I ask my students not to use their cell phones in class, I want them to really be engaged with my class, or as I tell them, "If you're going to be here you might as well really be here." It's the difference between simply going through life and fully experiencing it. As I come close to the end of this book, there is a temptation for me to "just finish it," to "just get 'er done." But that would be writing the book without really being engaged in my writing. This book will be much more engaging for you if I am fully engaged in my writing. In a nutshell, happy people are not simply active people; they tend to be engaged in their activities. In their relationships, they are engaged with the people they relate to. In their occupations, they are fully engaged in their tasks. Even when they are at play, rather than just "vegging out," they tend to choose activities that engage them, both in mind and body.

When we discuss happiness at work, we discover that people who have a sense of *calling* in their work have a tendency to be much more satisfied with their occupations. People who feel called to their careers believe that they were made for their jobs. It occurs to me that this calling perspective may relate to other life domains as well. When I feel called to a particular leisure activity, or called to certain relationships, this is bound to infuse these domains with more meaning, and hence this should foster increased engagement in these areas. Future research may want to apply the calling perspective to life domains beyond satisfaction at work.

People who don't just go through life but are actively engaged with life should savor the benefits that come their way (Bryant & Veroff, 2007). Indeed, how you savor the good things in your life matters to your happiness, and I look forward to more studies that might illuminate the psychological processes of savoring. I can just drink my daily latte because that's what I always do and that's a pleasure I'm entitled to, or I can really taste, experience, and savor my drink. *Savoring* enhances enjoyment of benefits, and thus promotes SWB as well. Being engaged with life means that I will try to savor all the good that comes my way.

In this we can also see the importance of *simple pleasures* to SWB. Recall that it's the frequency more than the intensity of positive emotional experiences that is important to your happiness. I can wait for a trip to Maui to be happy, or I can enjoy the simple pleasures in my life that I encounter every day. It is precisely because simple pleasures are so frequent and immediate that they become much more crucial to my happiness than spectacular pleasures. But in order for simple pleasures to really have an impact on my well-being, I need to actually be engaged in these events. I need to savor my simple pleasures to fully enjoy them. Simple pleasures matter to your happiness but, even here, engagement matters.

In short, happy people are fully engaged with life. Recall the study we review earlier in the book where people report much more joy when dancing than with any other leisure group activity (Hills & Argyle, 1998). For me, this result is a revealing picture of the happy life. When we dance with life—when we are fully engaged in the activities of our lives—we will invariably be satisfied with life. When I dance with my wife it fully stimulates my senses, my thinking, my emotions, and my body. When I am fully engaged in my work, my play, my relationships, and my religion, that is when I am truly flourishing. Engagement matters to your happiness. In Chris Peterson's wonderful words (2006, p.309), "We know the dance is wonderful when all participate, so how do we get everyone onto the floor?"

NEGATIVE EMOTIONS MATTER

And now, we need to look at how negative emotions matter to the good life. Just as with positive emotions, negative emotions have a purpose, and when they are functioning well in our lives, they help us to live well. In order to flourish, it is vital to experience and not to avoid the unpleasant emotions in our lives. Indeed, one of the consistent characteristics of those suffering from emotional disorders is that they try to avoid negative emotions and, ironically, this is one of the things that keeps them unhappy (Moses & Barlow, 2006). People who spend a great deal of effort in suppressing unwanted thoughts paradoxically end up dwelling on those unpleasant thoughts. In order to be happy, you have to be willing to be anxious, angry, and sad. Accepting our negative emotions frees us from having to feel good all of the time. Here, we should be quick to heed Diener and Biswas-Diener's wise advice (2008, p. 209): "The moral imperative to be constantly cheerful can feel oppressive."

So why can't we just avoid all the unpleasant emotions in our lives? In short, we can't dodge all unpleasant emotions because we can't avoid all unpleasant situations in life. Happiness results, in part, from using your emotions adaptively. Although negative emotions can easily become maladaptive, they are largely adaptive and can be crucial to our happiness when we use them appropriately. Both negative and positive emotions prepare us for some adaptive activity. So if you're anxious about an upcoming test, that anxiety is preparing you for some adaptive activity to deal with the threat. If all you do is worry about the test, that wouldn't be adaptive. But if your anxiety prompts you to study for the test, that should help you do well on the test, which might support your happiness. If you don't experience any anxiety about the upcoming test, however, you probably won't study for the test, you'll probably do poorly on the test, and that won't make you very happy. Even negative emotions matter to your happiness, and when you can accept them and use them to help you live well, unpleasant emotions can help foster your enduring happiness.

HAPPINESS INTELLIGENCE MATTERS

There has been much discussion about emotional intelligence in psychology; however, there is a type of emotional intelligence that I believe is crucial to your well-being: *happiness intelligence*. In short, happiness intelligence is having accurate knowledge about happiness, and being able to use that knowledge effectively in your life. To illustrate, individuals high in happiness intelligence accurately understand the things that really make them happy over the long run. People low in happiness intelligence might believe that if they get a new house, move to a new city, or get a new husband, then they'd finally be happy. Those high in happiness intelligence, on the other hand, would recognize that getting a new, higher paying job might not make them happier if it takes away from their relationships and their leisure life.

So what are the important components of happiness intelligence? The answer to that question would likely be a book in itself, but I propose that accurate affective forecasting is the key to happiness intelligence. Accurate happiness forecasting matters to your happiness. Recall in Chapter 6 that we explored several affective forecasting errors that should bear on your happiness. People high in happiness intelligence should comprehend these errors and be able to avoid them. For instance, if I understand the *impact bias,* I'll know that I tend to overestimate the intensity and duration of my emotional responses to events. Sometimes people avoid things that might be potentially good in their lives because they overestimate how terrible it would feel if things don't come out the way they had hoped. At times we refrain from doing good things that might have negative consequences because of *immune neglect;* we underestimate how effective our psychological immune system is at handling adverse circumstances.

On occasion we make decisions that are not conducive to our happiness because of the *focusing illusion;* we focus on one salient aspect of a choice, and make our decision based on that feature while ignoring other important characteristics of that choice. So those low in happiness intelligence might decide to move to California because they "know" the sunny weather will make them happy. But in the process they forget to consider the crowds, how expensive it is to live there, and that they are moving away from all their friends. Sometimes we buy something that is more than we can afford because we assume that how much we want that thing is reflective of how much we will like that thing. This is the *want-for-like confusion* and unless we are aware of this affective forecasting error, it may be damaging to our happiness.

There are several other happiness forecasting errors that we examined in Chapter 6; however, the point is that people high in happiness intelligence should grasp these natural tendencies in human thinking, and avoiding these mistakes should bode well for their happiness. So I conclude this chapter with the affective forecasting error that might be most essential to your happiness: *social neglect*. Research demonstrates that we tend to neglect just how much social interactions—even with strangers—are important to our happiness. In short, people who are high in happiness intelligence should comprehend that "others matter."

AND FINALLY . . .

To conclude, I want to leave you with some good news and some bad news. First, let me give you two pieces of good news. The good news about positive psychology is that happiness matters. Your pursuit of happiness is not ill-founded; it's not a foolish pursuit; it's not a quest that is bound to backfire. Indeed, research suggests that there are many desirable consequences from having an enduring sense that "life is good." And the second piece of good news makes the first even more significant: You can change your happiness. Studies consistently show that there are positive activities that you can participate in that can boost your SWB. The good news is that if you aren't extremely happy right now, there are things that you can do to improve your happiness.

But here's the bad news, if indeed this is bad news: It isn't easy to make enduring changes to your happiness. If you're unhappy, there's a good reason that you're not happy and, more than likely, that reason relates to habitual aspects of your life-style. Long-standing habits are not easy to change and, probably, it won't be easy to change your happiness either. In Seligman, Steen, Park, and Peterson's (2005) study of positive psychology interventions, they found that one treatment boosted happiness much more than all the others: the *gratitude visit*. But remember that the happiness of those who completed the gratitude visit was back to baseline in 3 months. It's not that the gratitude visit is a bad approach to changing your happiness. The moral of this story is that because your current happiness is based on your lifestyle— your consistent habitual pattern of intentional activities—it's very unlikely that one gratitude expression can make you permanently happier. You can't just count your blessings once, sign up for one dance class, go to church once, buy one latte for someone, or do one loving-kindness meditation (LKM) and expect to be happier ever after. "What is clear is that if we are to change our typical level of happiness, it will not be through quick fixes or one-shot interventions," observed Chris Peterson (2006, p. 307): "We will need to change permanently our lives and our lifestyles, just as if we were trying to change our weight or level of aerobic fitness." You can change your happiness, but the change will not be easy.

Although your journey to increased happiness may be difficult, this trek need not be overly unpleasant. It's probably better to view your pursuit of happiness as a journey rather than a destination (Diener & Biswas-Diener, 2008), but it's a road worth traveling nonetheless. Research on positive psychology interventions suggests that those most in need of particular treatments have the most to gain from them (see Chapter 7). If you are overweight, you probably have more to gain from an exercise program than someone who is close to a healthy weight level. But that doesn't mean that the exercise program will be easy. Indeed, it will be more difficult for an overweight person to jog for a mile than someone who is close to their ideal weight. So it is with happiness. If you're not a very grateful person now, it's probably more difficult for you to count your blessings than for someone who is already grateful. But the good news is that the ungrateful person has more happiness to gain from a counting blessings exercise than someone who is already pretty grateful. The road of happiness may not be an easy road, but the road is there to be found, and there is much to gain from its travels.

"True contentment is a thing as active as agriculture," wrote Chesterton, "It is the power of getting out of any situation all that there is in it" (2008, para 6). In this essay where Chesterton compares our two divergent uses of the word *content*, he argues that one can just go through life, or one can get all the content that can be gotten out of the experiences of life.

> A man might have gone "through" a plum pudding as a bullet might go through a plum pudding; it depends on the size of the pudding—and the man. But the awful and sacred question is "Has the pudding been through him?" Has he tasted, appreciated, and absorbed the solid pudding, with its three dimensions and its three thousand tastes and smells? (Chesterton, 2008, para 6)

Through this example of experiencing a plum pudding, Chesterton highlights a very important principle of the happy lifestyle. I can just "go through" the many experiences of my life, but it's not likely to leave me very fulfilled. The flourishing life makes sure that the experiences of my life actually go through me. It is pretty easy to mindlessly eat a delicious dessert; it is far more difficult to engage with the dessert, to truly taste, appreciate, and absorb the dessert. It is certainly more difficult to engage with the experiences in my life—to let life go through me rather than just going through life—but it is far more fulfilling as well.

So as I close this book my final encouragement to you is to resist the path of least resistance. If you tend to be somewhat introverted, the easiest thing is to continue to stay alone. It will be more difficult to increase your engagement with others, but it will be more fulfilling as well. If you find that your leisure hours are filled with passive activities such as watching television, the easiest thing will be for you to continue on that path. It will be much more difficult to pursue active social activities or new hobbies, but you'll find that you're more likely to be satisfied with your life. If you find that you are consistently preoccupied with your own needs and happiness, the path of least resistance will be for you to continue to be self-focused. It won't be easy to think more about the needs of others, but it is likely to be more rewarding. No, the change in your lifestyle that might be required to enhance your happiness is not likely to be easy; however, it will be well worth the effort, and my hope is that you will continue on this journey.

REFERENCES

Baumeister, R. F., Bratslavsky, E., Finkenauer, C., & Vohs, K. D. (2001). Bad is stronger than good. *Review of General Psychology, 5,* 323–370.

Bryant, F. B., & Veroff, J. (2007). *Savoring: A new model of positive experience.* Mahwah, NJ: Lawrence Erlbaum.

Chesterton, G. K. (1986). Heretics. In D. Dooley (Ed.), *G. K. Chesterton: Collected works* (pp. 37–207). San Francisco, CA: Ignatius Press. (Original work published 1905)

Chesterton, G. K. (2008). A miscellany of men. In G. K. Chesterton (Ed.), *The contented man.* Retrieved from http://www.gutenberg. org/files/ 2015/ 2015-h/2015-h.htm#link2H_4_0037

Diener, E., & Biswas-Diener, R. (2008). *Happiness: Unlocking the mysteries of psychological wealth.* Malden, MA: Blackwell.

Fredrickson, B. L. (2008). Promoting positive affect. In M. Eid & R. J. Larsen (Eds.), *The science of subjective well-being* (pp. 449–468). New York, NY: Guilford Press.

Hills, P., & Argyle, M. (1998). Positive moods derived from leisure and their relationship to happiness and personality. *Personality and Individual Differences, 30,* 595–608.

Konkler, J. G., Nienhuis, A., Hutchinson, D. E., Vance, P., & Watkins, P. C. (2015, May). *Security and gratitude: Secure attachment priming enhances gratitude.* Poster presented at the meeting of the Annual Convention of the Western Psychological Association, Las Vegas, NV.

Lewis, C. S. (1963). *Letters to Malcolm: Chiefly on prayer.* San Diego, CA: Harcourt Brace Jovanovich.

Lewis, C. S. (2001). *The abolition of man.* New York, NY: HarperCollins. (Original work published 1944)

Lyubomirsky, S., King, L., & Diener, E. (2005). The benefits of frequent positive affect: Does happiness lead to success? *Psychological Bulletin, 131,* 803–855.

Lyubomirsky, S., & Layous, K. (2013). How do simple activities increase well-being? *Current Directions in Psychological Science, 22,* 57–62.

Mauss, I. B., Tamir, M., Anderson, C. L., & Savino, N. S. (2011). Can seeking happiness make people unhappy? Paradoxical effects of valuing happiness. *Emotion, 11,* 807–815. doi:10.1037/a0022010

Myers, D. G. (1992). *The pursuit of happiness: Discovering the pathway to fulfillment, well-being, and enduring personal joy.* New York, NY: Avon Books.

Peterson, C. (2006). *A primer in positive psychology.* New York, NY: Oxford University Press.

Ryan, R. M., & Deci, E. L. (2000). Self-determination theory and the facilitations of intrinsic motivation, social development, and well-being. *American Psychologist, 55,* 68–78.

Seligman, M. E. P., Steen, T. A., Park, N., & Peterson, C. (2005). Positive psychology progress: Empirical validation of interventions. *American Psychologist, 60,* 410–421.

Watkins, P. C. (2014). *Gratitude and the good life: Toward a psychology of appreciation.* Dordrecht, The Netherlands: Springer.

Watkins, P. C., Solom, R., McCurrach, D., & Hutchison, D. E. (2014, May). *Narcissism and cynicism inhibit gratitude: A prospective study.* Poster presented at the meeting of the Annual Convention of the Association for Psychological Science, San Francisco, CA.

Index

9 780826 126979